FAMILY PRACTICE:

A Problem-Based Learning Approach

Heather Coleman

Don Collins

Tara Collins

eddie bowers publishing co., inc.

Exclusive marketing and distributor rights for
U.K., Eire, and Continental Europe held by:

Gazelle Book Services Limited
Falcon House
Queen Square
Lancaster
LA1 1RN
U.K.

---

eddie bowers publishing co., inc.
P. O. Box 130
Peosta, Iowa 52068 USA

www.eddiebowerspublishing.com

ISBN 1-57879-062-X

Printed in the United States of America.

9 8 7 6 5 4 3 2 1

Contents

Acknowledgements

Many people have contributed to the creation of this book through support, suggestions, and experience and we would like to thank each and every one for the faith they had in the writing of this book. First, we would like to thank Eddie Bowers for seeing this book through to the finish. His personable approach to publishing has been much appreciated. We would also like to thank Tom LaMarre for the faith he had in us and connecting us with Eddie Bowers Publishing. We have appreciated our association with Tom over the years. In addition, without the feedback and enthusiasm of our students, we would never have learned so much about Problem-Based Learning and how students can profit from this approach and the experiential exercises. Our children, Tara, Michael, and Ryan have been patient while we wrote the book. Our friends allowed us to use their names in the cases in the text and they did so with great humor. The families that we have seen throughout our careers have deepened our appreciation of the struggles of living. Our families of origin saw us through our growing up. We dedicate this book to the memory of our fathers - Dr. William Charles Gordon Collins and Major Harold Ralph Coleman.

Preface for Students

This book is about preparing you for your first encounters working with families in the role of a generalist family worker. It is intended to help you understand what generalist family work means and prepare you to become a competent generalist family work practitioner. This book is a practical, how to, workbook to be used by both the student and instructor in a course teaching family practice. It is expected that a deeper understanding of theories will be learned primarily through reading. The reference section at the end of the book should prove helpful. We are most concerned with the theory and making it become "alive" in the classroom by designing the class as a practical hands on experience for the student.

Maximizing student learning requires a critical examination of teaching methods. Teaching and learning is a challenge in the helping professions, in part because we need a balance between the acquisition of knowledge and the application of that knowledge to practice. An underlying premise of this book, then, is that classroom learning needs to locate a balance between theory acquisition and the application of knowledge to practice. Problem-Based Learning (PBL) with an experiential focus can assist in the process.

PBL, enhanced with practice experience and assignments designed to focus on learning, is an effective way of stimulating student-centered learning in a context where students critically analyze problems, yet feel safe doing so. It is congruent with the values and processes of family work because it capitalizes on the inherent strength and abilities of students to direct their own learning. As a mirror image process, students will empower families much in the same way they have been empowered. Students are largely responsible for their own learning in PBL, which is an empowering process for them.

Student-centered learning drives PBL such that students learn to critically analyze problems in a small group setting. A common definition of PBL is, "… the learning that results from the process of working toward the understanding or resolution of a problem. The problem is encountered first in the learning process and serves as a stimulus for applying problem-solving and reasoning skills, as well as for the search for information needed to understand the mechanisms responsible for the problem and how it might be resolved" (Barrows, 1985). In PBL, learners actively *construct* knowledge. They also take what they learn and decide how it fits in other settings. While learning is predominantly the outgrowth of learners' actions, classroom structure can enable and foster constructive learning. The major assumption of PBL is that learners are intrinsically motivated to solve problems, and when challenged, they will learn what is required to solve a problem successfully (McKeachie, 2002). Thus, students do not go to class to be entertained or to "bank" knowledge required for future uses (Friere, 2000). Banking information is too static. Instead, learning is more fluid and students learn how to navigate and work with relevant information and discard that which is irrelevant.

Our students have been excellent teachers. We have been impressed with their enthusiasm and openness to new learning experiences. They have convinced us that we need to evaluate our teaching, much in the same way that we expect students to evaluate their practice. Their feedback suggests to us that PBL is an effective approach to learning. *"I really enjoyed this class and the style. It honestly made learning about the different theories more interesting and fun. Since it made me want to be in class, it really helped facilitate learning. I think more classes should follow this class's lead."*

The recommended approach in this book is based on our students' feedback. The overarching goal of this book is that the "family" experience learned in the classroom will be reproduced in real family work situations that students will be familiar with. We thus encourage this approach to learning about family practice.

Preface for Instructors

Each chapter of this book represents a three-hour class. The instructor can follow each chapter as a week course schedule, combine chapters, or spend more than one week on a particular chapter. We have used this format for a number of years and found the need to be flexible as it often depends on the comfort level of the whole class and how fast or slow to move as well not all programs offer three hour classes over twelve weeks, for example some programs have two hour classes yet over sixteen weeks thus the text material needs to be modified to fit the teaching hour format being used.

What we would like to emphasize is the experiential and problem-based learning format where students are given ample opportunity for hands on experience to integrate the theory with practice. As well, not all programs offer three-hour classes over twelve weeks. For example, some programs have two-hour classes over sixteen weeks. Thus the text material needs to be modified to fit the teaching hour format being used.

Chapter 1 **Table of Contents**

GENERALIST FAMILY WORK

Chapter 1

Generalist Family Work

Chapter Coverage

- Starting a Problem-Based Learning (PDL) Family Class
- An Overview of Families and Family Diversity
- Definition of Family
- Historical Overview of Family Work
- Introduction to Generalist Family Work
- Forming Family Problem-Based Groups

Introduction

One of the most interesting and challenging parts of generalist practice is working with families. Scary for some, certainly an adventure for all, yet a most meaningful type of human service practice. In this book, we present a step-by-step process for learning generalist family work. We want this book to be a guide to learn about families so that by the end of the course you will feel comfortable seeing families.

Learning human service work is challenging on many fronts. Human service work is broad and diverse and students must gain a theoretical understanding of the many layers of helping. Teaching and learning in the human services often takes the form of theory. Besides understanding the many theories, students must also practice ethically and competently, reflecting on how values and life experiences affect practice. This means developing the ability to transform learning into competent work by combining theory, self-reflection and awareness, and professional skills and values, and transform all into competent practice. Competent practice demands the *thoughtful* application of skills to aid clients with their psychosocial problems. However, many of the qualities of a good worker cannot be taught in a traditional didactic (lecture) format (Patterson, Williams, Grauf-Grounds, & Chamow, 1998).

We therefore recommend taking an experiential approach to learning family work, accompanied by presentation of theory and exercises designed to aid in the transfer of family theory to practice. This book thus incorporates Problem-Based Learning (PBL). One of the premises of PBL is that students, as adult learners, complement their understanding of theory with pertinent reading. They then bring new learning into the classroom to solve problems and address issues related to families. This book includes theory about family work and in-class structured experiences for students to practice their skills, integrate theory, and develop critical thinking skills.

As with other teachers, we have struggled with how to help our students develop the full range of knowledge, skills, and values. After much investigation and reflection, we believe that we have discovered an effective way of teaching theory that can easily be blended with learning practice skills. This approach, based on a modified PBL teaching method, uses family cases and experiential learning supplemented with traditional lectures to teach family practice. Assignments are geared toward the integration of theory, skills and values. Our students tell us that this is a very effective approach. Thus, we first describe how we use PBL and integrate it with teaching a family course. In this chapter, we also share the experiences of our students in learning family practice skills.

Problem-Based Learning (PBL)

We start this journey by first introducing Problem-Based Learning and how we have used it to teach our family classes over the past several years. Students inform us that this approach stimulates learning and they learned a great deal about families and family practice. Their feedback has convinced us that PBL is an effective way of educating beginning professionals about family work. We have discovered that PBL removes students from a passive learning process, with the professor lecturing and students taking notes, and places students in the center of the educational journey. Because it is essential that students understand PBL before jumping into the process, we first discuss the approach and provide the rationale for using it.

Essentially, students form different "family" groups and role-play each week, based on specific theory. The format *demands* a commitment from all "family" members; much in the same way that real-life family work demands a commitment from family members. In this way, student experiences parallel "real life" by echoing the trials and tribulations of working intimately and continuously with a family from beginning to end. Students learn many other things. They learn the importance of motivation, both as a student and family member. They learn what it is like to run out of steam and what needs to be done to remain on task. They learn about family dynamics and what it is like to be on the receiving end of an intervention. They learn to apply theory to practice. Finally, they learn practice skills and become comfortable working with families before they encounter their first family.

Each family class consists of two parts. In the first part of class, students deal with theoretical material. In the second half of class, students receive instructions to help them connect theory and practice through specially designed family role-plays. Assignments apply to the PBL "family" groupings and include such topics as completing a family assessment, Genograms and Ecomaps, integrating weekly theory and practice scenarios, and formulating interventions. We have also found that weekly logs in which students reflect on theory and connect with their weekly sessions are particularly useful. Outside the classroom, students read and reflect, and integrate relevant theory with what transpired in their role-plays.

We recommend a blend of lecture on foundation family theory for undergraduates, combined with reading, assignments, and experiential exercises with a family of the students' creation. Students develop family groupings, which they keep for the entire course. We share with you what our students have told us about learning in this way. After presenting PBL, the book then presents relevant family theory and practice. Each chapter is sprinkled with exercises throughout to help students reflect upon and practice theory. These in-class exercises will be helpful even if the class does not take a PBL format. At the end of each chapter, we provide exercises for use in a class that uses Problem-Based Learning.

This format carries with it several expectations of students. First, students must take responsibility for learning. They must commit to their family work group because, as with an actual family, if one member is not committed, every other member is impacted. Parallels between the student learning process and the dynamics of family work quickly emerge. For example, a student not showing up for class parallels the same impact as family members not attending family sessions. Students might lose momentum, again much the same way that family members might. The instructor needs to be sensitive to the parallels and help students identify similarities and possible solutions.

Exercise 1.1

Life as a Student

(In Class)

Reflect on what it has been like for you as a student in your different classes. What were some of the learning challenges that you faced as you progressed through a class? Once you have done this, draw parallels between your experience as a student and what the issues might be for family members.

Student Issues	Family Member Issues
e.g., Motivation	Continuing family work, showing up for appointments
1.	
2.	
3.	
4.	

Students are also expected to stay focused on the work, rather than, as one student reported, "... *chatting about the weekend*." Therefore, ground rules must first be established in each group committing to the work. For example, attendance is crucial and attendance should be part of the ground rules.

Exercise 1.2

Ground Rules
(In Class)

Ground rules guiding family work, similar to cooperative student learning, must be established in the beginning-working phase. One important ground rule is attendance. List some other ground rules that are important to make with your group at the outset of your course. Compare these with ground rules that might be important for families.

Student Ground Rules	Family Work Ground Rules
e.g., Attendance	Attendance
a.	
b.	
c.	
d.	

In our classes, students reported being pleased, not only with what they learned but also pleased with their new abilities. "*I think problem-based learning helped me to understand that I was capable of learning on my own, with support from students and professors.*" However, students must be prepared to take charge of their learning. "*As a student I had to take a lot of responsibility, instead of sitting back and just listening. I think I assumed much more responsibility for my own learning in this approach. However, it was worth the amount of work I put in. Problem-Based Learning definitely depends on how much effort students put into it.*" Others echoed this opinion. "*This course is the only one where I have ever had so much control over what I learned. I really liked this. I think it is very important to take responsibility for what we learned. I think it made us gain the skill of incorporating what we learned into actual practice which is very valuable.*" Despite the demand for commitment and hard work, students reported having fun learning in this way. "*It was a fun way of learning. It was useful in practicing interviewing and family counseling skills.*" This feedback shows us that student empowerment is vital to the learning process. Again, can you translate the value of empowerment into family work?

The role of the instructor is vital in helping the small groups be successful. However, the role is different in that students, rather than the instructor, dominate the learning process. The traditional approach to PBL is that each group is assigned a tutor, which is expensive. However, slight modifications will work. For example, it is possible for the instructor to spend some time in each small group every week. "*The instructors' role was essential to keep the sessions running smoothly and the groups on topic.*" Students tell us that the time spent in small groups was useful, "*I loved when the instructors came into our working groups because we finally benefited from the process instead of just chatting.*"

Students need to develop skills to connect theory with practice. Feedback tells us that the format enabled them to create linkages. One student, for example, told us, "*I liked that we were not sitting in a classroom for three hours listening to someone talk. I think it's much better when you can apply the knowledge in a practical manner.*" Another said, "*I enjoyed being able to practice what I learned that day in class right away.*" Others were happy that they had a chance to practice before seeing a "real" family, relieved that they were not "*thrown to the wolves immediately.*" Rather, they had the opportunity to first understand family dynamics and develop skills first in a safe learning environment. Students were satisfied. "*When the group put the ideas into practice it was great to see that the interventions did work.*"

Learning did not stop at one course. Students transferred knowledge to other settings. For example, one student noted, "*I was able to apply the theory to other classes and other classes I was able to apply to this class. What I learned in this course helped me make connections with other courses in the program and be more independent in my learning in other courses.*" In the process, students take charge of their learning, rather than relying on being fed information by the instructor. They also developed critical thinking skills. One student told us, "*It* (PBL) *forces you to think critically. The individual has to take ownership for learning. What you learn is based on how much you want to put in.*" Another discovered that there was no clear-cut answer to problems, remarking, "*Thinking in other ways was new to me and sometimes challenging. It was difficult to generate a multitude of solutions.*" Some students, whose learning styles were more passive, experienced anxiety in the initial stages of the course. The expectations were new to many and anxiety usually persisted until students became acclimatized to the new andragogical (as opposed to pedagogical) style. Discussing experiences in class was helpful.

We also believe that it is important that students transfer their learning from the classroom to practice. Students verified that learning transfer happened. One student, for example, reported that, "*PBL gave me excellent insight into what families and social workers experience. I enjoyed being able to bring the theory to life and practicing applying it.*"

Our students have been excellent teachers. We have been impressed with their enthusiasm and openness to new learning experiences. They have convinced us that we need to evaluate our teaching, in the same way that we expect students to evaluate their practice. Their feedback suggests to us that PBL is an effective approach to learning. "*I really enjoyed this class and the style. It honestly made learning about the different theories more interesting and fun. Since it made me want to be in class, it really helped facilitate learning. I think more classes should follow this class's lead.*"

The recommended approach in this book is based on our students' feedback. The overarching goal of this book is that the "family" experience learned in the classroom will be reproduced in real family work situations. We thus encourage this approach to learning about family practice. However, this book contains enough in-class structured learning experiences for instructors who do not use a PBL approach.

Understanding PBL

PBL, enhanced with practice and assignments designed to focus learning, is effective in stimulating student-centered learning in a context where students critically analyze problems, yet feel safe doing so. It fits with the values and processes of family work because it capitalizes on the inherent strength and abilities of students to direct their own learning. As a mirror image process, students learn to empower families much in the same way they have been empowered in class.

The seeds of PBL were planted in the early years of medical schools, and later, discovery learning and the development of simulations in the 1960s enriched it (McKeachie, 2002). It is now a recognized teaching method in medical schools across the world. Other professional educational programs are now adapting and implementing PBL in their curricula. This book builds upon the PBL tradition by formalizing it in a family practice class.

Student-centered learning drives PBL and learners actively *construct* knowledge. Learning is the outgrowth of students' actions but classroom structure fosters and deepens it. The central belief of PBL is that learners are motivated to solve problems, and when challenged, will learn what is required to solve a problem successfully (McKeachie, 2002). Thus, students do not go to class to be entertained or to "bank" knowledge (Friere, 1970). Banking information is too static. Instead, learning is fluid and students learn to navigate and work with relevant information and discard that which is irrelevant.

Learning through traditional methods (lecturing, for example) works with a small range of learning styles and is therefore of limited use. In traditional lectures, problems only illustrate theory through case examples. By comparison, in PBL, cases fuel deeper learning wherein students resolve problem situations in small groups. Instead of being a *commodity*, knowledge is a *process* that imparts both information and the *ability* to discover and synthesize information. The crux of our approach to PBL is the application of theory to practice (which, in our example, occurs through family scenarios). An additional benefit is that what students learn in a classroom setting can be more easily transferred to situations outside the classroom.

Transfer of learning is an important goal of professional education. After all, if classroom work is to be relevant, it matters that students use it in practice. While everyone believes in the importance of transfer of learning, there is growing recognition of a "transfer problem" in professional education. One question needs to be asked about learning and the same question can be posed to clients. "How do you make certain that what you have learned in this class (or this program) will be used in other settings?"

Despite the assumption that learners will use the knowledge and skills, research tells us that transfer is "hit and miss." Questions of learning transfer must be addressed in every class. Transfer demands the fluid use of old learning in new situations. Another way to understand transfer is the application of learning in a real work performance. The ability to bridge the gap between training and application contexts is the core of professional education. Classroom learning can include practice skills taught in a situated learning context. Evidence exists that one can 'teach for transfer' in some situations.

Exercise 1.3

Learning Transfer
(In Class)

Transferring learning is central to professional education. Essentially, there are several circumstances in which learning can be transferred: from one setting to another (classroom to practice), from one time to another (after your program has ended), and from one person (client) to another. Reflect back on 5 things you have learned that you think are important to keep and describe *how* you can transfer your learning in each of these circumstances.

Learning's to Keep	How I Made My Learning Transfer

1.

2.

3.

4.

5.

From One Time to Another

1.

2.

3.

4.

5.

From One Person to Another

1.

2.

3.

4.

5.

Process of PBL

Problem-based learning creates optimal conditions to transfer learning from the classroom to practice. Family students can learn both theory and practice in the classroom in a manner that allows then to apply this knowledge in simulations that parallel real life families with problems.

PBL occurs in several stages:

1. Problem identification: Problems form the backbone of student learning. Students must learn about concepts related to the problem and be prepared to go beyond the presenting details. In addition, group members need to develop a clear definition of the problem.

If you decide to use a PBL approach, we recommend breaking students into small groups of approximately 5-6 students. The class might want to decide the best way to break into groups. One method is to cluster groups according to similar interests based on family problems. We recommend that problems be simple. Examples of problems that our students have developed include child welfare concerns, blending issues of a gay/ lesbian family, family illness, or disability. Clustering work groups by problem captures the imagination and motivation of students. Another way to cluster the groups is by student self-selection, but this risks producing social, rather than work groups. Once students create a family, they assume family roles upon which they base weekly role-plays. One member fills the role of family worker.

To derive maximum benefit, problems parallel, as accurately as possible, situations that family workers could encounter in practice. (We have found that the problem evolves as the family sessions progress and as assignments pertinent to special family areas are tackled.) Family demographics such as developmental stages, life circumstances, culture, and social networks need to be spelled. Family members receive a name and a history. Students quickly learn, as they get into their roles and learn theory, that the family problem includes theoretical, philosophical, practice, and ethical issues at the same time. From our experience, these elements naturally arise in the family scenarios.

2. Knowledge building: Family groupings spend the first couple of sessions creating and structuring family dynamics and solidifying their familiarity with the presenting problem. Classroom lectures orient the groups to the learning approach and to theories of family practice. Each week, a new topic is covered and groups base their role-plays on weekly topics. Students are provided with weekly work sheets stemming from the weekly lecture (the exercises in each of these chapters). Once the group defines the problem, they compare and contrast new knowledge with pre-existing knowledge. In addition to classroom lectures, students read outside the classroom. Students reflect on what happened in their role-plays in specially designed assignments. They must be prepared to handle conflicting or ambiguous information because real-life is never clear-cut.

3. Assessment and beginning intervention plans: In the next stage, the PBL group generates an assessment of their family and formulates beginning intervention plans based on their assessments. Each week students are presented with a new issue (e.g., Diversity, Genogram, Ecomap, assessment, intervention issues). Themes are selected based on the theory that students need in the development of family skills. Once students address the issues presented to them, they integrate the problems with what they have discovered and the factors that may help finding a solution. Then, initial solutions are posed based on what has been discovered, making debriefing of the role-play necessary.

4. Specific intervention plans: As the groups are exposed to more theory, they develop detailed intervention plans. What has to be done? How? Who is involved in the solution? When it should happen? Where should the solution be implemented? The group revisits and revises the final solution (and may even generate new problems). The solution should include a course of action and ways to monitor and evaluate it once it has been adopted.

After small group work each week, classroom discussion can be used to consolidate the learning. We find that the different groups are curious about what goes on in the other "families." Usually, we have a short debriefing period in the larger class at the end of each weekly role-play. Students are enthusiastic to introduce themselves and their families to the larger class.

With this approach, learning is embedded within a context as opposed to subject-based learning where learning is dissociated from meaningful contexts. Family work is context-based and so should the learning of it be. Because students work closely with key concepts and come up with practical solutions, the analysis and resolution results in strengthened knowledge and problem-solving skills. Teaching this way requires that learning move beyond fascination with a case to an appreciation of the general principle behind it.

The following exercise is designed to help you pinpoint your learning style as it pertains to PBL and decide what you need to do to develop skills for independent learning. How did you fare? After the exercise we move on to discuss family theory.

Getting Ready for Problem-Based Learning Approach in Your Family Class

Exercise 1.4

Examining Your Learning Style
(In class)

We have used the PBL approach successfully in teaching our family classes for the past several years. However, it is a new form of learning for many students placing new demands on them. In order to benefit fully from what PBL can offer, it is first necessary to reflect on *how* you have learned in the past and what you are used to. The following questions are designed to help you reflect and make plans for a new style of learning:

1. Most of my classes have been: (a) lecture format; (b) independent study (c) passive learning (d) other [describe] ____________________

2. Outside of class: (a) I study less than what I should (b) I study what I have been told to (b) I go beyond what is expected of me; (c) I do not do much work outside the classroom.

3. My preferred way of learning is: ____________________

4. Things that would block my self-directed learning include:
   a.
   b.
   c.
   d.
   e.

5. My feelings about being less reliant on the instructor are: ____________________

6. In the small family groups described above, I can be task-centered, (yes) (no)

7. Explain ____________________

8. My feelings about role-playing ____________________

9. What I think about the PBL approach described in this chapter

____

Family Work and Family Diversity

It is high time we gave up on our traditional concept of family and expanded our very definition of the term (Carter & McGoldrick, 1999).

Typical of most human service programs, students bring a diversity of family backgrounds and experiences to the classroom. Classes might consist of students, either from the past or in the present, from single-parent families, gay/lesbian families, with a sole partner, living with extended family members, mixed racial families, blended families, long distance commuter relationship families, traditional nuclear families, polygamous families, and a range of diverse family structures based upon culture, race and religious backgrounds.

Before getting down to the "nuts and bolts" of family theory, it is important to first appreciate the complexity of the concept "family" both in regards to diversity and in terms of developing a working definition of family. Other types of families include a combination of some or all family types as listed below:

- Interracial (e.g., Black - White)
- Interfaith (e.g., Protestant - Muslim; polygamous)
- Interethnic (e.g., Irish-Chinese)
- Gay & Lesbian (e.g., homosexual/bisexual men and women)
- Adoptive (e.g., where one or more children are adopted legally)
- Foster families (e.g., where one or more children are fostered, either formally or informally)
- Homogeneous families (e.g., with shared characteristics/transracial/physical and/or mental challenges)
- Advanced Reproductive Technology (e.g., in vitro/donor fertilization)
- Intergenerational (e.g., Grandparent)
- Physically/Mentally Challenged (e.g., wheelchair bound/Down's Syndrome)
- Extended Kin (e.g., aunts, uncles, grandparents)
- What have we missed? Families assume so many diverse forms and compositions, the list provided above surely misses some issues. Provide examples of 5 variations that are not included in this list.

1) ____________

2) ____________

3) ____________

4) ____________

5) ____________

Exercise 1.5

Getting Started
(In class)

Students are instructed to read the course outline and formally going over the class format and expectations. Appendix 1.1 (page 305) contains a sample course outline based on a problem-based approach to learning. Note that transfer of learning is an objective embedded in the outline.

Immediately following the discussion of the course outline, it is time to start the "hands on" experiential teaching and learning. Go around the room and ask students to introduce themselves, including describing their family background family (family of origin and/or current family). Other questions to answer might include: (1) how is your family unique; (2) what is special about your family; (3) what embarrasses you most about your family; (4) add your own question for introducing your family. Instructors can include themselves in family introductions.

From this introduction, note the diversity within the room and discuss the range of diverse family structures represented. Make a list of the family structures represented by members of the class. In discussing diversity, it is important to emphasize the diverse family structures that students may encounter in their family worker roles. What were the unique experiences of students living in each diverse family form? How did each family form benefit or disadvantage its members?

List of Family Structures

1.

2.

3.

4.

5.

Exercise 1.6

Definition of Family[1]

(In Class)

Create your own definition for the following terms and then have a group discussion of these definitions:

Nuclear family:

Family of origin:

Family of procreation:

Extended family:

Blended family:

Adoptive family:

Single-parent family:

What is not a family:

Provide a comprehensive, yet succinct definition of family:

Family Defined

The single term for family did not come into existence until the early fifteenth century. The word comes from the Latin word *familia*, which means household (McCown & Johnson, 1993). One current definition of family is: "A family is a social group that may or may not include one or more children (e.g., childless couples), who may or may not have been born in their wedlock (e.g., adopted children, or children by one adult partner of a previous union). The relationship of the adults may or may not have its origin in marriage (e.g., common-law couples); they may or may not occupy the same residence (e.g., commuting couples). The adults may or may not cohabit sexually, and the relationship may or may not involve such socially patterned feelings as love, attraction, piety, and awe" (Eichler, 1988, p. 4). This definition is quite a mouthful! From this definition, which is quite comprehensive, we need to ask, "What is *not* a family?" A more compact working definition of family might be: *Any two or more people who consider themselves a family are a family*!

Exercise 1.7

Your Family Defined

(In Class)

Using your own family, develop a personalized definition of family. How well does this definition fit into the Eichler (1998)? Now define family based on the unit provided by one set of grandparents. Share your definition with the class.

Definition:

The definition of family is also culture-based. For example, the dominant Western Anglo definition identifies the family as a nuclear unit, whereas North American Indian families and many other cultures such as Mexican include an expanded kin network. Asian families focus on ancestors and Italians embrace several generations of extended kin as their family group (McGoldrick & Giordano, 1996).

Practice and Policy Implications of Definition

Why does the definition of "family" matter? Isn't this just an academic exercise? Given the range of possibilities of what is considered a family, devising a comprehensive, yet precise and meaningful definition can be a challenge. The definition has real consequences for people in their daily life.

In fact, many policies and agency services rely on a particular definition of family. For example, to qualify for assistance, people must fit with the definition of family determined by Temporary Assistance to Needy Families (TANF). What kind of unit does not qualify for TANF? Health insurance must have an operational definition of family, as does child protective services, and some family counseling agencies.

Therefore, the services provided by agencies depend upon a particular definition of family. Does a gay/lesbian couple that has adopted or surrogated a child, or formed a unit after the breakup of a heterosexual union with children constitute, a family? A debate has erupted in North America about whether to legally recognize gay/lesbian marriages as marital partners and various states are now legalizing gay/lesbian unions. Many couples have come to Canada from the United States to get married, although when they return home, their respective states refused to acknowledge their unions.

Most family workers would agree that this example is a family, yet the governments of many countries across the world, including the United States, would disagree that including a gay/lesbian couple in the definition of a "family" is acceptable or constitutes a "true" family. What about an adult who has informally agreed to parent a child, without going through formal adoption or fostering procedures? In some countries across the world and among some religious groups, polygamy is practiced and we have had students in our classes from polygamous families. Yet, many governments refuse to recognize them as families and this refusal spills over to social policy. For example, would a place of employment extend health benefits to families where there is more than one wife? Would all agencies offer services to any grouping where its members consider it a family?

Exercise 1.8

Definition of Family
(In Class)

Agency-level definition: Contact five family-serving agencies in your community to obtain their definition of family. Reflect on whom these definitions include as well as exclude. Bring these definitions back to the class and discuss whose interests are being served as well as regulated. What are the practice implications of these definitions? How will each of these definitions benefit or disadvantage clients that you might be working with?

Agency Name and Family Definition

1.

2.

3.

4.

5.

Policy-level definition: Investigate five policies that impact families. They could include, but are not confined to, TANF, health insurance providers, child protection, etc. Bring these definitions back to class and discuss the values behind these definitions. In addition, critically reflect upon what power interests are served through these definitions. Who is advantaged and who is disadvantaged through these definitions?

Policy and Policy Level Definition

1.

2.

3.

4 .

5.

The legal definition of *family* therefore affects service delivery and social policy. Certainly, the definition of family has political implications. However, it must be remembered that definitions are *social constructions* that come from a particular value bias on the part of who is doing the defining. Any definition of family (and many other social phenomena) is determined by those in power who have a special interest in making certain that one definition is imposed and universally accepted. Yet, there are no universal truths. Many single concepts and abstract terms contain enormous political implications. Going back to the word "family" for example, the family has been the focus of a major political battle. Tied into the definition are beliefs about gender roles, sexual orientation, culture, economic issues (e.g., women working), religious values, and so on. If you deconstruct the traditional nuclear family, you can uncover some very interesting value biases.

Some politicians are adamant about "family values." What do family values really mean? Some politicians, for example, criticize the existence of single parent families. Others are bothered that women work outside the home, saying that they take employment away from men. At the same time, single-parent women on welfare have been targeted, claiming that they have children just to increase their benefits. One author suggested finding these women husbands - that would solve the "problem," whatever the problem is. The question can also be asked, "in whose interest is it have children?" In the words of Carter and McGoldrick (1999a), "the backlash forces in our society use code terms such as "family values" to imply that traditional nuclear families are the only valid families" (p. 13).

We encourage you, as a critical and reflective worker, to be skeptical about "facts." The best question to ask when learning new information or reflecting on old information is, "*Whose interest does this definition serve (fact, opinion, policy, etc.)*?" Each definition supports one interest group while disadvantaging others. Family workers are very aware of person-in-environment because they are sensitive to the context in which clients live. Family workers are also aware of how social contexts contribute to or relieve problems. (The person-in-environment or ecological perspective is discussed in more detail in Chapter 7). What is also true is that *knowledge* also develops and is embedded within a particular political, historical, and social context. Where does knowledge come from? *Knowledge is a resource that gives the developer and the owner social power and control.*

Definitions are embedded in *language.* Language is indispensable in family work since it forms the foundation of what and how we communicate. Language both creates images of the world and represents how we see the world. Words are powerful. Yet we seldom stop to reflect on *what* we are saying and *how* we are saying it. It is important to ask how the words we use coincide with what they are intended to describe. Language and observation are related. The relationship is clearest when words describe concrete things: chair, table, car, book, pen, etc. However, it is more difficult to develop such clarity when the concepts are more abstract. Think of more abstract terms: Family - male - female - success - mother - father… .

Besides biases surrounding family structure, society also has biases about family life. Many families receiving assistance from social service agencies are poor, vulnerable, disadvantaged or multiproblem. They are often blamed for their problems and are considered a drag on society, rather than the other way around - that society has failed to help them be the best they can.

Exercise 1.9

Social or Family Problems

(In Class)

Coontz (1996) challenged the belief that family breakup causes social problems. Instead, she argued that the failure of governments to guarantee a quality of life for its citizens is responsible for family breakup by creating stress on families. Take either side of the argument and debate in class.

This is a long way of saying, *how family workers conceptualize a family and its problems matter*. Workers must be open to the many possibilities of what a family is and also be aware of their personal biases. The following exercise is intended to help you go beyond current "accepted" definitions of family and understand the implications for accepting uncritically the definition of family.

Exercise 1.10

Whom to Include in a Definition of Family

(In Class)

Decide whom to include in a definition of *family*. Who should *not* be included in this definition? Include a rationale for whom to include and exclude in this definition. What are the practice and policy implications of your particular definition? Discuss in class.

Write out family definition and rationale for it:

The family is taking on a different face from families of the past. Changes include an increase in single-person households, female-led single parent families, families where there are two wage earners, divorce rate, age at time of the first marriage, an increase in remarriage. People are also now having fewer children today than one or two generations ago. Just because families are different does not mean that they are inferior.

Exercise 1.11

Family Changes

(In class)

The discussion provided above captures only some of the changes families have undergone over the past four decades. What other changes in families can you think of? How have these changes affected the definition of family? What do you think the family of the future will look like? Brainstorm in class.

List other changes

a.

b .

c.

Historical Overview of Family Work

A brief review of the history of family work reveals the deep historical roots that the various professions have in working with families. The earliest family work dates back to the late 1900s, starting in England with the 'friendly visitor' who was the precursor to modern clinical social worker. The friendly visitor primarily focused on helping poor families by going into their homes and offering moral advice. Mary Richmond, the grandmother of clinical social work, created the first school of social work to train social workers. Part of the emphasis was on developing a more scientific way to assess families. At the same time Jane Addams, another key founder of social work, was instrumental in the creation of settlement houses. Settlement houses educated families, and were a precursor to present-day parent training programs.

It was not until the late 1950s that family work moved beyond assessment and advice-giving to therapy. Most of the early work emerged from Palo Alto California with studies of communication patterns within families. Virginia Satir, a social worker had a major impact on family theory and skills. Family therapy became prominent in the 1960s with many different approaches including the Communicative/Experiential approach advocated by Virginia Satir, the Structural approach by Salvador Minuchin, and the Intergenerational approach by Murray Bowen. Other major family therapy approaches include: cognitive behavioral, problem-solving, strategic approaches and more recently, the narrative, solution focused and feminist approaches. Some approaches are discussed in more detail in Chapter 11.

Exercise 1.12

Family Trends
(In Class)

Discuss in class: What kinds of social conditions do today's families face compared with your parents, grandparents and even great grandparents? What are the positive and negative influences now and then? Do the current family forms contribute to social problems or do social problems place too much stress on families? How well does society support families? What do families need today that society is not providing?

Generalist Family Work

The National accrediting body for baccalaureate and master's programs in social work called The Council on Social Work Education (CSWE) in the United States and The Canadian Association of Schools of Social Work (CASSW) in Canada, requires that all bachelor's programs educate their students about *generalist* social work practice. A *generalist* social worker is trained to use the general problem-solving process to assess and intervene in the problems confronting individuals, families, groups, organizations, and communities. A generalist family worker, using a problem-solving approach, may focus directly on working with family members but at the same time is always aware of the larger systems that impact family functioning, both directly and indirectly. These larger systems include: the larger extended family, family friends, work and educational settings, neighborhoods, social agencies, religious institutions, social polices and laws, to name a few and are discussed in greater detail in Chapters 7 and 12.

Exercise 1.13

Beliefs About Families and Family Life

(In Class)

List five values you have about families that may affect your family work (e.g., mothers should not work, divorce laws should be tightened, getting married should be more difficult, anyone who wants to have a child should be licensed, etc.)

Value — Anticipated impact on family work

1.
2.
3.
4.
5.

Propose a solution for what you can do to adjust your biases to make working with families more constructive.

Solution:

Exercise 1.14

Family Functions: Why Do Families Exist

(In Class)

Why do people form family units. List five benefits of families for its members and five benefits for society:

Members — Society

1.

2.

3.

4.

5.

Who benefits? Discuss in small groups and present the responses to the entire class.

General Instructions for Forming Family Problem-Learning Groups

It is important that students understand the rationale and teaching objectives in using the case-based form of PBL. Having explained problem-based learning, students should discuss the format before forming family groups of between five to six students. There are several ways to form a family group and students have different preferences for doing so. Some prefer to form a family based upon a common problem area. Others prefer to group by selecting the members first and then formulating the problem. Sometimes members in the same class have different preferences in how they form their group and group formation can accommodate both preferences.

Once formed, each group invents their "family" and family "problem." We caution students not to use families and related problems too similar to what they have experienced in their personal lives. Students are expected to assume a family role and play out this role within the "family" for the remainder of the term. One person will assume the role of the family worker while other group members assume a different but unique family role.

Several options exist regarding these roles: (1) the first option is for people to remain in the same role for the entire term. The benefit of remaining within the role same role is that students get an in-depth understanding of the nuances of family work from one vantage. If remaining in the same role, it is critical to debrief what it is like for other family members in their role over the term. This will help you to understand the impact of the family work on individual family members. This information is not only necessary for family members. It is also important information for the family worker. (2) Another option is to switch roles *only* if your group is stuck or loses momentum. [Nevertheless, working through being *stuck* is also a valuable learning experience]. Throughout the semester, students can alternate roles within the family group so that all students can experience being the family social worker and various family members. If this is the case, again, debriefing after each family session is still important. (3) The final option is to switch roles within the family group so that all students will have the experience of being a family social worker and a family member. We have tried all three options. One author prefers the first option while the other author prefers the last. Your group needs to settle on a tentative plan at the outset.

Each week, the class meets with the large class at the beginning of the class where they are exposed to foundation concepts and theories of that particular week. In addition, each week, groups will be provided with a standard set of instructions related to weekly themes. During the second part of the class, students break into family groups and role-play based on the theme of the week. If there is only one instructor, s/he briefly goes into each group to facilitate the process, make certain that the groups are on task, and to help with any learning blocks. Longer times can be spent in sessions where groups are stuck.

Every week, but particularly at the beginning of the course, the experience should be briefly discussed before the class breaks into the small groups to deal with any learning blocks. Course assignments capture and formalize the work done in the family groups and include a combination of assessment, intervention, and practice knowledge (Appendix 1.1). At the end of every role-play, the small groups and larger class debrief the experience. At the end of the term, class members should also complete a questionnaire about what the PBL process was like for them (Appendix 1.3).

Debriefing at the end of each role-play is essential. We provide some general guidelines around which debriefing can be structured:

Guidelines for Debriefing

- What was the main part we learned today? How does this learning relate to theory?
- Did the group stay on task? If not, why? What needs to happen in order for the group to improve its focus? How does the group function in terms of group dynamics?
- What can be used in practice?
- What is it like for members to be responsible for their learning?
- What was the experience of individual family members and what contributed to these experiences?

Exercise 1.15

Forming Family Problem-Learning Groups
(PBL Worksheet)

Today the family group will build the foundation for learning over the next term. This will necessitate breaking into family groups of five to six students. Each group will create its own family unit and "problem" using group interest and past experience. In this first week, students will also construct their family composition and start to create details of a family history. One student fills the role of a family worker while other members assume the role of a member of the family.
Before creating the family, it is first necessary to make some ground rules for how you are going to operate over the term. We suggest that the following ground rules be decided upon:

1. Am I prepared to focus on my learning and pledge to the group that I will take this learning seriously? What does this mean in terms of my attendance, cooperation with others, and staying on task?
2. Will our group members stay in the same role throughout the term or will we switch roles? (This ground rule might be re-negotiated at several points in the term)
3. What can we do if someone gets off task in a group?
4. At what point should we call in the instructor to help us get past blocks to our learning?
5. Who will be the timekeeper to ensure that we role-play and then guide the debriefing (about 5-10 minutes in each session)?

In the first week, the group will begin to develop an understanding of the dynamics surrounding the "presenting problem" and the relationship of each family member to this problem. Do not expect that your family will be fully operational by the first week since over the next several weeks, the groups will solidify details and family patterns. In the creation of families, students should focus on the personality development in their role as well as interactions with other family members. They should also develop a unique understanding of what brings the family to this agency. Decide what agency is working with this family.

(continued)

A crucial aspect of generalist family work (and any other types of generalist practice) is working with *patterns*. These patterns appear in many areas of family life such as circular patterns of communication, roles (to be discussed in more detail in Chapter 6), daily behavior, interaction with larger systems, how people solve problems, etc. Generalist family work involves making these patterns explicit and helping people overcome deficits in their social functioning both within and outside the family. You should make note of family deficits, conflicts and *strengths*. If you neglect family strengths, there will be little leverage upon which to create positive solutions with the family.
While the next few classes will focus on patterns, now is the time to get repetitive patterns to gel within your family group. This is a tall order and it will not happen in one session. It is paramount to keep the momentum going, so it is important for students to immerse in the role as much as is realistically possible.

While the family is forming by creating patterns and developing a past, the social worker will not intervene with the family, but will assist in developing content for the role-plays and family issues. The job of the worker is to help to construct the family and help make sense of the family problems within the context of the services of the agency. You will want a good fit between what the family needs and what the agency has to offer. To do so, the family worker must select the most appropriate agency for this family.

Continue this role-play developing the family for approximately 45 minutes. Spend 10 further minutes reflecting the following questions:

1. How does the role I am assuming with the family "feel" to me?
2. How are your personal perspectives of the issues unique to your role?
3. Express your feelings about your family based on the particular role you are assuming.
4. How is help sought for this particular family? Try to develop a sense of what it would be like for this family to seek help.

For the last part of class, the small groups can reconvene with the large group and members briefly describe their family groups and debrief the experience. [2]

Chapter Summary

In this chapter, we explored the necessity of integrating theory and practice. Beginning family workers need to feel comfortable working with families and PBL provides a good structure in which to develop the necessary skills and comfort level before students see their first family. Family workers must be cognizant of the need to transfer learning from the classroom to practice and make plans for how they can do so. These plans can be bolstered through carefully designed classes and critical reflection.

The implications of critically understanding the importance of something as simple as formulating a definition of "family" can help students understand special interests groups in society as well as issues related to power and oppression. These special interest groups determine which family structures will be valued and supported and which family structures will be disregarded or oppressed through laws, agency service foci, or social opinion. Thus, some family units are privileged over others. However, family definitions are merely social constructions, not social facts. Certain family groups benefit from societal beliefs about families.

The next chapter builds upon understanding family diversity. Diversity comes in many forms but we focus on cultural diversity and diversity relating to sexual orientation.

[1] Definitions for family terms can be found in Appendix 1.2

[2] **Note to instructor**: You may not cover all the material and exercises in the chapters within your class time limits. Material can be put over to the next class.

Chapter 2 **Table of Contents**

DIVERSITY

Chapter 2

Diversity

Without our cultures, we simply would not know how to feel.
(Scheper-Hughes, 1992)

Chapter Coverage

- Influence of Cultural Background
- Ways to Become Culturally Competent
- Culturally Based Assumptions
- Culturally Effective Helping
- Gay/Lesbian Families

Introduction

We discuss diversity at the beginning of the book because diversity affects every aspect of family functioning. Minority and immigrant families in North America live in a social context that is often a different world. In addition, they may experience hardships related to living in a harsh and oppressive environment, both in terms of resources and of goodness-of-fit. Families that are different from mainstream society often suffer at the hands of the dominant group, through racism, sexism, heterosexism, and ethnocentrism. Often we measure individuals and families through the standards of the mainstream culture without consideration of the uniqueness of their culture or of the inherent strengths embedded within each cultural group. In an ethnocentric view, that which is merely different becomes "abnormal," "inferior," or "pathological." Cultural biases surface when meeting with a client who may not think, talk, act, or behave like the worker and sometimes we believe that workers need to change families to fit into the system.

The enormous and complex task of understanding diversity is difficult yet necessary. If you cannot speak the language (used figuratively and literally), how can you do the work? Developing multicultural awareness and sensitivity is a necessary task for all helping professionals.

Simply, diversity is the state or quality of being different. However, by labeling diversity as different, we need to ask "Different than what?" We do not want to give the message that diverse families are the "other" because they do not conform to mainstream patterns. What we hope to accomplish is to create awareness of the many dimensions along which families exist. Many kinds of diverse families exist such as culturally diverse families, families diverse in structure and origin such as single parent families, families with adopted children, multicultural families, families that are diverse because of transgenerational issues, families that are diverse due to individual characteristics such as physical/mentally challenges, and diverse families due to sexual orientation. Most of the world's population lives by non-Western perspectives. Nevertheless, most of what we know is based on a North American and Eurocentric approach to teaching, research, and theory. Effective work involves removing our blinders and open up our minds to other possibilities. The current trend toward globalization makes this necessity.

Regardless of how diverse families appear on the surface, they all share certain commonalties. For example, family-of-origin influences all families. Families from an ethnic group share common ancestors and many families bring a unique history based on social and cultural heritage. As the number of immigrants to North America increases, the multicultural face of the continent is changing. In fact, "every family's background is multicultural" (McGoldrick & Giordano, 1996, p. 5). In Chapter 4, we encourage students to construct a cultural Genogram to identify their unique ancestral heritage. Included in this heritage are issues related to shame and pride. A family's cultural history contains unique experiences concerning the pressure of acculturation to a North American context.

Cultural sensitivity and cultural awareness are necessary traits of effective family work. Awareness is a cognitive process through which workers become aware of different cultural expressions. On the other hand, cultural sensitivity is an affective process wherein worker emotions are brought in play in a respectful way (Daughhetee, 2001). Awareness and sensitivity to the diversity of a family strengthens competence. Recognizing both uniqueness and commonalties normalizes the psychosocial stressors placed upon a family. It also alerts workers to the unique views, expressions, and rituals within families that do not fit into the "traditional" family that has pervaded mainstream thinking.

The task of being both sensitive to and aware of differences (and similarities) is daunting. Workers cannot stop at cultural awareness, although this task alone is a tall order. For example, McGoldrick, Giordano, and Pearce (1996), discuss families from over 40 different cultures. They also cite the 1990 Census in the United States identifying 95 racial and ethnic categories. Learning the intricacies of 95 cultures as well as your own would take three lifetimes of study. Many times a culture involves beliefs and behaviors that are taken for granted and not made explicit. These rules are similar to family rules. As such, without making them explicit, people might identify with one or more ethnic or cultural groups, but have little awareness of its intricacies. Thus, it is difficult to have awareness of one's own culture and by extension, developing awareness about other cultures can be a monumental task. Awareness of other cultures is more than just having a checklist of behaviors and beliefs, although this is a start.

Exercise 2.1

Starting a Multicultural Checklist

(In Class)

Select three ethnic groups. Write down five characteristics of each that you are aware of. Share your list with your classmates.

Ethnic Group

1.______________ 2.______________ 3.____________

Characteristics

1.

2.

3.

4.

5.

Cultural sensitivity occurs at a deeper level. It requires awareness of your culture and of the culture of others. Beyond this, you need to understand your biases and prejudices that may interfere with family work, potential sources of feelings of superiority or inferiority, and recognition of how a particular worldview and behavioral patterns block effective understanding of another's world. These shortcomings have dominated family work for many years. For example, without understanding the extended kin and community network of Aboriginal families, child welfare workers entered the homes of Aboriginal peoples and removed their children *en masse*. The Aboriginal parenting style was interpreted as neglect, leading to the cultural genocide of the North American Indian culture (Coleman, Unrau, & Manyfingers, 2001). You are challenged to develop the appropriate level of knowledge, skills, and attitudes that contribute to effective family work with all families.

Developing multicultural competence will help you work more effectively with members of other cultures in several ways. First, it will eliminate potential sources of misunderstanding. When working with families from different cultures, we expect clients to enter our world and play by our rules. We even assume that everyone plays by the same rules: Not only is this *not* the case, it is also unfair and puts our clients at a disadvantage in family work. We cannot assume that everyone knows the rules. Collaboration works best.

Exercise 2.2

Misunderstanding

(In Class)

Recall one interaction with a person from another culture where there has been some misunderstanding. What was the misunderstanding about? How does this misunderstanding highlight different world views?

Rather than expecting families to enter your world, it is up to you to enter theirs. Moreover, understanding the nuances of different cultures will help you develop more accurate assessments and tailor interventions that best match the cultural style of a particular family.

Exercise 2.3

Matching the Cultural Background of Workers and Clients

(In Class)

Most people agree that coming from the same cultural background as clients creates both advantages and disadvantages in the helping process. Make a list of what you consider are advantages and disadvantages of coming from the same cultural background as your client. Once you have made you list, pick a side. Join up with members of the class who share your opinion and debate in class.

Advantages

1.

2.

3.

Disadvantages

1.

2.

3.

Influence of Cultural Background

Thus, an essential task is the development of cultural competence. While such competence requires a lifetime of study and experience, there is no time like the present in which to start. The starting point is to learn to identify, accept, understand, and respect differences through an ongoing self-assessment and continuous accumulation of cultural knowledge (Kilpatrick & Holland, 1999). Family workers need to acknowledge the natural tendency to view situations through their own cultural lens. Once we do this, we can move past biases. At the same time, you will accept that we will probably never fully understand the experiences of another, regardless of whether they are like us or differ by some important characteristic such as culture, sexual orientation, religion and so on. Having acknowledged the differences, the family worker can also acknowledge the commonalties that draw human beings and families together, instead of the differences that create division, discord, and conflict.

Exercise 2.4

Teaching About Your Cultural Background
(In Class)

Identify the key features of your cultural background. Take five minutes to teach your classmates about your cultural heritage.

Key Features:

a.

b.

c.

d.

How are we to understand our culture and the cultures of others? Learning about other cultures is full of dilemmas. If we provide a checklist, we risk perpetuating stereotypes. On the other hand, if we fail to recognize differences (and hence uniqueness) we are in danger of being color- and culture-blind. What if during our self-reflection, we uncover biases and prejudices that need to be challenged and then eliminated through open discussion and receiving a reality check? Are we then labeled racist and will this label stick forever? Alternatively, do we allow an open discussion in the classroom with the potential for hurtful words to be spoken about different groups? We need to create safe classrooms and still allow room to be challenged and learn from being challenged. How do we understand and acknowledge the values of other cultures when these cultures also have values that discriminate against others. For example, we recall one classroom discussion where the topic focused on diversity. The class had acknowledged the importance of respecting multicultural diversity. The discussion then moved onto homosexuality and the same students that expected others to be sensitive to their culture claimed that homosexuality was unacceptable in their culture and that they should not therefore be expected to accept homosexuality. How can we accept cultures that run counter to our own convictions, such as cultures that are patriarchal and which we believe oppress women? It depends, we suppose, on how you want to "slice it."

Exercise 2.5

Debating Cultural Dilemmas
(In Class)

Just because a culture espouses certain values or beliefs does not make them sacrosanct. All cultural practices are not ethical. Every intervention we make is value laden. We must not use notions of neutrality or "deconstruction" to shy away from committing ourselves to the values we believe in. We must have the courage of our convictions, even while realizing that we can never be too certain that our perspective is the "correct" one. This means that we must learn to tolerate ambiguities and continue to question our stance in relation to the position and values of our clients. And we must be especially careful about the power differential if we are part of the dominant group, since the voices of those who are marginalized are harder to hear. The disenfranchised need more support to have their position heard than those who feel they are entitled because theirs are the dominant values.

In addressing racism, we must also deal with the oppression of women of color. This cannot be blamed solely on White society, for patriarchy is deeply embedded in African, Asian, and Latino cultures. We must work for the right of every person to a voice and a sense of safety and belonging. We must challenge those who argue: Let cultural groups "speak for themselves." This ignores the issue of who speaks for their group, which is usually determined by patriarchal and class factors.[1]

Every culture has its own values that conflict. Using the quote from above, select two possible opposing values that might create difficulty for you agreeing with a particular culture (e.g. gender equality versus the right of a culture to be patriarchal). Debate the conflicting values in class (E.g., In order to be cultural sensitive you have to accept a particular cultures patriarchal biases versus no culture is perfect and we should not accept any cultural value that oppresses a certain subgroup).

Perhaps developing multicultural competence is so challenging because culture is embedded in every fiber of living, and contains so many dimensions. However, just because a task is difficult does not mean that it should be avoided. It is beyond the scope of this book to provide a checklist of behaviors and beliefs embedded in every culture. We instead refer you to some excellent resources contained in the bibliography. We also encourage your classmates to play a crucial role in your learning. We will try, however, to point out some of the dimensions with which culture can be understood.

Ethnic identity may be expressed through gender, roles, communication style, and the degree to which family members are expected to separate from other family members. Cultural background also determines patterns of communication and the use of words. For example, a belief in keeping things "private in the family" or how certain subjects are communicated, are passed on from generation to generation. The following table and subsequent discussion points out some of the many dimensions of culture.

Table 2.1

Dimensions of Culture

Cultural identity
Belief systems
Differences between and within groups
World view
History of a culture, including history of colonization
Communicating meaning and the use of language including self-expressiveness
History of migration
Beliefs about family and family structure
Beliefs about children within the family
Family life cycle issues and cultural rituals related to life cycle
Partnering
Kinship bonds
Gender roles
Social values
Religion and spirituality
Sense of community and social supports
Intermarriage
Cultural expressions related to dress, food, music, and the arts
Work and education
Beliefs about social troubles and help-seeking behavior, including the use of indigenous and traditional healing practices
Cultural rules governing social behavior

Let us briefly examine each of these dimensions. Once you have an idea of what these dimensions are, try to apply them to your own culture.

Cultural Identity

While everyone's family identity is multicultural, we still identify ourselves within a particular ethnic or cultural group (McGoldrick & Giordano, 1996). Few cultures are homogeneous and we must recognize subtleties of cultural identity. For example, North American Indians identify most with their tribe or clan (Sutton & Broken Nose, 1996). Cultural identity is strengthened through language and religion.

Exercise 2.6

Ethnic Identity
(In Class)

Most people have multiple ethnic backgrounds. Stop and reflect on the number of different ethnic and cultural ancestors in your background. What group do you most identify with? How does this multiple heritage play out in your present family with yourself and your siblings?

Exercise 2.7

Cultural Beliefs
(In Class)

Identify five beliefs that you have that can be attributed to your culture (e.g., beliefs about family, gender, relationship to the community, etc.). How do the beliefs differ from your classmates? What beliefs could contribute to misunderstanding with other cultures?

Beliefs

1.

2.

3.

4.

5.

Differences Between and Within Groups

We often think that ethnic groups are homogeneous - that every member and subgroup is the same. In fact, ethic groups contain much heterogeneity. Furthermore, we need to dispel the notion that ethnicity only pertains to people of color (Giordano & McGoldrick, 1996). For example, the Latino culture might include Mexicans, Puerto Ricans, Cubans, Dominicans, Central Americans, and South Americans, each with their own unique history and cultural patterns (Garcia-Preto, 1996).

Exercise 2.8

Cultural Heterogeneity
(In Class)

Have two members from the same culture take five minutes each to introduce their culture to the class. Each should prepare and present separately. What similarities and differences stand out?

World View

Geopolitical history greatly influences world view. One model of cultural differences suggests that cultures differ in their relationship with others, their relationship with nature, and their relationship with time. History of invasion and war in country-of-origin, harsh climates, and even political regimes all influence a culture's character. For example, German history shows a country, situated in the middle of Europe, confined to borders, necessitating that people live together within a small area, contributing to a highly structured society (Winawer & Wetzel, 1996). The Irish, too, have been influenced by their geography and history (McGoldrick, 1996) such that they have lived through British domination and oppression, and harsh living conditions, all contributing to adaptability through humor, a rebellious spirit, and courage (p. 545).

Exercise 2.9

Geopolitical Influences on Culture
(In Class)

Pinpoint the country of your ancestors. Then identify the major political and geographical influences from that country and speculate upon their influences on your cultural character.

Country of your ancestors____________________

Political and geographical influences and their influence on your cultural character

a.

b.

c.

d.

History of a Culture, Including History of Colonization

Every culture has a history. Sometimes the history is a source of pride while for others culture is a source of shame. Many cultures have had a history of colonization affecting their beliefs about involvement with a family worker from mainstream culture. Most disturbing is the history of cultural genocide that North American Indians experienced. Other cultures have experienced a history of colonization from the British, French, Spanish, and Dutch, depending upon the location of the home country.

Exercise 2.10

History of Your Culture
(In Class)

Identify some important historical factors and events in your culture's background? How have these events impacted your sense of identity? What are the cultural sources of pride and what are the cultural sources of shame for you? How do these factors contribute to your sense of pride and shame about your culture? How have these events affected your attitude toward cultures with which your culture has encountered in the past?

Historical Factors

a.

b.

c.

d.

Communicating Meaning and the Use of Language

It is through communication that cultural traditions, beliefs, and worldviews are transmitted to younger generations. Communication is an important means of self-expression. Yet, much cross-cultural misunderstanding occurs because meaning is communicated differently through words and nonverbal expressions. McGoldrick and Giordano (1996) identify how some cultures use talk - the Chinese communicate through food, the Irish communicate through poetry or humor, while Italians use communication to convey emotional intensity of an experience. North American Indian families listen and use silence to convey respect (Sutton & Broken Nose, 1996). In Mexican families, communication is indirect, implicit, or covert, fitting well with Mexicans' emphasis on family harmony and getting along (Falicov, 1996). The Irish are good with words, but have a talent for verbal obfuscation through innuendo, ambiguity, and metaphor (McGoldrick, 1996). Their communication is also indirect and the use of "I" is discouraged (p. 176). Communication styles might also differ in a family where the younger generation has learned English faster than parents. In the Anglo culture, constraint, decorum, logic and stoicism is the preferred mode of expression (Giordano & McGoldrick, 1996, p. 428).

We are also familiar with the different greeting customs. In some cultures, hugs and kisses are part of the greeting process, while in others the same type greeting is uncomfortable. Initial family worker impressions of a client's nonverbal behavior should therefore be tentative until the family worker learns more about the personal, social, and cultural background of the client. When unfamiliar with a culture, we recommend admitting this and respectfully asking families to teach you. Not only will this approach show respect and humility, it will also help equalize the relationship between you and your family. One of the best ways to become familiar with another culture is to ask questions that convey an open and honest interest in learning more (Coleman, Unrau, & Manyfingers, 2001). Most clients will appreciate being asked questions about their culture.

Family workers who follow the practices and beliefs of the mainstream culture may not understand when ethnic families communicate in ways that are familiar to them but unfamiliar to you. Through learning about other cultures, family workers must be aware and sensitive to the factors that affect both the verbal and nonverbal behavior. In family social work, we assume that behavior occurs within a family context. Similarly, the patterns of behavior and social expression of a particular family must be placed within a wider cultural context. Personal, familial, cultural, and social background affect the worldview and behaviors of families and their members and need to be factored into the assessment and understanding of nonverbal and verbal behavior. In some cultures (such as the Anglo culture), avoidance of eye contact suggests dishonesty or lack of social skills. In another culture (such as Native American or Puerto Rican women), the same behavior suggests that the person is listening but comes from a culture where eye contact is considered impolite. Similarly, talking face-to-face may be a sign of interest and concern or disrespect, depending on the culture.

Exercise 2.11

Communication Styles: Role-Playing Different Communication Styles.
(In Class)

Break into groups of two. Each member will select one of the following communication styles and initiate a conversation about the weather, lasting for five minutes. These different communication styles include: (1) speaking quickly, minimizing personal body space, and being somewhat aggressive and disregarding the reactions of the listener; (2) speaking very slowly, maximizing personal body space, being submissive, respectful and sensitive to the reactions of the listener; (3) using indirect communication, avoidance of feelings and eye contact; (4) speaking with feelings and being direct.

First, debrief the experience with your partner. Then share your experiences with the rest of the class.

History of Migration

All people in North America except for Native American people have a recent history of migration to North America. Learning about a family's migration experience reveals a lot much about their resources, social class, and aspirations (Bibb & Casimir, 1996). The history of migration brings with it special issues for each ethnic group. For example, it makes a difference if people came to North America willingly versus immigrating due to persecution, war, or capture from the home country (as was the experience of African Americans). The stage of the family life cycle at time of migration also affects the family and migration might add an extra stage to the life cycle of immigrant families (McGoldrick & Giordano, 1996). It can also create role-reversal between parents and children (Lee, 1996). Many immigrants also leave family members behind. Others come with young children who acculturate more quickly than parents, threatening the traditional family hierarchy (p. 17). Adherence to traditional views and behaviors is impacted by social class and length of time since immigration (Almeida, 1996). It is not unusual for new immigrants to remain closely knit with their families and cultural group in the new country. Over time, groups gradually adopt the customs of the new land.

Exercise 2.12

History of Migration
(In Class)

Select one or two branches of your family tree and discuss the reasons for that part of your family coming to North America. How has this history affected your attitudes toward your new country?

Beliefs About Family, Family Structure, and Kinship Bonds

Families are the basic social unit in any society and it is difficult to conceive of any culture in which the family is not a cornerstone. Nevertheless, the expression of "family" varies. As mentioned in Chapter 1, different family structures do not fit into the "traditional" definition of family, and many variations are due to ethnic and cultural differences. Various cultures include extended kin, community, or even ancestors in their concept of family. In the American Indian family, for example, no terms exist for "in-law" and grandparents are central figures in family life (Sutton & Broken Nose, 1996). African Americans also place great emphasis on the family, in part because of homeland traditions, but also because slavery necessitated that the family includes the extended family (Black, 1996). For some, Genograms (Chapter 4) can be complex since not all families conform to bloodlines (Moore Hines & Boyd-Franklin, 1996). Therefore workers must explore who is considered to be a "significant other."

In some cultures, family issues are private and members are reluctant to enter family work for this reason. Family hierarchies are also important to consider, most notably the role of gender and elders. In addition, different emphases are placed on the husband-wife dyad versus the parent-child dyad. In Asian families, the parent-child bond receives the most emphasis (Lee, 1996). By comparison, in Arab families, the most common family structure is patriarchal where "men are given specific duties toward their wives and children, wives are given instruction as to how to treat their husbands, and children are advised to honor their mothers" (Abbudabbeh, 1996, p. 328).

Beliefs About Children and Child Rearing

The meaning and role of children also differ according to culture, as do child rearing practices. Many new immigrants to North America believe in obedience from their children and may discipline them accordingly. One example is in Irish families where children are expected to be seen and not heard, and not be praised too much (Giordano & McGoldrick, 1996). The nature of disciplinary practices also varies from one cultural group to another. In American Indian families, child rearing is laissez faire and elders act as role models through which children learn. Alternatively, other cultures might believe in physical discipline, at times clashing with child abuse legislation. In the German culture, children are raised with structure, limits on spatial exploration, and precise schedules (Winawer & Wetzel, 1996, p. 507). By comparison, Irish child discipline includes ridicule, belittling and shaming (McGoldrick, 1996). In some cultures, male children are preferred over female children.

Exercise 2.13

Child Rearing Practices in Your Family
(In Class)

Describe the beliefs about children and child rearing practices from your family-of-origin? Can you identify any beliefs or child rearing practices that are culturally based?

Beliefs about children and child rearing from family-of-origin

a.

b.

c.

d.

Culturally based beliefs

a.

b.

c.

Family life Cycle Issues and Cultural Rituals Related to Life Cycle

As mentioned, migrating can add an extra stage to the family life cycle. In addition, different life cycle stages are more prominent or expressed differently in some cultures than in others. For example, in the Mexican family, there is a longer period of interdependence between mother and child and a more relaxed attitude about children becoming self-reliant (Falicov, 1996, p. 178). Other cultures, such as the Irish, place great emphasis on death, as we see in wakes.

Partnering

Partnering takes many forms and romantic love is not a universal concept. In the history of slavery, marriage was forbidden (Moore Hines & Boyd Franklin, 1996). Culture also determines dating customs (Mahmoud, 1996). Others might still abide by customs of arranged marriages. Sometimes members marry outside of their religious group and depending on the group, intermarriage may or may not be acceptable. When two people from different cultures marry, the door is open for misunderstanding and the couple must navigate many issues. In addition, biracial children have a unique set of issues with which to contend. Among some groups, such as Arabs, marriage occurs within the same lineage (e.g., cousins) (Abudabbeh, 1996).

Exercise 2.14

Inter-Racial or Inter-Ethnic Marriage
(In Class)

What is the history and/or pattern of intermarriage in your family over the past three generations? How has this affected your cultural identity?

Gender Roles

Gender roles are central to family structure and are largely determined by culture. Many cultures still follow traditional gender roles, a fact that is difficult for those from a feminist tradition to understand. Men and women assume different roles in the family, such as nurturer or disciplinarian such as in Asian families (Lee, 1996). In Muslim families, gender roles also follow a traditional path and the sexes are segregated for most social and religious occasions (Mahmoud, 1996).

Exercise 2.15

Gender Roles
(In Class)

Describe the gender roles in your family. What beliefs about gender are culturally based?

Gender Roles

a.

b.

c

d.

e.

Social Values, Sense of Community, and Social Supports

Basically, orientation to the sense of community exists on a continuum - individualism to communalism. The mainstream American value is that of individualism. Another American value is that people should be independent. Other cultures such as the North American Indian value sharing and community responsibility. The concept of community may lead a family worker to include friends and community members in family work. We need to know about the indigenous support systems of different cultural communities and be prepared to make the appropriate referrals.

Religion and Spirituality

Not long ago, Christianity was the impetus behind many colonizing efforts and one tenet of Christianity was to preach to the unconverted. (This in fact is still a feature of many Christian sects). The role of religion or spirituality plays a large role in the lives of most ethnic groups. Both have been the source of much misunderstanding when viewed from the lens of another group. Religion plays a role in such things as family structure, gender roles, and beliefs about childrearing. In addition, "ethnicity often has a religious character, while religious life may be largely influenced by ethnic customs and rituals" (Giordano & McGoldrick, 1996, p. 435). For example, in many Muslim families, traditional gender roles are the norm (Mahmoud, 1996). Awareness of the importance and value of religion in each family is crucial before working with any cultural group, since interventions must be sensitive and geared toward the particular belief-systems of the family.

Exercise 2.16

Religion
(In Class)

What is your religious background? How connected is your religion to your cultural background? What have our religious teaching taught you about family, gender, and social values?

Cultural Expressions Related to Dress, Food, Music, and the Arts

It is through food and music that many people are first introduced to a new culture and eating at ethnic restaurants is an enjoyable pastime of many North Americans.

Exercise 2.17

Multicultural Day
(In Class)

Have a multicultural potluck lunch in class. Students are instructed to bring in one ethnic food, dress in ethnic attire, and bring in cultural artifacts (e.g., a CD with music from their cultural group).

Work, Education, and Social Class

Cultures place different emphases on work and education. For example, Moore-Hines and Boyd-Franklin (1996) state that African Americans traditionally place great emphasis on work and education. Therefore poor school performance might be the presenting problem in these families. Asian American family's value hard work and unemployment can create intense stress (Lee, 1996). Anglos and Germans typically embrace the work ethic, whereas Italian immigrants have a negative view of upward social mobility (Giordano & McGoldrick, 1996b).

Beliefs About Social Troubles and Help-Seeking Behavior, Including the Use of Indigenous and Traditional Healing Practices

Studies in ethnicity reveal that people differ in:

1. Their experience of emotional pain;
2. What they label as a symptom;
3. How they communicate about their pain or symptoms;
4. Their beliefs about the cause of the difficulties;
5. Their attitudes toward helpers;
6. The intervention they expect (McGoldrick & Giordano, 1996, p. 9).

Therefore, it cannot be assumed that every client holds the same beliefs about receiving help. Moreover, we need to challenge the assumption that formal counseling is more important than informal support systems. Ethnic minority clients may not know what counseling is, how it can help, what to do, or what to expect (Zane, Nagayama Hall, Young, & Nunez, 2004).

Many cultural groups turn first to family and friends before formal helpers and others believe in self-reliance. Alternatively, members of some groups might turn to doctors rather than mental health services. For many, counseling is the last choice. Different cultures bring with them different value orientations and behaviors that affect how they present in family work. For example, in the Native Indian custom, families come to counseling with the expectation that the worker will give them practical and concrete advice (Sutton & Broken Nose, 1996). Alternatively, African American families might think that counseling is for "crazy people" (Moore-Hines and Boyd-Franklin, 1996). Attitude toward family work is also influenced by a certain group's history. For example, in cultures that have experienced a history of oppression or genocide, members would understandably mistrust workers from the oppressive group.

Exercise 2.18

Cultural Expressions of Pain
(In Class)

Reflect upon your multicultural heritage and identify the major cultural/ethnic group(s) that is part of your background. Select an influential person from your family and describe how that person expressed anger, joy, sadness, disappointment, frustration, and emotional pain. How do your observations connect with cultural expressions of pain?

Anger

Joy

Sadness

Disappointment

Frustration

Emotional pain

Attitude toward seeking help

Culture not only affects how people communicate, it also produces unique "noises." For example, ethnicity interacts with economics, race, class, religion, politics, geography, the length of time since migration, a group's specific historical experience, and the degree of discrimination it has experienced (McGoldrick & Giordano, 1996, p. 2). Additionally, the proportion of non-whites who are poor is larger than that of whites (Davis & Proctor, 1989). A biased or prejudiced view might lead some to conclude that these different groups are poor through their own inertia, laziness, or incompetence, and that the solution to their poverty would be to "pull themselves up by their bootstraps." A sensitive understanding would lead one down a path of understanding how prejudice, oppression, exploitation, and even genocide have disadvantaged some groups such that opportunities for self-expression and self-actualization are lacking in a social system dominated by a white heterosexual Anglo socio political system within which only those who subscribe to these mainstream values and behaviors can flourish. Your journey might even lead to the conclusion that many people are enjoying a high quality of life through the toils of people on the bottom of the social rung. This phenomenon is referred to as "the invisible knapsack of privilege" (McGoldrick & Giordano, 1996, p. 15). Think about it.

Exercise 2.19

Taking a Look Around You
(In Class)

The purpose of this exercise is to help you understand how culture structures the world around you. Look at how cultural diversity is manifested around you. Select 10 professions or occupations that you encounter every day, such as sales clerk, doctor, taxi driver, waitress or waiter, politician, etc. Make a list of the ethnic and gender composition in each profession. Compare your findings with those of your classmates. Can you identify any patterns? What are the implications for family work? Share your observations with those of your classmates.

List of professions or occupations and ethnic and gender composition

1.

2.

3.

4.

5.

6.

7.

8.

9.

10.

Exercise 2.20

Family Status
(In Class)

How does ethnicity and culture affect your family in terms of: social status, gender roles, communication patterns, beliefs about family, and role of extended family

Social status

Gender roles

Communication patterns

Beliefs about the meaning of family

Role of extended family

Help-seeking behavior

Relationship to time

Relationships with others

Beliefs about the expression of personal problems

How might some of these behaviors and beliefs be perceived by the mainstream culture?

Ways to Become Culturally Competent

The first step in developing cultural competence is discarding the belief that your way of doing things is the only way. We need to approach learning about other cultures with curiosity and an open mind. We also need to feel comfortable talking to other people about their culture and be prepared to ask questions and listen. It also means discarding ethnocentric beliefs, biases, and prejudices. These are equally important behaviors whether you come from the dominant or a minority culture. We also need to understand culture as a major organizing principle in life and be prepared to adapt our rules and beliefs to accommodate those with whom we are working. Above all, we must start with awareness and make sensitivity our goal. Doing so enables us to challenge unfairness embedded in racism, sexism, elitism, heterosexism and any other differences that can negatively affect the quality of life for anyone.

We also need to understand our impediments against working cross culturally. Language is often a major impediment. Other impediments include holding rigidly onto our cultural values at the expense of learning about other possibilities. We also need to guard against our countertransference such that our prejudices allow us to prejudge or unfairly judge members of other cultural groups. We also must watch for how clients react to our cultural background and be willing to open the door for client-worker exploration of these issues.

Exercise 2.21

Your Cultural Heritage
(In Class)

Break into groups of about four students. Each student will educate other members about his or her own cultural identity and heritage. To do this, go around the room and discuss the following questions as they pertain to each student personally. At the beginning of the session, estimate how long it will take to cover the heritage of everyone in the group. Assign a timekeeper to keep everyone on task.

Describe yourself ethnically and culturally.

Relate who in your family experience influenced your sense of ethnic and cultural identity.

What are the unique cultural practices that you learned from your culture?

Discuss which groups other than your own you think you understand the best.

Explore which characteristics of your cultural group you like most and which you like the least.

Discuss how you think your own family would react to having to go to family therapy and what kind of approach they prefer.

Diversity Issues with Gay/Lesbian Families

Popular culture has historically portrayed lesbians and gay men as denizens of a subculture world divorced from "the family." (Johnson and Colucci, 2004)

In Chapter 1, we referred to the debate of including gay and lesbian families in the definition of family. Johnson and Colucci (2004) contend that lesbians and gays are bicultural and for this reason we include them as a continuance of our discussion on cultural diversity. We believe that gay/lesbian couples should be included in the definition of family, and that partners should be entitled to the same rights and benefits as other families. One definition of gay and lesbian families is a family that includes "… at least one lesbian or gay adult or two or more adults with a same-sex orientation who are rearing a child" (Jordan, Hunter, Rycraft, & Vandiver, 2003, p. 313).

While many of the issues discussed in this book applies to any couple, gay and lesbian families face a unique set of challenges. However, the reactions of society to these families are considerably different. Most states criminalize the sexual behaviors of gay and lesbian people. Social policy also discriminates against these unions such that they are not included in work benefits and health insurance. Their union is not officially or legally recognized. Following this, they have no legal protection or set of socially prescribed rituals to guide them (Johnson & Colucci, 2004, p. 351). The first vignette in the film *If These Walls Could Talk* depicts an older lesbian couple where one woman suffers a stroke and dies. The hospital refused her partner the right to decide about funeral arrangements and the house they had been living in together for years was given to the deceased woman's nephew because he was the closest next-of-kin. The woman left no will and neither the state nor the nephew recognized the relationship.

Gay and lesbian couples not only suffer from social discrimination. They also often encounter conflict with their families when they decide to come out. Nevertheless, the process of coming out is affected by characteristics of their families' such as willingness to allow differentiation of members, the degree of openness or closedness, and management of differences (Johnson & Colucci, 2004, p. 351). The family's response will affect the couple's relationship. The cultural background of the couple also affects behavior and well-being.

Heterosexism exerts unique pressures on gays and lesbians. We know of gays and lesbians who have married heterosexual partners and had children with them. Reasons for marrying are varied but if an individual later decides to come out, s/he and their current family unit encounter a host of challenges. However, gender roles still influence the relationship such that money and power might enter into gay men's relationships, while lesbians strive to equalize that power (Johnson & Colucci, 2004).

For these reasons, the gay and lesbian community has formed closely-knit communities from which they receive support, acceptance, sustenance, and belonging. Nevertheless, these communities might not be structured around children. However, just as we cannot assume that members of the same cultural group are homogeneous, neither can we assume that every gay or lesbian family is the same. Therefore, when working with gay and lesbian families, the worker needs to inquire about relationships with one another, with the gay community, and with the community-at-large. While gay and lesbian couples are vulnerable to the same relationship challenges as heterosexual couples, they also face many more ecological challenges, not the least of which is heterosexism (Jordan, Hunter, Rycraft, & Vandiver, 2003). The lack of social acceptance and support from families and others creates additional stress.

If a couple decides to have children, other difficulties can arise. The first issue is how to conceive, but with modern reproductive technologies, many options are available. Adoption is another possibility, but this option may be limited because of state laws. If they do have children, they encounter difficulties receiving validation. Gay men and lesbians might also bring to their relationship children from a previous heterosexual union. Nonetheless, one parent in a gay/lesbian relationship is not biologically related to the child, blurring roles (Johnson & Colucci, 2004; Jordan, Hunter, Rycraft, & Vandiver, 2003).

While the life cycle format applies to gay men and lesbians, the life cycle must be modified for them (Slater, 1995, cited in Johnson & Colucci, 2004, pp. 347-348). The reasons for this are five-fold. First, parenting is not the *raison d'etre* of homosexual family life. Second, the definition of family usually revolves around blood and legal ties, which clearly does not exist for these families. Third, the family life cycle models suggest that a function of intergenerational relationships revolves around the transmission of norms, rituals, and values from generation to generation. Fourth, family rituals often punctuate key life passages within a family. Fifth, language fails to capture some of the key aspects of lesbian and gay life (e.g., in-law).

Exercise 2.22

Gay and Lesbian Families

(In Class)

Just as you might have biases and prejudices against different cultural groups, you might also have prejudices against gay and lesbian families. In this exercise, you should reflect on what these prejudices are. You may have brought prejudices from your cultural or religious background. Decide whether you believe that gay and lesbian couples should receive the same social benefits of heterosexual couples. Assume the opposite side of your argument and debate in class.

List Prejudices

1.

2.

3.

Exercise 2.23

Ethnicity and Families
(PBL Worksheet)

Today you are going to spend time in the PBL group dealing with the family's cultural identity and heritage. The worker will assume the role of a worker who wants to understand the family's culture better. To do this, go around the room and discuss the following questions as they pertain to the family. At the beginning of the session, estimate how long it will take to cover the heritage of everyone in the group. Assign a timekeeper to keep everyone on task.

Describe the family ethnically and culturally.

Relate who in your family experience influenced your sense of ethnic and cultural identity
Discuss which groups other than your own you think you understand the best
Explore which characteristics of your cultural group you like most and which you like the least

Discuss how you think your own family would react to having to go to family therapy and what kind of approach they prefer

After your group has done this part of the exercise, and if there is time, process what you have all learned about the family's culture and how the family's issues and work interacts with its ethnic identity. How does this identity affect the family work you are doing with this family.

Chapter Summary

In this chapter, we looked at the influence of diversity on family life. You are challenged to develop cultural awareness and cultural sensitivity for your future family worker role. While cultures are heterogeneous, cultures share commonalities based upon a number of dimensions. Some argue that gay/lesbian families have a unique culture. Cultural competence is a demanding task for family workers, but is needed in order to work cross culturally.

[1] McGoldrick, M., & Giordano, J. (1996). Overview: Ethnicity and family therapy. In M. McGoldrick, J Giordano & J. Pearce (Eds.). Ethnicity and family therapy (pp. 1-30). New York: Guildford Press.

Chapter 3 **Table of Contents**

STARTING WORK WITH THE FAMILY

Chapter 3

Starting Work with the Family

Anticipation is the best defense.
(Karl Menninger)

Chapter Coverage

- Preparing for the Family Interview
- Empowerment
- Starting the Family Interview
- Engagement
- Stages of Change
- Basic Interviewing Skills
- Principles of Effective Communication

Introduction

In this chapter, we outline concrete steps to help you get started with your family interview. We emphasize the importance of trying to gain the cooperation of the entire family unit. We also encourage you to prepare for the family interview by developing a basic understanding of the family and by getting ready emotionally and conceptually for the tasks that lie ahead. Empowerment is the central message that you need to convey to every family member, although it can be tricky.

Family members may not be at the same place in the first family interview, complicating contracting and goal setting. With ongoing practice and by using interviewing and communication skills, you are taking the first step in creating change in the family.

Steps in conducting the first interview:

1. Mental preparation
   a. role of theory
   b. reading previous case notes
   c. deciding who to involve in the first interview
   d. scheduling the first meeting
2. Introductions
   a. setting the stage: conveying the purpose of the agency, your role, setting the stage for what you can do
   b. starting to join with family members
3. Gathering information
   a. finding out family beliefs about the problem
   b. exploring the family's expectations
   c. listening and observing
   d. asking questions
   e. structured assessment
4. Problem identification and goal setting
5. Contracting

Preparing for an Interview Before the Interview

New family workers often feel anxious about seeing their first, second and even third family. Common concerns include, "What should I do?" and "How should I proceed?" Workers feel compelled to "do something" and hope that the "something" they do will be effective and even impressive. In the words of Alfred Kadushin (1997):

To know is to be prepared; to be prepared is to experience reduced anxiety; to reduce anxiety is to increase the interviewer's freedom to be fully responsive to the interviewee.

Family work begins before the first meeting. We agree that planning and reflection at the outset will help you feel at ease and free to be fully responsive to the family. Family work is demanding and without both physical and mental alertness, opportunities will be lost. However, because families operate according to established patterns, if you miss one opportunity, others will later emerge.

Several tasks confront the family worker *before* the first family contact. Preparation takes many forms but much is mental. First, family workers must be equipped with theory about family dynamics, as well as interviewing skills and self-awareness. Theory will sharpen the focus and guide the work. Two aspects of theory need to be considered: general knowledge about family dynamics and knowledge about a specific problem area. Family workers must also be equipped with concrete tools such as a referral form, an agency mandate, family rooms, and even play equipment. The referral form will contain basic information about the family, such as presenting problem, referral source, and who is in the family. If the family has been at the agency previously, case notes will be available. The presenting problem in the referral form will shed light on what theory to brush up on before the interview. File notes by other workers about the history and problems, as well as what interventions were tried can be useful. Nevertheless, workers new to a family still need to formulate their own opinions. In the words of one expert, families "do not write their own stories. Once they enter the institutional network and a case history is opened, society does the editing" (Minuchin, Colapinto, & Minuchin, 1998, p. 23).

Exercise 3.1

Using Existing Case Notes

(In Class)

Write the pros and the cons of relying on existing cases notes before seeing a family. How would using these notes impact your work? Compare your answers with your classmates.

Pro's | Con's

One of the initial challenges is getting every family member to show up for the first interview. The worker conveys expectations about attendance usually by telephone. You are at a disadvantage because the telephone only allows one-on-one contact, and the person at the other end must be able and willing to rally other family members to come to the first interview. One way of conveying this message is to say, "My agency's philosophy is that families are important in treatment and we expect every family member to be present for at least the first interview." Can you think of other possible lines? What could be some reasons for family members to not attend the first interview? How can you address each of these reasons?

Exercise 3.2

Gaining Full Family Participation

(In Class)

Gaining full family participation for the first interview can be difficult. Write down some possible reasons why different family members might refuse to come in for the first family meeting. What could the worker do to address these reasons?

Reason | Worker Responses

Worker self-awareness is another essential of family worker skill. This entails the worker reflecting on his or her personal family experience to sort out biases and personal baggage. These life experiences will no doubt come into play in family work. Sometimes, they contribute to *countertransference* (when the client reminds the client of someone or issue in their own lives), which plays a role in how you engage with individual family members and deal with the issues. For example, if the worker grew up in a family troubled by substance abuse, the experience can affect how the worker approaches similar family situations. The worker might think that s/he has found the perfect solution in such situations, but it is important to remember that every family is unique. Having experienced a similar issue is both a curse and a blessing. Self-awareness can help you understand when your "buttons are being pushed" and remove blind spots that interfere with family work. To deal with "blind spots" and buttons, we advise talking this over with your supervisor and/or a therapist.

Exercise 3.3

Blind Spots and Buttons
(In Class)

The purpose of this exercise is to help you identify your blind spots and buttons. Try to visualize your family-of-origin (remembering that no family is perfect). What were the predominant characteristics and issues of your family? For some, your family might appear quite "normal." If this is the case, exaggerate the issues to an extent that if they were severe, they would have made the family seek help. For others, the history of family issues might be more apparent:

If you were to give your family a "Presenting Problem," what would this problem be?

If you speculated on the origin and dynamics of this problem, where would you place it?

Who would be the most likely person in the family who manifested this problem?

How has this issue affected you in terms of your beliefs about families and family work?

What do you need to do to develop a more neutral view of the issue?

Exercise 3.4

Help or Hindrance?
(In Class)

One longstanding debate in the helping professions is whether someone who has experienced a particular life issue (e.g., sexual abuse, drug dependence) is in a better position to help a client with similar issues than a helper who has not had such experiences. List the pros and cons of having had the same difficulty as the client. Pick a side and debate in class.

Pro's	Con's

Physical Setting

A family interview can take place anywhere - in the family's home (the kitchen, the living room), in an institution (at the bedside, the family worker's office), or in a community agency (in an interviewing room or an office).

If the family worker defines an interview as the process through which a range of information, including basic demographic data, family history, social history, and critical family incidents, is gained and worked with, then some settings are more appropriate for an interview than others. In selecting the setting, family workers need to consider the advantages and disadvantages of each possibility. You should be flexible in selecting settings that are appropriate for the purpose of the interview, meet the needs of family members, and matches the mandate of your agency.

Exercise 3.5

Home Versus Office Setting
(In Class)

Family workers can see families in many different settings. Each setting has both benefits and drawbacks, both to the worker and the family. List the advantages/disadvantages of family interviews in the home compared to an office setting.

Home-Based Interview		Office-Interview	
Advantages	Disadvantages	Advantages	Disadvantages

Setting Up an Interviewing Room

If you are interviewing a family in a home (see Chapter 10), setting up the interviewing room is less within your control as it is within the control of the family. Yet it is important to encourage the family to meet with few distractions, for example, away from the TV or at least with the television turned off.

In an office, it is also important to be aware of the set up. Are toys available for young children? Are there enough chairs with sizes appropriate to the family members? Do you want to arrange chairs in a particular order, perhaps for videotaping? Is it important where you sit as a family worker? Some family workers believe that where they sit is important (sometimes out of safety concerns) and 'protect' their chair by placing a book on it. Others believe that where they sit is less of an issue than where family members sit. In fact, allowing family members to choose where to sit will yield useful information about family dynamics.

The Stone Family

The following case, the Stone family, is used throughout the book to highlight issues being presented. Many of the exercises refer to this family. More information about this case is presented in appropriate chapters. However to get started this is the information you have received initially about the family:

CASE 3.1

The Stone Family

You are a family worker with Juvenile Court and have received a referral to see the Stone family. The referral form states that 15-year old Michael has been in trouble with the law recently. This is his first offense. He was charged and convicted with beating a homeless man and videotaping it for a website. He is the oldest child in a family of two children. His sister Mary is two years younger and has had no difficulties and does well in school. His mother Linda and stepfather John have been married for 6 years. Michael's biological father is not on the scene and Michael does not remember him. Your role is to continue seeing the family, first for an assessment. The court has ordered ongoing family work for the Stone family.

Exercise 3.6

First Meeting
(In Class)

Break into small groups and role-play greeting the Stone family described above. One student will assume the role of family worker. The group is to imagine the family coming to you where they enter an imaginary waiting room. Starting from the waiting room, the worker is to bring the family to a family interviewing room and get ready to start the family session. This session will continue for approximately ten minutes. The group should appoint a recorder to take verbatim notes.

After the role-play, in a large group, describe precisely how each worker introduced him or herself, to whom, first, second and so on. Did introductions occur in the waiting room to each family member, or family as a whole? Did they talk to the family on the way to the interviewing room, to whom? Did they do a general introduction in the waiting room and individual introductions in the interviewing room? To whom did they introduce themselves first? How did they start the actual interview? Did they explain the room set up? Did they explain their role, the purpose of the interview? How did they now proceed? All of these issues are discussed below.

Exercise 3.7

Family Interview Materials
(In Class)

Create a list of materials that you could use in a family interview. Break down the materials used for the various ages of family members. Beside each item provide a rationale or purpose for why you would include it. Compile a list based on the input from the entire class. (Adapted from Collins, Jordan & Coleman, 1999)

Family Members	Materials Used
Infant -	
Toddler -	
Pre-schooler -	
Public school child -	
Pre-teen -	
Young adolescent -	
Older adolescent -	
Parent -	
Family as a whole -	

Empowerment: Introductions

Introductions contain subtle messages. The message that we are most concerned with is that of *empowerment.* Empowerment opens the door for clients to have control over their lives; the power of members to share their ideas; the power to be valued as important; the power to own thoughts, feelings and behaviors. Empowerment fits with research suggesting that collaboration and feelings of affirmation relate to positive outcomes (Orlinsky, Ronnestad, & Willutzki, 2004). Thus, the message that workers need to convey is that the family-worker relationship is a partnership. Remember that, "the first contact with the agency establishes the tone of everything that follows, and consequently is crucial" (Minuchin, Colapinto, & Minuchin, 1998, p. 68).

Let us move onto the initial contact with the family in the waiting room. While there is no right or wrong way to introduce yourself, you have choices. You need to be mindful of these options and the implications of selecting one over another. It is crucial to be *intentional* in your decisions. *In fact, one way of viewing the helping process is that it is simply a series of decisions*. Enhanced awareness, knowledge, and skills enable you to make better decisions.

We suggest that when families are in a waiting room, a general introduction is most appropriate. "Is this the Stone family? Would you please follow me to the interviewing room?" We might avoid initiating small talk on the way to the interviewing room unless directly spoken to and then we would answer briefly. One of the authors had the experience of commenting on the weather and having a client become very agitated in the hallway because of the foul weather. Similarly, a question to a client about finding a convenient parking space elicited swearing in the hallway about how difficult it was to find a parking spot at our clinic. I have learned the hard way to avoid small talk!

Upon entering the interviewing room, the formal introduction and engagement process begins. You could spend a couple of minutes settling the family, but the longer this lasts, the more difficult it is to get down to work. Now reflect back on the Stone family consisting of a father, mother, teenaged son, and teenage daughter. The family was referred to you because of problems presented by the son. Think about whom first to introduce yourself, and the implications of the options available. You have *five* choices: 1) father, 2) mother, 3) son, 4) daughter, and 5) the family as a whole. In considering these options, let us look at how empowerment might play out with this family.

If you take a traditional family perspective, you would introduce yourself to the father first, momentarily empowering him. In this case, you are subtly conveying that you acknowledge his status in the family. This is where introductions get tricky because while you are empowering the father, you are also disempowering other family members! On the other hand, fathers are sometimes reluctant to participate in family work and it may be strategic at the outset to engage him by first empowering him and trying to gain his commitment to family work. Moreover, many cultures follow a traditional view of fathers as the "head" of a household.

On the other hand, if you take a feminist view, you might introduce yourself to the mother first, acknowledging her importance and believing in the empowerment of women. Since mothers often initiate referrals to family work, recognizing her first acknowledges the family member who seems most concerned about what is happening. However, the flipside is that she may be the one feeling most responsible and guilty for family problems. Mothers are often blamed for "family problems." In the words of one feminist therapist: "Mothers are the switchboard of the family" (Goldner, 1985b). By introducing yourself to her first, you may be inadvertently implying that you consider her role as central in the development of the problem. At the same time, you might momentarily disempower other family members, and if this was a "traditional" family, you may be alienating the father 'right off the bat'!

If your approach is child-focused, you might introduce yourself first to the teenager. You may believe this person is the target of the family's anger and blame and needs positive affirmation. You might wonder if Michael's difficulties are the result of his role within the family or you could have questions about if Michael's behavior contributed to the family difficulties. At this moment, you are unaware of the details behind his issues. Your intent is simply to 'connect with' this young person and convey that someone is supportive and willing to listen. Again, this tact may backfire because the teen may feel that your introduction to him first points a finger at him and makes him the focus of more unwanted attention.

Another other option is to start introductions with the daughter, who has not been identified (yet!) as a problem. You note that the daughter has no known problems, is a good student, and is younger than Michael. Can you foresee any difficulties in starting with Mary?

Exercise 3.8

Implications for Mary

Discuss the implications of starting introductions with Mary first. What are the advantages? Disadvantages? Share your opinions with the rest of the class.

Advantages	Disadvantages

An alternative introduction is to the family as a whole, letting family members introduce themselves. For example, "Hello, my name is Mary Richmond and I am the family worker. I'd like to meet everyone one in the family. Who would like to go first?" You then wait to see who takes the initiative. Through this invitation, you empower the entire family unit and allow the group to reveal its typical way of interaction. Approaching introductions this way provides valuable information because you observe who jumps in and takes control, who first, and how individual family members are introduced. However, even this approach has a price. Families who come for counseling have problems and problematic ways of relating. Do you want to validate these problematic ways of relating? Is not the purpose of family work to change their problematic family patterns to helpful family patterns? Maybe you want to 'shake up' existing family patterns from moment one, not empower them. We suggest waiting to do so until you know more about this family.

A final choice is to start with the youngest child and work up by chronological age. Using this example, we first introduce ourselves to the daughter, the son, the mother, and finally, the father (assuming he is the oldest). By introducing yourself to the youngest first, you are taking a child-centered approach, empowering the youngest member. You want to convey the message that even the thoughts, feelings, and behaviors of the youngest person are valued. Of course, you are again momentarily disempowering other family members and need to weigh the cost. The primary task at this stage is to ensure that each family member receives equal airtime and respect, enabling them to talk, express their views about family dynamics, and relate what brought them into the agency.

This discussion needs further emphasis. Because empowerment issues are subtle, you could use any of these introductions. Each approach has a unique impact on the family. The most important thing is that whatever choice you make, it needs to be conscious, factoring in the potential benefits and costs. We recognize that with so many pitfalls about something as simple as introductions, students might feel paralyzed. (That is why we are advocating an experiential problem-based learning approach so you can experience these issues first and then critically reflect upon them in your small group before you see your first family. You need to make mistakes in a safe environment and sort through the issues.)

Starting the Family Interview

After the initial introduction, instrumental issues need to be addressed. These instrumental issues include:

- your role
- the length of the interview
- the purpose of the first interview
- required paper work
- if the interview is being observed or taped as well as the consent forms
- billing information
- issues related to confidentiality

Family members should also be asked if they have questions or concerns. Once these issues have been clarified, the next step is to move into the formal assessment and problem solving processes. In the section below, we explain the next stage of the interview, finding a starting line.

Families come to counseling for assistance in dealing with specific problems. These problems cause distress, hurt, and human suffering. It would be unusual for every member to not be distressed about a particular issue, but show it in a unique way. A problem focus differs from issues around unresolved feelings (a psychodynamic family model), changing oppressive life stories (a narrative model), dealing with low self esteem (a communicative model), or dealing with oppression (a feminist model). While it well may be that all of these issues will be addressed in the work ahead, initially we start with a focus on the presenting problem.

Thus, the first line after introductions might be:

"What concerns or problems have brought you here for help?"

— or —

"I am very interested in hearing about the issues that you are coming here for. Where would you like to start?"

Exercise 3.9

Other Starting Lines
(In Class)

Write down five possible lines to get the first interview started. Once you have completed this exercise, share your responses with the rest of the class.

1.

2.

3.

4.

5.

Useful responses from the class:

1.

2.

3.

4.

5.

As with introductions, you must decide how to start. The first line should concern what each person perceives as the reason why the family is there. All of the caveats presented in the previous section apply here. Regardless of which family member you start with, it is important to eventually allow each family member a voice. Therefore, do not stop at getting <u>one</u> person's opinion. Move onto the next person and get his or her opinion, until you have asked every family member. Remember that at this early stage, some family members might feel intimidated about speaking openly and honestly. Asking this question or similar questions to the entire family gives you useful assessment information. Noting who takes the lead, for example, provides cues about family dynamics. Do the parents speak for the children, or does everyone have the autonomy to speak for himself or herself? How do the perceptions of the "problem" or other family issues differ among family members? How do family members handle disagreement? Is one family member blamed or scapegoated? These observations are the first step in making sense of this complex group of people. Remember that this initial conversation with a family is exploratory. The family has yet to commit to work, they have not decided whether they trust you, or even whether they think they have a problem that you can help them with.

Once each family member has offered an opinion about the problem, we recommend that you next find common ground among the various family opinions. Moving the problem away from the "person with the problem" and finding common ground will further the process. It will take the "heat" off the "person with the problem" and show empathy with family members who are distressed at their family's troubles. For example, you might say, "Mother, I hear you say …, Father, I hear you say, Michael, I hear you say … and Mary, you seem to be saying ….I can see how what is going on in your family is very upsetting to *all* of you. I would like to explore more about your family issues so *we* can work together and help make *everyone* feel better about what is going on." A first step in engaging the family is acknowledging anger and/or their pain. Notice how this summary bridges the divergent views of family members and unites them in a common concern, without blaming one person.

Some members might be guarded about showing anger and pain. It is at this time that some family members might express reluctance about participating in family work in the future. They might say something like, "I don't know what this has to do with me. Michael made his own bed, let him lie in it." First, you need to decide whether this person's involvement is necessary. Often it is. Then you can respond conveying that, "You are a very important person in Michael's life and we need your input. Without your involvement, helping Michael will be very difficult."

Exercise 3.10

Getting Family Member Support
(In Class)

In Exercise 3.2 (pg. 55), we asked you to come up with reasons why family members would not attend the first interview. Now imagine a situation where a family member might be reluctant to *continue* with family work after the first session. Write down reasons for this reluctance and beside the reason, provide a response that you can give in return. Share your answers with the rest of the class.

Reason for the Reluctance	Possible Worker Response

Exercise 3.11

Introducing the Purpose
(In Class)

Compile a list of five possible opening statements that you can use to introduce the purpose of family work. Share your list with the class.

1.

2.

3.

4.

5.

Engagement

Engagement involves the formation of a working relationship. The working relationship is important in any culture, although its qualities will depend upon the family's unique cultural and individual characteristics.

Engagement starts at the first moment of contact. During engagement, a beginning relationship characterized by trust, respect, warmth, acceptance, and human wisdom (Lambert & Ogles, 2004) develops between the family worker and family members. The family's perception of the worker's credibility and other qualities is particularly critical since a positive relationship will determine the role investment of family members in the work (Orlinsky, Ronnestad, & Willutzki, 2004). First impressions also give the family worker and family members the opportunity to check out one another. While the family worker should be sensitive to the particular cultural aspects of family dynamics, *ideally* the entire family should be present for the first interview. Engagement is so vital because *negative* change (i.e., deterioration) is associated with lack of empathy, underestimation of client problem severity, and negative countertransference (Lambert & Ogles, 2004). It is the *client's* perception of empathy, not the worker's, that is most meaningful (Orlinsky, Ronnestad, & Willutzki, 2004).

Exercise 3.12

Who Can I Open Up To?
(In Class)

Imagine the biggest secret you have - one that you have never told anyone, one that you would never tell in public or one that is just too embarrassing to talk about. Write this secret down on a piece of paper. (As you do this, you will not know what is to become of your secret and how it is going to be used.[1]) Reflect on what would make a family have difficulty telling you their secret. Then, answer the following questions:

Why have I not told anyone my secret?

What do I need from someone else to talk about this secret with him or her?

What conditions need to exist in order for this secret to be told?

What qualities must this other person have?

What are your feelings about telling this stranger your secret?

What must happen (concretely) before you would be prepared to talk to this stranger about your family secret?

Now that you have answered these questions, share your answer to the six questions with the rest of the class. No, you do not have to tell your secret. Now answer the following questions:

What are the implications of your answer for working with intimate family difficulties?

What characteristics and behaviors will you need to bring to the family in order to work with their issues?

[1]Adapted from Collins, Jordan, & Coleman, 1999.

(Tear up this piece of paper at the conclusion of the exercise.)

Engagement occurs when opinions are being shaped - the worker forms opinions about the family and the family forms opinions about the worker. Rapport building occurs in this initial phase, and it is through rapport that perceived barriers begin to disappear. These barriers stem from preexisting ideas, reservations, and reluctances that the family and the family worker have about each other and the helping process. The quality of the relationship with the family is the foundation of family work and it develops through rapport. Rapport is the vehicle through which understanding grows and develops. Mutual understanding enables the family worker and family to relax and focus on the necessary tasks.

Engagement is neither time-limited nor static. It is contingent on the individuals involved and on the evolution of the relationship. Engagement also depends on the nature of the issues within the context of the family. Thus, the urgency of need drives engagement process. The particular agency may control the pacing and policies governing intervention are important elements in working with families. For example, in shelters for domestic violence or child welfare, work must be initiated immediately and progress rapidly. In family preservation programs, agency philosophy determines the window of intervention. (These programs are brief but intense.) In addition, funding issues dictate how long the family worker may work with a particular family.

Another aspect of engagement is the establishment of ground rules. The clarity of these rules paves the way for future focused work. Understanding rules also bolsters the investment of each member in entering into the ongoing relationship. Mutual understanding equalizes the partnership, removing some of the authoritative tone. Congruent with the belief about mutuality, the family worker and the family jointly determine the essentials of their relationship together.

Exercise 3.13

Ground Rules
(In Class)

Make a list of ground rules that should form the foundation of family work, both for the worker and family. Discuss in class.

List of Ground Rules

a.

b.

c.

d.

New family workers often want a concrete formula telling them what to say and do in specific situations. There are no recipes and while we often teach students to "start where the client is," we blend this adage with "start where the worker is" (Hartman & Laird, 1983), because many things determine how engagement will unfold. The family worker represents a particular agency mandate. The worker also brings to an interview, knowledge, skills, personal experience, and authority with which to carry out his or her role combined with self-awareness and awareness of purpose. Included in this awareness is the worker's ability to self-reflect critically. Families, on the other hand, bring to the agency a motivation level, unique perspective about their issues, and varying abilities to do the work.

Therefore, the family first has to agree that a particular problem requires family intervention. Beginning workers often proceed as though all family members believe the same thing about these issues and that they are invested equally in change. However, each family member starts at a unique place. The family must also connect with an agency for assistance and how they came to the agency affects the course of work. Finally, the agency must decide whether the family's problem fits its mandate. Each factor affects family work. Sometimes, the court mandates a family's initial contact with the agency. Even though the family begins as involuntary clients, with skill family workers can get the family to commit to the work. We discuss involuntary clients in more detail later in this chapter.

Assessment starts during engagement and can only unfold in an atmosphere in which people feel safe. We recall the impressions of one student who was learning counseling for the first time. She was startled about the intrusiveness of working so intimately with people. We recommend that you take her observations to heart and remember, that, as with sharing your secret (in Exercise 3.12), you are walking on sacred client territory and respect will go a long way in allowing the family sufficient space and safety in which to work through their difficult and painful issues.

During the early stages of work, you take a neutral stance without confronting anyone too early or making premature interpretations until you have a stronger sense of what are the issues and contributing dynamics (Collins, Jordan, & Coleman, 1999). (Families accept confrontation better when the relationship is firmly established.) Minuchin (1974) labels the early phase "joining" wherein you connect with each famiy member and the family as a whole. Of course, workers must use common sense because in high-risk situations, such as violence, quick action must be taken. On the other hand, neutrality must not be perceived as condoning unacceptable behaviors. Through joining, the social distance between the family worker and family decreases. Others refer to the importance of the *therapeutic alliance* and advise that the quality of this relationship is fundamental to positive change (Clarkin & Levy, 2004). The quality of the relationship is crucial to *each* family member for without a strong relationship, the work will not be accomplished. A strong relationship is indispensable in working with ethnic minority and low-income clients (Clarkin & Levy, 2004; Minuchin, Colapinto & Minuchin, 1998).

Exercise 3.14

Confidentiality

(In Class)

Role-play with another student a discussion of confidentiality with a family. What information are you obligated to pass on? Can you guarantee *absolute confidentiality*? Will your supervisor, teacher, or peers be privy to the work that you will be doing with the family? Discuss in large class. How would you handle information that one person wants to remain confidential but affects the rest of the family?

Exercise 3.15

Catastrophic Expectations

(In Class)

Most workers have "catastrophic expectations" about the worst that can happen during a family interview. What kinds of situations would cause you the greatest amount of anxiety during a family situation? Devise two possible responses for responding to these situations.

Write a list of potential situations from a first family interview that would be difficult for you to deal with. Share your list with your classmates.

Situation	Responses
1.	1. 2.
2.	1. 2.
3.	1. 2.
4.	1. 2.
5.	1. 2.

Exercise 3.16

Focusing on the Client

(In Class)

Think of a particular person and problem you have had difficulty dealing with in the past. First, describe the difficulty then list some things you could do to establish rapport with this person. What are some ways that you could show this person that you are focusing on them, rather than on yourself?

Difficulty	Establishing Rapport	Focusing Words

The Next Step: Problem Identification

During early work, the family worker gathers information to clarify family issues and problems. Obtaining this information sows the seeds for assessment of family dynamics. However, it is important to develop a framework within which to understand family functioning. Dynamics might include communication patterns, family power hierarchies, and closeness of relationships. Without a framework, observations will be disjointed and senseless. Interviewing will no doubt uncover the complexity of this particular family. As families join with the family worker, all will learn about family functioning and develop deeper insight.

Throughout work, family members learn from each other. As Satir once suggested, "The family is the main learning context for individual behavior, thoughts, and feelings" (1990, p. 35). Family members continue this vital learning process as they become better able to see and understand family dynamics that previously eluded them. It is only when the once obscure and invisible areas become explicit that the issues can be openly addressed. Consequently, family interaction sheds light on the issues causing distress. With this information flushed into the open, the family worker can direct the family to focus on key issues. The family worker must listen attentively. Listening is a skill that enables the family worker to direct family members to pinpoint and unify concerns.

Finally, the worker has the responsibility of ensuring equal participation of each family member, conveying the message that everyone is respected equally. The family worker has the difficult task of ensuring that the interview is balanced to prevent family members from feeling that they are not respected, that their views are insignificant, or that they will be in trouble for their opinions outside the family work.

Six Steps to Engagement

Engagement can be accomplished in six steps:

1. Connect with every family member one at a time

Remember empowerment. It is important initially to balance your questions and talk time equally with all family members. For example, if you ask one family member to talk about their work or schooling, you should also ask other family members the same or a similar question.

> **Example:** *I have just spent a few minutes asking Mary about her school, her likes and dislikes, I would now like to ask you Michael about your school.*

2. Acknowledge individual family members perception of the problem

It is important to ask all family members what they perceive to be concerns in the family. Once the varied perceptions have been solicited, the worker can list the different perceptions of the concerns or problems. At this point, it is common for every family member see the problem from a unique vantage and you might wonder if you will ever get the family to see eye-to-eye. This makes the next step very important, although it is a bit trickier.

> **Example:** *A number of problems have been identified by this family, including Michael's hostile behavior to a homeless person, Mother feeling depressed a lot, Dad feeling overwhelmed yet not overly involved with the family. Do you all agree with this list and are there other problems or concerns?*

3. Connect the problem to show its relationship to every family member

You need to define problems in a way that connects the problem with every family member (see Chapters 5 and 6 for further detail). This is where you frame the issue as a family problem, rather than blaming one person. Often, "the problem" is that all family members are upset about what is going on and would like to improve the situation for themselves and others.

> **Example:** *I sense a connection of these problems. This family all seems overwhelmed and worried right now as well as not sure what to do. You all are reacting in different ways, mom being depressed, Michael angry, Dad and Mary overwhelmed yet distant. You all are hurting and yet I believe by being here want to help all of yourselves to be a better family.*

4. Start to create goals that include the entire family unit.

This involves the process of discussing with the family what they would like to see changed. These wishes form the basis for establishing goals and clarifying what needs to happen to accomplish them. Beginning workers are often idealistic about goals and it is important to be realistic. For example, it is probably not realistic to believe that a single course of family work will inoculate a family forever from future problems (Lambert & Ogles, 2004). At the same time, it is important not to be so pessimistic that goals undershoot a family's capabilities. It is reasonable to expect that, with focus and hard work, families will reach their goals and maintain their gains after the work has ended.

> **Example:** *What would it look like if this family were working better together? How would everyone change?*

5. Develop a preliminary intervention plan and initiate a tentative contract

Listing these goals verbally precedes the development of formal contract. Contracts with families cover four issues:

- Treatment context - where and when the work is to take place;
- Treatment modality - form of work such as individual or family work as well as the theoretical approach;
- Timing - how long each session should be and how long the overall work will be (dosage);
- Compensation - payment for the worker (Orlinsky, Ronnestad, & Willutzki, 2004).

Essentially, a contract entails making explicit the "business" of the work. Many of these contractual issues are spelled out, in large part, by the worker's agency. Once the parameters of intervention set by the agency are made explicit, the contract is further informed by the needs of the family and the abilities of the worker. A contract demands that the worker and client agree on problem priorities and when clients are involuntary, the working agreement with the client should be different than the one provided by the agency mandate (Ivanoff, Blythe, & Tripodi, 1994).

> **Example:** *Let us now see if we can all come to an agreement on what we would like to see changed in this family, including how long we think it will take. One common issue raised is that this family is overwhelmed with feelings. Would you agree to look at how family members express their feelings and develop supportive ways to help each other?*

6. Clarify family expectations

Because people from different groups and cultures have different expectations about the helping process its is important at this point to clarify what the family expects to happen. This can include a discussion of family and worker roles.

> **Example:** *I would like to ask you how do you see me be most helpful to you, that is, what role would you like me to play in helping this family?*

Stages of Change and Involuntary Clients

Family work can be challenging because family members often have different perceptions about why they are seeing a family worker, what they think needs to be done about the "problem," and how prepared members are to do something to create that change. Moreover, there might be motivational incongruence between the worker and client. The Transtheoretical approach sheds light on how change unfolds (Prochaska, 1995). It is a particularly useful model for understanding the complexities of family change and how individuals within the same family might be in different places in the change process. Members may believe that another family member needs to change his or her behavior but not themselves.

The stage of change that clients are in is an important focus. For example, research suggests that the factor that most consistently predicts outcome is client willingness and ability to become actively involved in the change process (Clarkin & Levy, 2004). Stage-related variables are powerful predictors of successful termination (Prochaska, DiClemente & Norcross, 1992). While their initial work was in the field of addictions (smoking cessation), the Stages of Change process has now been applied to a wide range of problems.

The stages of change are described in more detail in the following section.

Basically, change unfolds over the following six stages (Prochaska, 1995):

1. Precontemplation
2. Contemplation
3. Preparation
4. Action
5. Maintenance
6. Termination

1. ***Precontemplation Stage:*** When a person has no intention of changing or might be unaware that there is a problem or think that the problem belongs to someone else. Others may have told them that they have a problem and that they should change, but at this stage, have no intention of doing so. The metaphor used by Miller, Duncan and Hubble (1997) is that the worker has not been invited into the client's house. If you were to put yourself in the client's shoes, what would need to happen for you to let the worker enter? People close to them have more awareness of the issues than they do. When people in this stage enter counseling, it is because others have pressured them to do so. The same is true when the problem is in the family. One member of the family often presents with a problem and others exert pressure to go for help. Sometimes all family members point fingers at each other or at one person but assume no personal responsibility. This is often the case when there is a substance abuse problem in the family. In the case of the Stone family, whom do you think recognizes the problem" Who would you think denies there is a problem? Who would be most resistant to recognize or modify the problem?

The goal is not to make clients change (even if you could). Your goal is to create a climate in which clients can consider, explore, and appreciate the pros or cons of admitting to the problem. Workers who are eager for change often get frustrated at this point and label people as resistant. Yet, people in this stage process less information about their problems, spend less time in self-reflection, have fewer emotional responses to the negative aspects of their problems, and fail to shift attention in the direction of overcoming their problems. Needless to say, cooperation is strongly related to positive outcome (Orlinksy, Ronnestad & Willutzki, 2004). The worker, at the entrance, needs to be friendly, engaging, and not overbearing. "It isn't that they can't see the solution. It is that they can't see the problem" (Prochaska & Norcross, 2003, p. 519).

Involuntary clients pose unique challenges in the Stages of Change Process. They may be involuntary through a court order. They may also be involuntary because of extreme pressure placed on them by family members. When clients are involuntary, workers should expect that they resent and resist being forced into counseling. They might respond with hostility and noncompliance (Ivanoff, Blythe, & Tripodi, 1994).

2. ***Contemplation Stage***: People begin to see that a problem exists and are thinking seriously about changing but have not yet committed to do so. Clients use words such as, "Yes...but!!" In addition, they may have only partially formulated a goal and how to reach it, and are uncertain about whether to make the necessary sacrifices. It is possible to be stuck here for a long time. The worker needs to believe that "Patience is a virtue" because the client can jump between the first and second stages. Listening, nudging, friendliness and empathy are more helpful than nagging, blaming, or arguing (Miller, Hubble, & Duncan, 1997). As with the first stage, the worker should be supportive and allow the client to explore issues without pressure. Above all, we recommend empathizing with the client. "I can understand why you would not want to make any drastic changes at this point in time."

3. ***Preparation***: Occurs when there is an intention and attempt at change, however weak. The client is making plans to change in the future. Clients may try on some behaviors that move them toward change to see how they fit. Rapport and good feelings grow and the therapeutic alliance strengthens allowing workers to help clients select goals and map out possible routes. Clients need to be active in choosing a change strategy because clients will better commit to action when it is their choice.

4. ***Action:*** Occurs when an individual takes concrete steps moving toward the goal that the client has formulated. People outside of the problem might start to notice changes. Individuals are in the action stage if they have successfully altered a problem behavior for between one day and six months (Prochaska & Norcross, 2003, p. 521).

5. ***Maintenance***: Where clients consolidate gains and plan relapse prevention. Maintenance is an important phase of change and we believe that workers often overlook it. Family workers need to ask, "What is success?" and "How do you know whether the work you have done has been effective?" These are two important questions since much research on intervention effectiveness and many agencies do not follow up after termination. Maintenance parallels student learning - teachers often ask how long students will remember what they have learned in the classroom? Unless students prepare to remember and transfer their learning outside the classroom, quite likely, little follows the student.

Part of maintenance is relapse prevention. Relapse prevention addresses the question, "What strategies can the family use to prevent falling back to problems behaviors?" For some, relapse is the rule rather than the exception. When relapse occurs, people feel embarrassed, shame, and guilt. It is important to help clients anticipate challenges that might spark relapse. The worker can help the family design plans for relapse prevention and determine what steps to take if relapse should occur.

6. ***Termination***: Occurs when the person is no longer tempted to engage in the problem behavior and feels confident and capable of not engaging in the problem behavior regardless of the situation or the provocation. Termination might be the ideal rather than the real.

Workers are often unaware that their families may not be as ready to change as they hope and many times clients are less eager to change their lives than workers. Accordingly, it is important to be realistic about client readiness for change. As you are seeing in your family role-play, it is important to make a mental note of where each individual family member is in the change process.

Exercise 3.17

Assessing What Stage of Change Individual Family Members Are In
(In Class)

Reflect on the individual family members in your PBL role-play family. What stage of change is each member in? What impact does this have on the family as a whole? Compare your answers with the rest of your group.

Member's Stage of Change	Impact
A	
B	
C	
D	
E	

Family Work Skills

Before discussing skills needed by family workers, we would like to make a few points. The first is that many factors contribute to success. These factors transcend the technical aspects of the work. Second, the characteristics of clients and workers (stages of change, personal resources, etc.) are important determinants of success. Finally, the relationship between the worker and the family, characterized by empathy and warmth are important, but alone are insufficient in creating change (Orlinsky, Ronnestad, & Willutzki, 2004). We would be remiss if the process was reduced to simple, technical, theoretical, or personal qualities. In the words of one adult who was abused as a childhood, "Theories only take you so far. I lived in constant fear and no theory and no worker can ever understand what I experienced as a kid." Nevertheless, work without thoughtful attention to the technical, and the theoretical, in tandem with the personal characteristics of the key players enhances effectiveness. Family work, as with all other kinds of helping, involves what the worker does in relation to what the client *perceives* is done.

Family workers need a combination of *conceptual* and *executive* (i.e., practical) skills. The conceptual skills are the map, the framework, the ability to understand behavior within a broader family and social context. Conceptual skills are like having a map in front of you that tells you about the terrain, direction and location of family problems. Practical skills give you the vehicle with which to arrive at the destination. These skills are like having a workable car and a valid driver's license. To accomplish the end, you cannot have one without the other.

Most interviewing courses focus on individuals. Some skills necessary for interviewing individuals are the same, but are used somewhat differently. The skills will be useful in accomplishing the tasks of family work The worker also demonstrates new behaviors to the family members. In addition to individual interviewing skills, basic interviewing skills necessary for family social work include:

- Listen carefully to family meanings that emerge from the shared understanding of family members.
- Be attuned to verbal and nonverbal communication. Sometimes communication is incongruent, indirect or masked, leaving room for misunderstanding;
- Be attuned to effective problem-solving;
- Promote family awareness and skills related to the conditions that contribute to effective family coping.
- Recognizing that every family member plays a single instrument, but together the family is an orchestra!

Making the Relationship Professional

The following rules can assist you to establish a professional working relationship with families (adapted from Kadushin & Kadushin, 1997):

- An interview is deliberate.

Example: *The purpose of today's interview is for us to get a better understanding of the issues being faced by this family.*

- The content of an interview connects with an explicit purpose.

Example: *I would like to get a better understanding of how this family functions (questions now asked guided by the Family Categories Schema* (Chapter 6).

- The family worker assumes responsibility for the content and direction of the interview.

> **Example:** *At this point I would like to discuss....*

- Relationships are structured (have rules) and time-limited (an explicit beginning, middle, and end).

> **Example:** *We only have ten minutes left today so I would like to summarize what we have talked about today and make plans until we see each other next.*

Effective Communication

The interview occurs within the embrace a special relationship in which every behavior contains a message. Therefore, all worker messages are deliberate. The worker helps the family learn deliberate communication as well. Communication takes place between the family worker and the family, and between family members. Communication can be quite complicated, and "You cannot *not* communicate." (Collins, Jordan Coleman, 1999)

Communication involves speaking with words and bodies (includes facial expressions, gestures, posture, and tone of voice).

Effective Communication is Clear, Direct, and Honest.

- Communication is clear where it is not masked. The communicator says what s/he means.

  Masked communication:

> **Example:** *I am feeling that men do not know how to raise children (A thought not a feeling).*

  Clear Communication:

> **Example:** *I am feeling frustrated as my husband is not home enough to support me.*

- Direct communication is sent toward the person to whom the message was intended. (Indirect messages fail to convey personal responsibility and avoids the expression of true feelings.)

  Indirect communication:

Example: *I just do not know what to do with Michael. He is just not helping out (When the key problem is lack of support from spouse John).*

Direct Communication:

Example: *I am angry with you John because you withdraw from me, instead of supporting me.*

- Honest communication conveys a message that accurately reflects the sender's thoughts, feelings, and behaviors.

Dishonest communication:

Example: *Nothing is the matter with me (Said with a scowl on Linda's face while she slams a door).*

Honest Communication:

Example: *I am angry with you right now for leaving a mess in the kitchen.*

The worker must model clear, honest and direct communication and help family members do likewise. The worker can use the words used by clients as the worker enters the client's world.

Core Conditions

Empathy, warmth, and genuineness (Lambert & Ogles, 2004; Miller, Duncan, & Hubble, 1997) are at the heart of effective helping. In tandem, these qualities establish a climate of trust and safety in which family members can begin to view their problems with new eyes.

According to some, almost 30 percent of change occurs through the quality of the worker-client relationship, whereas, theory and technique contribute only about 15 percent to change. Strong alliances occur when families see the worker as warm, trustworthy, nonjudgmental, empathetic, and honest (Miller, Duncan, & Hubble, 1997).

Empathy

Through empathy, the family worker shows the family that s/he understands client experiences, behaviors, and feelings *from the client's point of view*. Empathy must exist to allow relationships and rapport to grow. Empathy in family work can be tricky because being empathic with one person may be inadvertently discounting another member's feelings.

Example: *In cases where there has been sexual abuse of one of the children, family members may see empathy as agreeing with the excuses, denials, projections, and rationalizations offered by the perpetrator. However, agreeing with any of these puts the worker in conflict with the need to empathize with the victim. Empathy in this situation does not mean agreeing with the perpetrator. Rather, it could mean empathizing with the discomfort, embarrassment, or guilt of the perpetrator. Family workers "start where the client is," even when the client's perspective eventually needs to be challenged. It should be remembered that some ethnic groups do not focus on feelings directly and the worker must find culturally specific ways of seeing the world through another's eyes.*

Reflection of Feelings

Reflection of feelings is a concrete way of being empathic. Clients may be unaware of their feelings until they are made explicit. Validating feelings shows that the family worker is listening. Metaphorically, reflection of feelings is a mirror reflecting both content and affect. An accurate reflection can help clients sort out buried or mixed emotions and make the true underlying affect of one family member clearer to other members. Feelings are shown both verbally and nonverbally, necessitating that the worker look for incongruence between verbal and nonverbal expression (Collins, Jordan, & Coleman, 1999).

Example: *I see the tear in your eye and can sense the hurt you are now feeling.*

A client might verbally express comfort in the interview, but at the same time, the worker might observe nonverbal signs of discomfort such as a scowl or a rigid, closed posture. While reflections help build rapport and trust, some clients may be uncomfortable talking about feelings. For example, some people use intellectualization as a defense. It is important to vary the sentence stems used and to draw from a diverse range of feelings and words.

Example: *I hear what you are saying but wondering what you are feeling?*

Warmth

Warmth is the next core condition. It shows caring and acceptance. Worker warmth conveys worker acceptance, understanding, and interest. Through worker warmth, family members start to feel safe in the interview. Warmth gives life to the techniques that you use and gives the impression that people come first. Warmth is more than saying "I accept and care for you," and is shown verbally and nonverbally.

Example: *It is very difficult when you feel alone and there is no one there for you. I will be there for you and will help your family be there for you. Or I can hear the depth of your sadness. (A caring tone of voice is imperative)*

Genuineness

Genuineness refers to the honesty and congruency of the worker's behavior in terms of feelings and beliefs with the family. Genuineness is also sincerity, honesty, and unpretentious (Barker, 1995). Workers who are genuine are described as "down to earth."

Example: *I am momentarily stumped, yet with your help I am sure we will figure a way out of this issue.*

Exercise 3.18

Core Conditions
(In Class)

Provide examples of each of the following core conditions. For each core condition, try to create a response that conveys a good response using empathy, warmth, and genuineness.

Use the following statement to respond to: *I woke up this morning and thought, what's the use? Nothing is going right for me. The boss is on my case all the time, but I think it's her problem. I'm not enjoying my job one bit because of the politics and the hassles. Then I bring it home to my wife and kids. I don't know what's going to happen to us if I keep blowing up at them. It isn't even their fault.*

Empathy:

Warmth:

Genuineness:

Exercise 3.19

Feelings
(In Class)

Make as complete a list as possible of possible feeling words that can be used in empathic statements with adults and children.

Adult List

Child List

Exercise 3.20

Starting an Interview
(PBL Worksheet)

Today, you will formally begin to work with your PBL family in your first meeting. Start interviewing the family, progressing from introductions through to engagement and contracting. The family group will continue to build the foundation of their family group and adding to the details of a family history and interaction patterns. The group will also start to develop a beginning understanding of the dynamics surrounding the "presenting problem." You will spend the next several weeks solidifying details and family patterns.

A critical aspect of family work (and any other type of social work practice) is working with set *patterns.* These patterns are revealed in many areas of family life such as circular patterns of communication, roles, daily behavior, transactions, how people solve problems, etc. Much of family work involves making these patterns explicit, helping the family see the patterns and the role the patterns play in family difficulties, and helping people overcome deficits in their social functioning both within and outside the family. You will make note of deficits, conflicts and *strengths*. If you neglect developing family strengths, there will be no leverage upon which to work with the family.

While much of this class will be examining patterns based on the issues presented in the previous statement, now is the time to get these repetitive patterns to gel within your family group. This is a tall order and it will not happen in one session. It is important to keep the momentum going, so try to immerse yourself in the role as much as is realistically possible.

At this point, the worker will not do any intervention with the family. The job of the worker is to help to construct the family and help make sense of the family problems within the context of the services of the agency. In other words, you will want a good fit between what the family needs and what the agency has to offer.

The task today is to deal with the following issues:
Introductions of <u>all</u> family members involved, including the worker.
Articulate how <u>each</u> family member views:

- The family problem,
- What is causing the problem,
- The problem's impact on other family members, and
- What can be done to change the problem?

Checklist

- ✓ Make contact with every family member to make each feel special and unique.
- ✓ Get perceptions of all family members. Try to understand the subjective family experience.
- ✓ Clarify the problem, and avoid blaming and scapegoating.
- ✓ The family does not have to believe at this point that the source of the problem is the family dynamics. It is more important that the family understand how the problem affects them, their well-being, and their stress level.
- ✓ Develop a preliminary contract with the family - include in this contract the number of family meetings, who should attend, when the meetings will take place, and how they will know when things get better.

(continued)

- ✓ You will learn <u>how</u> to create changes in the family later; so do not feel pressure to change right now.
- ✓ The worker's job is to help the family understand why the family should work on the problem, rather than just the "Identified Patient."
- ✓ The worker must start to build a relationship with the family and its members

Continue your role-play for 45 minutes. Spend 10 minutes answering the following questions:

1. How does the role I am assuming with the family "feel" to me?
2. How are your personal perspectives of the issues unique to your role?
3. Express your feelings about your family based on the particular role you are assuming.
4. How is help sought for this particular family? Try to develop a sense of what it would be like for this family to seek help.

Chapter Summary

Family work involves a series of decision-making steps on the art of the worker. The family worker makes important decisions even before the first family contact. Each decision carries with it implications for members of the family. In the first interview, you must engage with every family member, listen to the unique perspective of each, and frame the family issue in such a way that the whole family can relate. Skills of working with families are more complex than those used in working with individuals. Nevertheless, the principles of effective communication must be employed.

Chapter 4 **Table of Contents**

THE GENOGRAM

Chapter 4

The Genogram

The family life has a history of its own. It is not what it happens to be at some particular moment or "in reference to some particular act," but it is what it is "on the whole."
(Mary Richmond, 1917-1964)

Chapter Coverage

- The Genogram
- Drawing a Genogram
- Incorporating Culture into the Genogram

Introduction

In this chapter we discuss the Genogram and how it can be used to engage and assess families. Genograms are required by many agencies. They use symbols to show the family constellation, intergenerational patterns, family structure, relationships, and important family events. They can help families understand repetitive patterns that appear in their families.

We build upon the work accomplished in the engagement phase and move to the next phase - assessment. An accurate assessment of the family situation will make your intervention focused and purposeful. Assessment involves making sense of how the family functions internally and externally. While a theoretical framework guides assessment, with greater exposure to more theories, workers recognize the limitations of each and move on to others (Patterson, Williams, Grauf-Grounds & Chamow, 1998). Many workers therefore start out by being generalist and then end up using an eclectic approach once exposed to the strengths and limitations of the theories.

During assessment, you observe and make sense of information provided by the family. In the earliest stages, the assessment is a "snapshot," but with ongoing contact with the family, the assessment becomes a "videotape" where assessment of here and now processes is possible. Assessment is a fluid process that continues throughout the work as the worker obtains and processes more and more information. Because assessment is ongoing, workers are advised to be open to other possibilities and not set their initial impressions in concrete. Initial impressions are only hypotheses and hunches to be tested and discarded if disproved.

It is through comprehensive assessment that an enormous amount of family information is placed within a structure that gives the information a meaning. The purpose of this chapter is to provide you with one framework in which to place this information and help understand the meaning of what you have discovered. Without structure, you would be overwhelmed with the mass of seemingly disjointed information you discover. Assessment allows the family worker to formulate a hypothesis about the family. Working with the family in a collaborative journey creates a partnership and it is not sufficient for only the worker to understand what is happening. As active participants, families can learn what to look for and how to make sense of where their discoveries take them. Understanding is a first step in change. Worker openness will aid relationship building and decrease suspicions about what the family worker is thinking. Developing the ability to order and place the information within a meaningful context is a crucial step in assisting families, and enables the worker to remain focused and give a clearer direction to all family members.

The *Genogram* is often the first tool used in assessment and is done by mapping family structures to depict family relationships and family history visually. The *Genogram* originated from early family systems thinking developed by Murray Bowen. His original instrument was based on the belief that family history repeats itself from generation to generation, referred to as the *multigenerational transmission of family patterns* (Bowen, 1978). Genograms also assess current levels of family functioning, generate hypotheses about family issues, and increase client awareness (Daughhetee, 2001).

The Genogram

Assessment tools serve several purposes: (1) to provide information about client functioning, (2) to help clients to understand client and family functioning, (3) discuss client problems, and (4) set client goals in a focused and structured way. Many family-serving agencies now require the use of a *Genogram* and it is standard fare in many family case files. Information in a *Genogram* should connect with the family's current functioning and generate hypotheses about where problems originate. Mapping them with the family is a good way of strengthening rapport. Through its use, family history becomes alive and members begin to understand themselves and their relationships in a different light. It also conveys a clear message that the work is specific and focused. McGoldrick and Gerson (1985) refer to the patterns as horizontal (the present family) and vertical (multigenerational) understanding. It also highlights important events in family history (e.g. births, marriages, separations, and deaths), relationship issues, intergenerational patterns, underlying belief systems and other family issues that need to be addressed. Other assessment tools usually supplement the *Genogram*, notably the *Ecomap* (See Chapter 7). The amount of material included in a Genogram depends on worker role and agency requirements. Graphics should include enough detail to show the family's complexity but be simple enough that it can be easily understood.

Reflecting back on our definition of "family," a *Genogram* captures who the family believes should be included in a particular family. Family members find that being active participants in *Genogram* construction is informative as they gain insight into family patterns and interactions.

How to Draw a Genogram

No universally accepted method of *Genogram* construction is available despite its universal use (See for example, Hartman & Laird, 1983; McGoldrick & Gerson, 1985; Wright & Leahey, 1994) although commonalities do exist. *Genogram* creation occurs in five stages: (1) engaging the family, (2) mapping family structure, (3) recording family information, (4) delineating family relationships, and (5) interpreting patterns. Nevertheless, there is basic agreement about what information should be included and how to record and interpret it. Genograms usually encompass three generations (i.e., grandparents, parents, and children), it is important to plan spacing ahead of time. Symbols are used because essential information is represented through shorthand. Some agencies have their own system of symbols, although most adhere to the typical standard symbols. Below are examples of the more common symbols contained in a *Genogram*:

Figure 4.1

Common Symbols for a Genogram

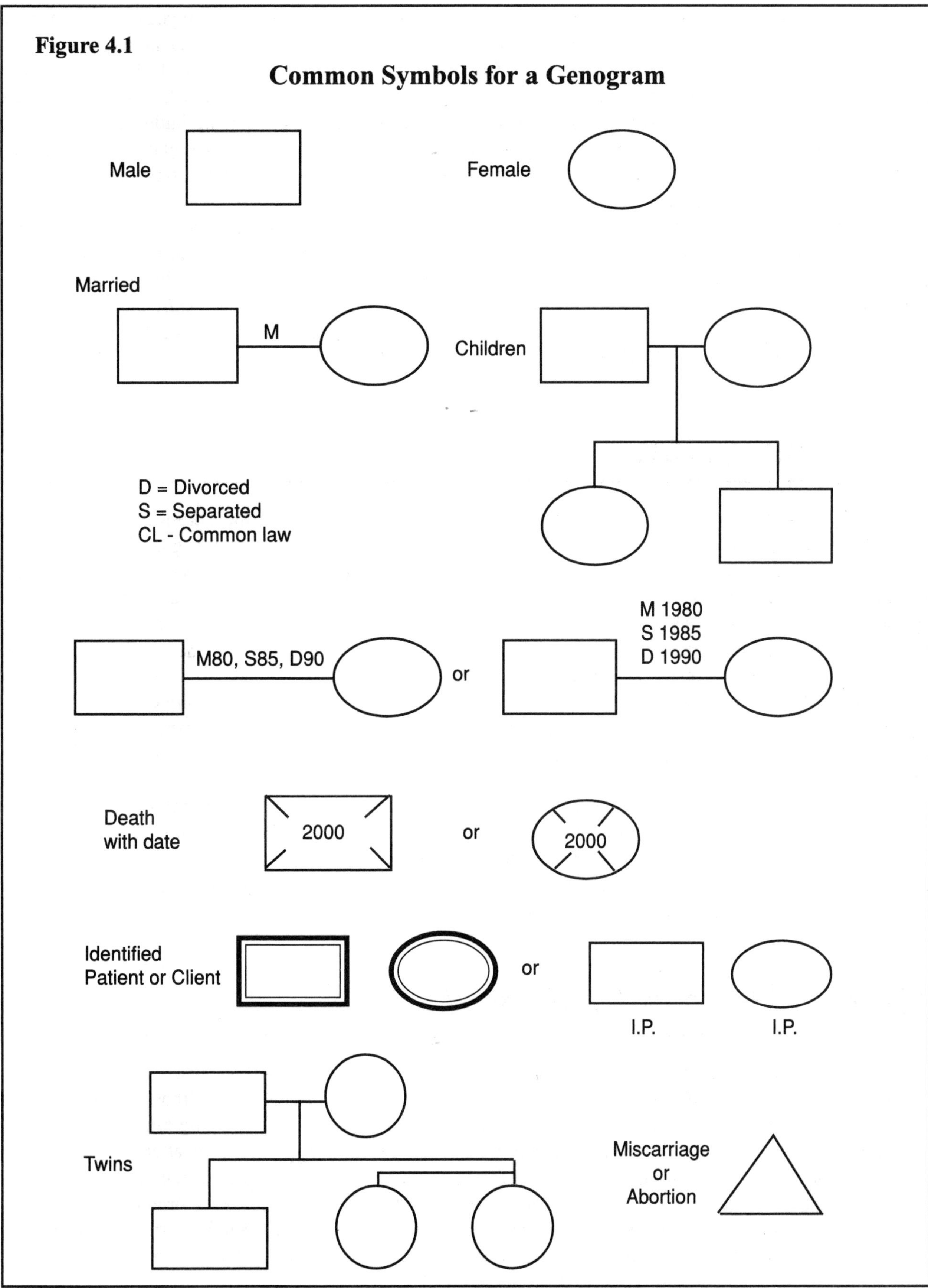

The *Genogram* presents all family relationships (legal, biological, consensual). A square or a circle represents each member. Squares denote males while circles denote females. Double lines around a figure depict the identified patient or index person — 'IP' for whom family work was initiated. Family members of one generation appear on the same horizontal line, in chronological order. One horizontal line represents conjugal relationships. Children appear on a different horizontal line below the parents, and are connected to the parental line with a vertical line. Children appear from left to right, beginning with the oldest child on the left moving to the youngest child on the right (McGoldrick & Gerson, 1985).

All family members must appear in the correct place on the *Genogram*, regardless of whether they are alive, deceased, or living outside the formal unit at that particular moment. Everyone who has ever been part of the family must be represented. Depending on the number of family members and the nature of interpersonal relationships, the final depiction can be detailed and complex and complexity is often the rule. Making the diagram clear, concise, and accurate is the responsibility of the family worker.

The worker structures and directs the exercise. The *Genogram* becomes quite dense when children have different parents, when the parents have had multiple partners, when there is a blended family, or when people outside the immediate family reside in the household. Space problems due to too much detail or very complex family structures, relationships and events can pose challenges. Intermarriage, foster placements, adoption, and lack of family agreement on the information also complicate the Genograms. It is therefore important to plan ahead and first ask the family how complicated its family tree is.

Once symbols have been included, family member's name and age are put inside the squares and circles. Outside the symbols, important characteristics such as health status, school, or occupational information should be inserted. If a family member is deceased, the year of death, the age and cause of death is recorded. This particular square or circle is marked with an "X." When the symbol for miscarriage is used, the sex of the child should be identified, if known. A sample of the Genogram for the Stone family is shown in Figure 4.3. Significant dates of birth, marriage, divorce, separation and significant events should also be noted. Divorce is represented with two slashes on the marital line. Common-law relationships and affairs join the two individuals with a dotted line, again with the dates. A dotted line encircles the current household.

There are several possible places to start. One place is the current household. Another is to draw the skeleton of the Genogram over three generations and then obtain demographic information, information about functioning and then critical family events (McGoldrick & Gerson, 1985).

Demographic information includes data on dates of important events, where people live, occupation, etc. Functional information concerns information about the medical, emotional, and behavioral functioning of family members (McGoldrick & Gerson, 1985, p. 19). Finally, critical family events include transitions, relationship changes, losses and successes (p. 19). A chronology of important family history might also be recorded as a list on the page.

The Genogram also reveals the nature of family relationships. Family members can report on how they see their relationships with others in the family. Different types of lines portray different types of relationships. The stronger and closer the relationship, the wider the line. Poor or conflictual relationships are depicted with a jagged line while distant relationships are shown by a dotted line. It is possible to have both a fused but conflictual relationship captured with a wide line with a jagged line through it. Questions such as "How would you describe your parents' marriage?" or "Who did you have the closest relationship with?" are examples of questions that describe the quality of family relationships.

If the Genogram becomes too detailed, the relationship patterns can be placed on a separate Genogram on another page. Relationship questions are varied. Examples include, "Who would you go to when you have a problem?" "What was your grandparents' relationship like?" "How would you describe your relationship with your oldest child?" "What kind of line should I draw between you and your husband?" "Husband, do you agree with this line?" As with other parts of the Genogram, you will find out that family members have different opinions. Different opinions are okay.

The family worker can also ask the adults about their perception of how their family of origin affects the current family, in particular, relationships with partners or their children. When doing family-of-origin work, the worker pays particular attention to themes and repetitive patterns that appear in the present family and have been passed down from previous generations. Examples of themes include:

- Males have the final say in major decisions affecting the family.
- Females take care of the children and household work.
- Youngest children are indulged while older children take care of them.
- Discipline is primarily physical.
- Demonstrating affection is not acceptable.

Exercise 4.1

Critical Family Events

(In Class)

Make a list of ten possible critical family events that might be included in a Genogram. Compare your list with your classmates.

1.

2.

3.

4.

5.

6.

7.

8.

9.

10.

Figure 4.2

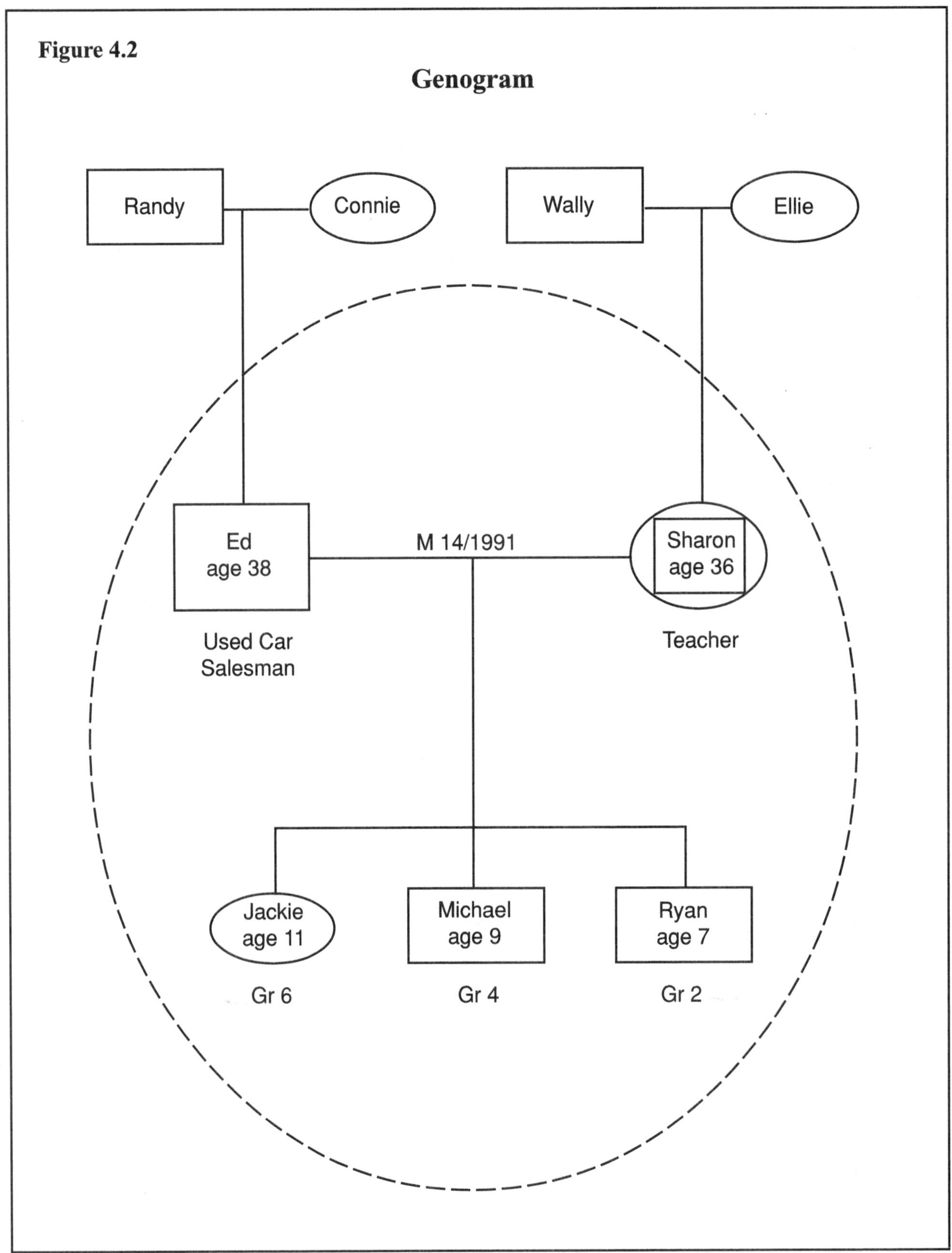
Genogram
Randy
Connie
Wally
Ellie
Ed
age 38
M 14/1991
Sharon
age 36
Used Car
Salesman
Teacher
Jackie
age 11
Michael
age 9
Ryan
age 7
Gr 6
Gr 4
Gr 2

Figure 4.3

Stone Family

Genogram

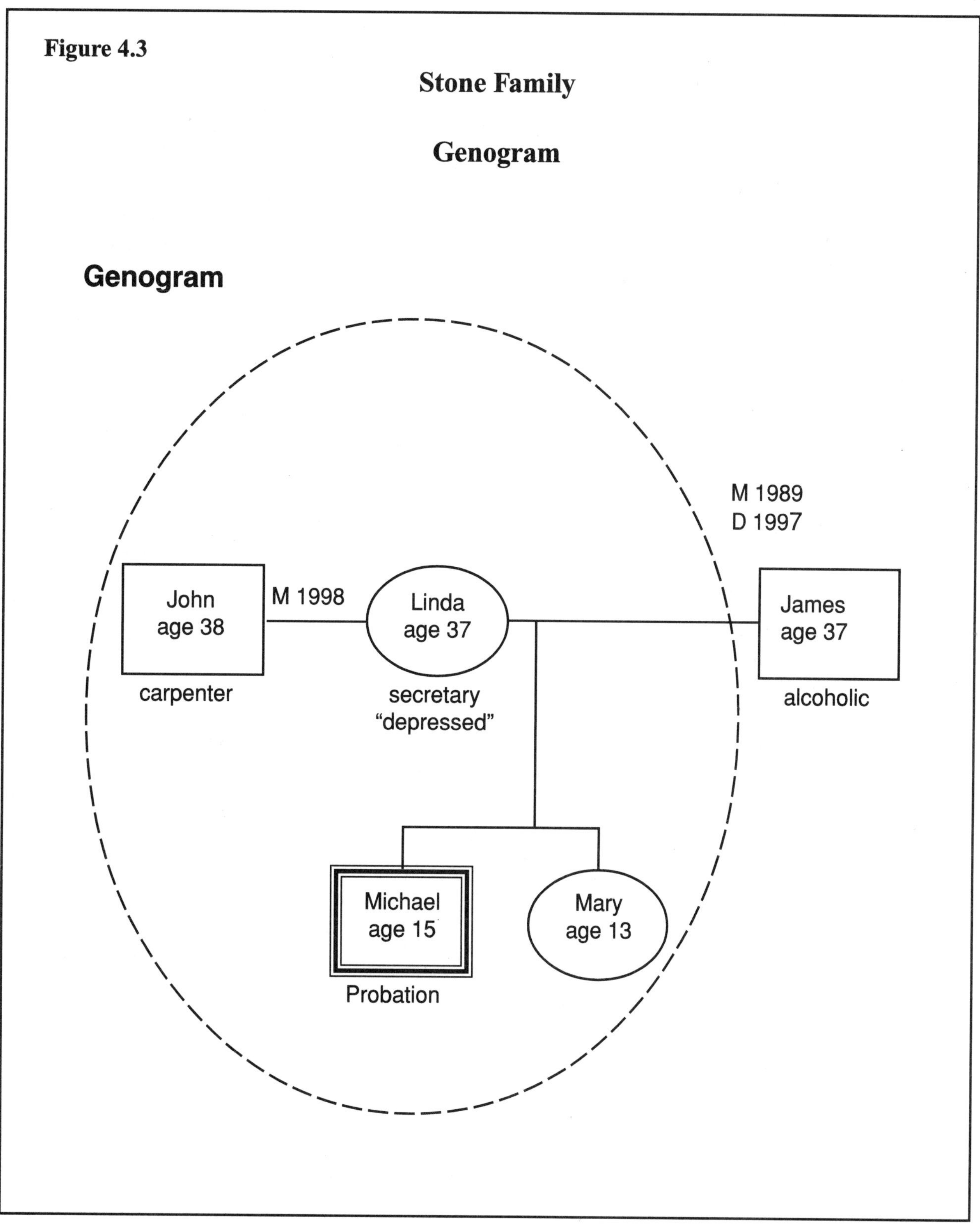

Gathering information for the *Genogram* occurs either in a conjoint family interview, or if seeing an individual, with one person. Remember, some information may be sensitive or painful, such as troubled relationships within the current family, especially if there are differing perceptions. Interviewing skills are as important in doing a Genogram as they are in all other phases of family work. Everyone who is present for the interview should provide input. You will need to decide whether to get the information from one family member or several. McGoldrick and Gerson (1985) recommend that the more people that provide information, the more reliable that information will be. Be prepared, however, to hear different versions since "...family members tell different stories about the same events" (p. 30). A basic family tree can be done quite quickly and efficiently, but creating depth will take longer.

McGoldrick and Gerson (1985, p. 30) suggest that the flow of information can spread in five different directions.

1. from the presenting problem to the larger context of the problem;
2. from the immediate household to the extended family and broader social systems;
3. from the present family situation to a historical chronology of family events;
4. from easy, non-threatening questions to questions that are difficult and anxiety-provoking;
5. from obvious facts to judgments about functioning and relationships to hypothesized family patterns.

Exercise 4.2

Formulating Questions
(In Class)

As we have mentioned it is important to prepare for a family interview. The purpose of this exercise is the help you plan ahead to do the Genogram with a family. Given McGoldrick's and Gerson's (1985) suggestion about direction in the interview, formulate some questions capturing each of the suggested directions:

Direction	Possible Questions
1. a. Presenting problem	
b. Larger context questions	
2. a. Immediate household	
b. Extended family and broader social systems	
3. a. Present family situation	
b. Historical chronology of events	
4. a. Easy questions about facts	
b. Difficult questions getting opinions about relationships	

Note that some of the questions provided below help people reflect on their parents (who are often *outside the room* and not in the current household). It is also important to get family members to talk about the current relationships *within the room*. The latter emphases help family members bridge the gap between the past and present.

Examples of General Questions in Constructing a Genogram

The following are some questions you can ask a family member about the family *Genogram* (Author unknown, n.d.):

- What was your relationship with each parent? Which parent were you closest to? Who did the disciplining?
- What was your relationship with each sibling? Who were you closest to? Now? Then?
- Who was the favorite child?
- Who was the black sheep?
- What were you appreciated for? Were you praised? What for? What were your parents proud of you for?
- What were you put-down for? What did they criticize you for?
- How did you make impact in you family? How did you get attention? How much influence did you have?
- What were/are the strengths of your family?
- What were/are the unresolved trouble spots?
- How much have you separated (physically, emotionally, etc.) from your family? How much have you achieved a sense of your own identity apart from them? Are you still trying to be the way they wanted you to be? Do you want to be like your father? Your mother? Do you want not to be like your father? Your mother?
- Do you see one as the "good" parent, and the other as the "bad" parent?
- If you could ask each of your family members one question, what would it be?
- What patterns and meanings from your family-of-origin have you kept? How are you the same as your parents and how are you different? What choices have you made in your parenting practices because of your upbringing?
- What connections do you see now between how you were raised and how you are raising your children now that we have looked at your experience growing up? What would you like to do differently?
- What meaning do you make of your upbringing now? How have you carried that sense in your upbringing into your current family?

Exercise 4.3

Constructing Questions Specific to a Presenting Problem
(In Class)

The questions presented above represent some general questions to ask during Genogram construction. Select a presenting problem (e.g., substance abuse, physical, sexual or emotional abuse, family illness), and devise 5 questions that would be important to ask during Genogram construction. Share your responses with the class.

Presenting Problems:_______________________________

Questions

1.

2.

3.

4.

5.

Questions to Ask Mother or Father[1]

- Describe your mother/father as a person.
- What were her/his attitudes towards: love, work, money, play, responsibility, sex, religion, achievement, etc.
- What did s/he value most?
- How did s/he express feelings: anger, hurt, love, fear, happiness, sadness, etc.
- Which feelings did s/he express most often, which least often?
- How did s/he express want, needs?
- How did your parent(s) treat you when you were growing up? How did you make sense of their relationship with you? What is the nature with your mother/father like now?
- How are you like your parents? How are you different from your parents? What choices have you made as a result of your relationship with your parents? How has your relationship with your mother/father impacted you now?
- What is the same and what is different right now in your parenting?
- Who in your current family reminds you of your mother/father? What is it about these two people that is similar? How does this perspective influence your relationship with X right now?

(continued)

General questions about the parental relationship[2]

- Who is/was the most powerful parent? Who was in charge of what?
- Was their relationship warm or cool?
- How well did they communicate? What did they talk about?
- How did they fight or argue, and how were fights resolved? Who won?
- What kind of relationship do you think they had?
- In what areas were they able to cooperate? Where did they compete?
- What were the rules (shoulds) about: male and female roles; closeness and intimacy; individuality and separateness?
- What were the trouble spots in the marriage?
- What was your mother like as a wife? Good and bad points?
- What was your father like as a husband? Good and bad points?
- What messages did you get about intimate relationships based on what you witnessed growing up?
- What did you learn about relationships in your childhood? How does this show up in your life now?

Exercise 4.4

Constructing Questions Specific to a Marital Issue
(In Class)

The questions listed zero-in on specific questions that can be asked to gather information about conjugal or intimate relationships. Select an issue pertinent to a conjugal relationship (e.g., divorce, remarriage, violence, expression of affection) and devise 5 specific questions that would be useful to ask during Genogram construction.

1.

2.

3.

4.

5.

Exercise 4.5

Drawing Your Own Genogram
(In class)

After understanding these suggestions for drawing a Genogram, take 30 minutes to draw your own Genogram, going back three generations. Use the questions provided as a general guide and develop further questions that pertain to your particular family setting. Include as much detail as possible. Take another 10 minutes to interpret your personal Genogram, including the repetitive patterns that stand out in your family and how your Genogram affects your current behavior and assumptions. Note what information you do not have. Figure out why you are missing this information.

Exercise 4.6

A Complex Genogram

(In Class)

The following family situation represents a very complex family structure. Below we provide a description of the people involved. Create a Genogram and compare your Genogram with your classmates.

JR 49, father, teacher, first married for 15 years, divorced now for 13 years, first wife was alcoholic.
Susan 46, JR's common law partner for the past 2 years, nurse.
Joanne 15, Susan's daughter from a previous relationship, grade 10, health problems.
(Susan and JR lived common law for 2 years yet Susan and Joanne in last month left the home because of it being too stressful, Susan and JR still "in love" just not living together full time.
John 19, JR's son from first marriage, living with JR, unemployed.
Linda 24, JR's daughter from first marriage, pregnant, living with JR.
Mark 25, Linda's common law boyfriend for past 1 year, living with JR, unemployed.
Darcy, 29, step daughter, from first wife's first marriage, in substance abuse treatment center.
Darcy's son Ryan age 10, living for past 8 months with JR who has legal custody.
Darcy's daughter Meagan age 8, living for past 8 months with JR who has legal custody.
Arnold, 46, friend of JR, living with JR for past 2 months, Arnold is separated from his wife and two children, Arnold is unemployed, also gay.

Genogram

Interpreting and Analyzing the Information on a Genogram

To summarize the principle for interpreting pattern repetition across generations, repetitive patterns of functioning, relationship, and family structure on a Genogram suggest the possibility of the patterns continuing in the present and into the future. Recognition of these patterns offers the possibility of helping family members alter these patterns (McGoldrick & Gerson, 1985, p. 83).

Family systems theory (Chapter 5) provides a useful framework within which to interpret *Genograms*. Several options are available for interpretation:

1. Understanding family structure:

What is the family structure? What does the information about siblings tell about the family? Is there any piece of the family structure that is unique to this family? What events or experiences have influenced the structure (e.g., divorce, extended kin)? You will want to explore issues related to family structure (e.g., loss, role overload, poverty). The latter list of issues is a good example of how theory and research can guide your practice. You will want to note if there are any intergenerational patterns. McGoldrick and Gerson (1985) suggest that patterns occur in functioning, relationship and family structure (p. 75). Note the similarities and differences on each side of the family tree.

Exercise 4.7

Family Structure Questions
(In Class)

Select a specific family structure (e.g., single parent, blended, extended, traditional) and make a list of the issues that need to be explored in doing a Genogram?

a.

b.

c.

d.

e.

2. Sibling Constellation:

Several issues are important to note when examining the sibling constellation. These include birth order, timing, gender, spacing of births, and relationship of siblings with one another. Another important focus is the birth order of the parents (e.g., oldest child partnering with youngest child, two oldest children partnering, etc.). Siblings that are close in age share many similar life experiences compared with those who have greater age differences (McGoldrick & Gerson, 1985). In addition, families might have special expectations for a particular child. You will also want to note whether there are any intergenerational patterns (e.g. substance abuse, health problems, affairs, etc).

3. Individual Functioning:

How do family members function in their lives? Are there any intergenerational patterns repeated, such as educational levels, illness, remarriage, education, alcoholism, criminal behavior, sexual abuse, domestic violence, etc.

4. Patterns of Relationships:

The nature of relationships is important to understand, both within a particular family constellation and across generations. Be on the lookout for triangulation in the current family and patterns of triangulation across generations (discussed in more detail in Chapter 5). (Basically, a triangle appears when a dyad, e.g., marital couple, brings a third party into the relationship, e.g., child).

5. Life Cycle Issues (discussed in Chapter 8):

Every family goes through different stages of development over the life cycle of a family. According to McGoldrick and Gerson (1985) "normative" expectations exist regarding ages at the time of marriage and child bearing. A Genogram sheds light on whether events and family transitions happened within the "norm" (recognizing that there is great variation from one family to another). What are the patterns (e.g., marrying later in life, length of the courtship, children not leaving home until later in life, expectations that children take care of parents, etc.)? It is also important to determine whether significant events overlap?

6. Life Events and Family Functioning:

Genograms can reveal trauma (e.g., untimely death), stresses (e.g., poverty), and the impact of historical events (e.g., The Great Depression, war). In addition, the Genogram can help flush out family resources - financial well being, work, etc.

Exercise 4.8

Analysis of Your Genogram
(In Class)

One way to analyze your own Genogram is to fill in the categories below. Take 20 minutes to complete this in class exercise. In your Genogram, what did you learn?

Gender roles:

Occupational messages:

Messages about education:

Messages about heterosexual relationships:

Messages about same-sex relationships:

Handling conflict:

Child discipline patterns:

Substance use/abuse:

Religion:

Mental health issues:

Other repetitive patterns:

Now synthesize the information in terms of how it plays out now in your life:

Exercise 4.9

Family Role-Play: Genogram Construction[3]
(PBL Worksheet)

Today the PBL groups will complete a Genogram on their role-play family. Guidelines from this chapter will serve as a framework. It is important for the family worker to obtain a picture of the family from every family member, without letting the parents dominate the discussion. The family worker should start out by introducing the purpose of the Genogram and the rules around its construction (e.g. no interruptions, everyone will get a chance for input, etc.).

However, parents might provide the initial input into the Genogram. It is also important not to "lose" the children while this is happening. Thus, the family worker can briefly ask the child(ren) what s/he thinks about what s/he has just heard...then move on again to the parents. One by one, each member should tell about his or her particular part of the family tree. Use a flip chart or blackboard to show the family the unfolding Genogram while you are drawing it. Toward the end, the family worker could elicit emerging patterns and write them down on the flip chart.

Incorporating Culture

As mentioned, the Genogram described above encapsulates family structures and patterns. The greater the detail, the more complex they become. However, they can also identify cultural issues in families. Using a Genogram in this way will help you understand the impact of culture on a family. Hardy and Laszloffy (1995) describe one way of incorporating culture into a Genogram. While the intent of their article was to train family therapists, their model can be adapted to capture cultural issues in which families you are working.

They suggest the following five steps in incorporating culture into a Genogram:

1. Define your culture of origin, including the major group(s) from which you have descended.
2. Identify the major organizing principles and pride/shame issues. Organizing principles are perceptions, beliefs, and behaviors that characterize a particular group. Pride/shame issues include those aspects of a culture that are designated as negative or positive.
3. Use one color to identify all the different groups of which you are a member. If your heritage includes American Indian, Chinese, Italian, British, etc. each one is represented in the circles.
4. Identify intercultural marriages and identify how organizing principles and pride/shame issues have blended in your family.
5. Create a legend to the Genogram that allows people to interpret its meaning.

Exercise 4.10

Doing a Cross Cultural Genogram
(In Class)

Pair up with another classmate. Interview each other for 10 minutes each doing a cross cultural Genogram. Use the five steps described above. What patterns do you see?

Chapter Summary

The Genogram is standard fare in many family-serving agencies. It is a map showing family structure, important family events, and relationship patterns across three generations. While each agency has developed its own symbols for Genograms, some common symbols are used almost universally. This chapter presents some useful dimensions to help in interpreting a Genogram. Genograms have evolved to the point where they can now capture unique cultural issues of pride and shame.

[1] When gathering information from a multigenerational perspective, family workers must recognize that different historical times carried with them differing social expectations. For example, in the early to mid Nineteenth Century, physical discipline of children was harsher than what is acceptable nowadays. Helping place particular beliefs within such a context can help families develop a deeper understanding of their issues.

[2] It is important to be sensitive to intergenerational boundaries while asking questions for the Genogram. For example, information about the parents' sexual relationship should be off-bounds to the children and should therefore not be asked during Genogram construction. Can you think of other questions that would not be appropriate to ask using this assessment tool?

[3] While the Genogram will be the same for each PBL family group, the analysis of the Genogram can be different for individual members of the family group in course assignment. The purpose of analyzing the Genogram independently is to encourage self-directed work and independent, critical thinking.

Chapter 5 **Table of Contents**

FAMILY SYSTEMS THEORY

Chapter 5

Family Systems Theory

Crisis is opportunity on the tail of a dragon
- Chinese proverb

Chapter Coverage

- Family Systems
- Basic Tenets of Family Systems
- Circular Causality

Introduction

In this chapter, we discuss family systems theory, which is central to understanding family dynamics and opens the door to different intervention possibilities. We pay particular attention to circular causality and describe how to apply this useful concept in family work.

Family Systems

The contributions of Minuchin, Bowen, Ackerman, Whitaker, Boszormenyi-Nagy, Lidz, the Palo Alto group, and others combined to change thinking about family problems. Rather than viewing problems as falling under the domain of the individual, family workers became increasingly aware of how problems sprout from family relationships. This thinking was influenced by general systems theory introduced in the 1930s by von Bertalanffy who formulated an encompassing theory rooted in biology and medicine. General systems theory emphasizes the interrelationships of parts to one another. When applied to families, general systems theory replaced the practice of focusing on individuals and explained how family members interact to form a broader picture. Out of this perspective came the belief that one could not understand any individual family member (part) without understanding how all family members (whole) function and relate together.

The Family as a System

The *process* through which all family members interact and function together is referred to as the family system. Taken to its logical conclusion, in general systems theory, each system is part of a larger system (for example, the community, which in turn is part of yet a larger societal system). Likewise, each system also consists of smaller systems, or subsystems. For example, the family system is composed of individuals, child subsystems or a parental subsystem. Accordingly, general systems theory is a good fit with the social work person-in-environment, ecological perspective (Chapter 7).

Family systems theory is founded on the understanding that each family is a unique social system. Problems are located, not with any single family member, but in the arena of family relationships and social interaction. Therefore, we say that a *system* (family) is a complex set of *elements* (family members and subsystems of family members) in *mutual interaction* (relationships formed through interaction). This belief departs from traditional counseling models where the problem is assessed as being an individual issue. When applied to families, systems theory allows family workers to view the family as a set of interconnected units.

In working with a family system it is important to recognize that behavior, interactions, and relationships are *reciprocal*, *patterned*, and *repetitive*. Relationships are reciprocal in that they have a mutual impact on members. Over time, transactions become patterned with predictable ways of members relating to each other, particularly when feeling stress. Patterns are repetitive as they occur regularly in a range of different situations yet in the same patterned manner (see circular causality later in this chapter). Family interactions are thus woven together to create a complex, but patterned and predictable family personality, with each family being unique. Through family systems theory, family workers can understand family dynamics, especially how members interact with others, thus providing the context for individual behavior. Family workers look for *what* and *how* something is happening, not *why*.

Recognizing *patterns* is the cornerstone of family systems theory. By patterns, we mean that the same thing happens repeatedly and becomes quite predictable. Predictable patterns contribute to family system stability so that the energy of family members is not wasted on mundane tasks. We know who is going to ask the children to do the dishes, put them to bed, or get them to do their homework. We are also quite certain about how the children are going to respond to these requests. When systems are stable, the familiar patterns within a family play an important role in keeping the family on an even keel. Family patterns also reveal patterns of affiliations, tensions, and hierarchies within the system (Minuchin, Colapinto, & Minuchin, 1998). Some family patterns are determined by ethnicity and culture. Behavior is explained through these ongoing, repetitive patterns, which both trigger and maintain behavior.

When a family has trouble, it is often because their repetitive patterns have produced inertia, but without an adequate response to the issue at hand. In this way, *the solution becomes the problem*. Because the patterns are habits, family members feel secure in the stability they provide. The habitual patterns might be hurtful to individuals and harmful to the family system, but because family members are unaware of or unskilled in other ways of responding, they are unable to change and the family is described as being stuck.

One of the most vivid metaphors that highlights systems concepts as applied to families is provided by Wright and Leahey (1994, p. 9) who suggest that when thinking about the family as a system, it is useful to compare it to a mobile. Visualize this mobile with four or five parts suspended from the ceiling, gently floating in the air. The unit is in balance, steady but moving. Some pieces are heavier and exert more influence on movement. A breeze catching one part of the mobile immediately influences the movement of every other piece, as the pace quickens with some pieces being unbalanced, moving chaotically. Gradually the whole exerts an influence in the errant part(s) and balance is restored but not before a change in the movement of the unit has occurred. Notice the fluidity, closeness, and distance among pieces, as well the impact of contact on one with another. One piece may persistently appear isolated from the others, yet the position of isolation is essential to the balancing of the entire system.

Exercise 5.1

Understanding Family Systems
(In Class)

As a child take time to reflect on your family and describe your family-of-origin as a family system. The following questions will guide your understanding:

List the members of your family system.

Identify family subsystems in your family. How were they divided — generation, gender, interests and functions?

Describe the family boundaries using an open to closed continuum.

Describe family relationships.

Describe the informal and formal roles assumed by each member of your family. Account for role conflicts and role clarity in this family.

What cultural influences affected the family?

Describe the predictable patterns of interactions and relationships. Select one predictable pattern and try to predict what would happen if it changed.

Beliefs of Systemic Family Work

Three guiding beliefs of family system work are:

1. Problems occur as the result of ongoing *patterns* of communication within the family;
2. Family crises creates both instability and opportunities for change; and,
3. Families function based on established rules. The rules governing families must be changed before problems can be addressed.

Family systems theory is a useful guide for understanding family dynamics. However, we caution workers that although family systems theory has been used as a general theory, it is seriously limited in its ability to explain serious family problems such as violence or sexual abuse. In addition, feminists have criticized family systems theory for its gender bias.

Six Family Systems Tenets

Several important family systems ideas are important. Six tenets are now widely accepted as the foundation of family systems theory and it is important to understand them as they pertain to families. These six key concepts include:

1. A family system is part of a larger social system and contains many other smaller subsystems. The triangle is one important family subsystem to be aware of and work with.
2. A change in one family member affects other family members and the family as a whole.
3. The family as a whole is greater than the sum of its parts.
4. Families work toward a balance between change and stability.
5. A family functions according to established rules of governance.
6. Family members' behaviors are circular rather than linear.

Tenet # 1: A family system is part of a larger social system and consists of many subsystems. The concept of triangles is an important family subsystem phenomenon.

This assumption is the entrée of family work thinking. An individual is part of several other family subsystems and the family is part of a larger social system. As mentioned in Chapter 7, family work appreciates the person-in-environment perspective. In addition, all living systems contain subsystems in relationship to other sub-systems.

Triangles are an important family systems concept. Triangles appear when a dyad (two people) relationship is under stress and a third party, often a child is drawn into the relationship to stabilize the situation. Triangles are not a preferred family subsystem because they do not allow the two people opportunity to deal with their issues (Carter & McGoldrick, 1999c). They usually appear when something negative is going on and are often harmful to the well-being of the third party. We discuss triangles in more detail at the end of this section.

The concept of boundaries is the next useful concept here. Invisible boundaries, like skin, surround individuals, subsystems, and the entire family unit, and demarcate who is included in the particular system or subsystem. Rules determine how boundaries are created and function. The nature of family boundaries varies according to culture, lifestyle, and other unique features of the particular family. Some families have well defined, clear boundaries, while in others the boundaries between the family and the outside world are fuzzy. Yet others have very fixed, impermeable boundaries, affecting who and what can enter. The same is true for boundaries around individuals or subsystems. As mentioned in Chapter 1, a family is defined by their boundaries that determine who is inside or outside the system. Services typically target individuals within family boundaries, although the permeability of a family's boundaries affects the ease to which services can be offered.

The nature of boundaries is unique to each family, but can generally be described as open or closed. Families with boundaries that are either too rigid or too open expose members to greater risk than do families with pliable yet discerning boundaries. Boundaries also exist within families and families should not only have flexible, clear boundaries and have well-established intergenerational boundaries. Families with rigid or closed external boundaries restrict the contact of members with the outside creating difficulty in accessing and using external resources and support. Such families have difficulty requesting or accepting external assistance, as members are isolated from potential sources of support. Alternatively, families with loose boundaries fail to regulate involvement with the outside world and individuals slip in and out of the family indiscriminately, regardless of the consequences to family members. We recall one family where the father was sexually abusing his teenaged daughter. He was very strict about her friendships with peers outside the family and tightly regulated her contact. On the other hand, we also recall a single parent family where people entered and exited the household indiscriminately. Three different men sexually abused the child in this family before child welfare received a report.

Some subsystem boundaries are more apparent than others are. When there are two parents in the family, for example, there should be a good boundary around the parental subsystem. The children should not be triangulated into this parental system, although it often happens. For example, the parent's sexual relationship should be kept within the dyad. Can you think of other issues that should remain in the parental subsystem? Similarly, sibling alliances often serve as a family subsystem with its own set of boundaries. The sexual abuse of a child by a parent occurs when intergenerational boundaries are too loose.

***Triangulation*:** In family systems theory, the interpersonal triangle is a key unit of analysis. All intimate relationships have the seeds of instability and sometimes require a third party to maintain stability. At first glance, this might seem to be paradoxical - that intimacy needs a third party! However, it makes common sense. The price of intimacy in any relationship is interpersonal tension and conflict because it is almost impossible for two people to exist in harmony all the time. When in conflict, people often rely on a third person (or different third persons, depending on the circumstances) for mediation, ventilation, or problem-solving assistance. Parents of more than one child are often called into their children's battles. *"Mommy, Randy is looking at me funny." "Daddy, Kate hit me. Mommy, Wally just stuck his tongue out at me."* These are examples sibling-parent triangles that are common in families. Parents who are sucked into these exchanges are unknowingly being triangulated into their children's relationships.

Figure 5.1

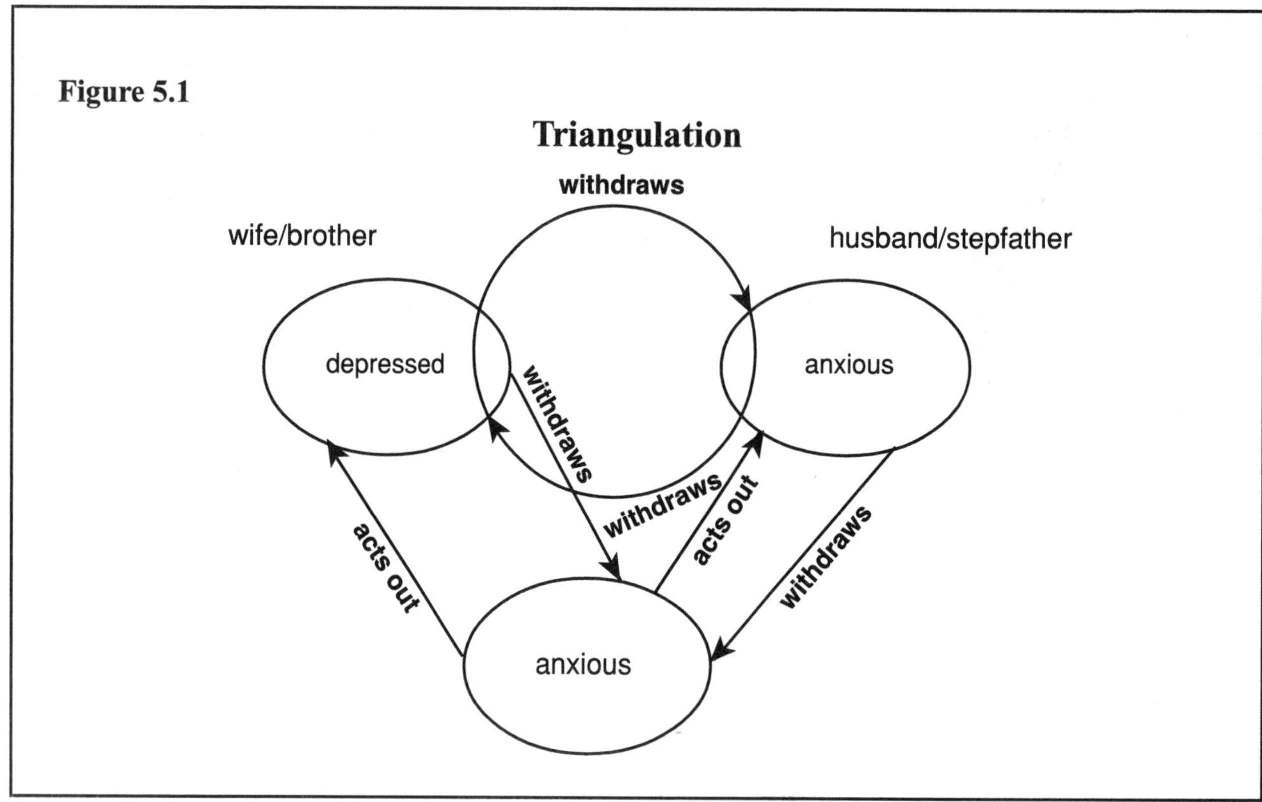

Family triangles are very common. For example, one triangle is that of the mother-father-child. Triangulation becomes problematic in families when adults who are in conflict draw in other family members (who are often weaker, such as the children), to maintain stability in their relationship. In these situations, triangulation serves a particular purpose - the third party is drawn in to provide support to one member, in opposition to another. In fact, the two members act as a coalition with one another against a common enemy. Sometimes, triangles are not patterned, but happen only fleetingly. It is when these triangles become patterned and hostile that they hurt the family system.

Detriangulation: Detriangulation involves strategies through which the family worker disrupts one triangle and opens up the family members to new, more functional alliances or triangles. Triangles are often difficult to break up since the patterns involved in the triangulation become entrenched (and hence patterned) over time. For example, a couple might focus on the misbehavior of a child rather than deal with their couple issues. Over time, the distraction due to focusing on a child rather than the relationship becomes an engrained pattern within the family structure. The child is scapegoated and may develop problems that warrant heightened attention. In fact, some conflict over discipline might actually be the result of marital problems that have sucked the child into the difficulties (Carter, 1999). There are many strategies the family worker can use to disrupt triangles within the family.

One way of de-triangulating is to use a "reversal," that is changing a habitual pattern by doing the opposite of the established pattern. Another method of detriangulation is ensuring that family members interact as dyads. This involves making certain that a third person does not jump into conflictual relationships, but instead allows the two other family members to work out the conflict on their own. Detriangulation also can occur by shifting alliances (i.e., who does what with whom). If the mother is always the one trying to get a child to comply with a command, change can be accomplished by having the father gain the child's compliance. When a couple is triangulated with a child as a means of avoiding issues in their relationship, they might be instructed to spend a certain amount of time together talking about whatever is on their minds that day without the third party present. If they need the assistance of a third party to bring an issue to resolution, they might be encouraged to talk with a different adult, including the family worker. Ideally, the couple should learn to deal with their issues directly and honestly. Alternatively, another adult family member could act as a supportive advice giver, removing the children from the conflictual relationship. In this way, members are guided into new functional attachments with nuclear or extended family members.

Strategies that contribute to members opening to new attachments can be pursued. The family worker should always encourage the development of new attachments that have the possibility of promoting a member's self and family well being. For example, working with a family with a stepfather who is always cross with his stepson and thus in a strained relationship with his wife is one example of a triangulated family. The wife feels capable and comfortable dealing with discipline issues with her son, yet backs away from this role since the husband is constantly trying to parent the adolescent. Detriangulation can be used by supporting the wife to be the disciplinarian of the son and encouraging the father to assume a supportive role of both his wife and son. The couple can be instructed to meet for thirty minutes during breakfast to discuss any anticipated parenting issues, the husband to give his suggestions and support, yet mother to be solely in charge of implementing the parenting rules she sees fit.

Exercise 5.2

Family Boundaries
(In Class)

Describe the family boundaries in your family of origin, using every system, subsystem, and triangle. What were the triangles in your family? Describe the nature of the boundaries between these subsystems. For example, are people under involved or over involved with each other?

Exercise 5.3

Boundaries
(In Class)

Pick a family you know. Draw a Genogram of the family and its sub-units and draw the types of boundaries around each. Further, discuss boundaries in relation to diverse family groups represented in your class. For example, are you discouraged from marrying someone outside your cultural, racial, or religious affiliation?

Genogram

Tenet # 2: A change in one family member affects other family members and the system as a whole

Central to understanding families as a social system is the idea that a change in one member of the family will affect every other family member as well as the entire family system. This assumption highlights a family response to change and the reaction to the family worker's attempts to stimulate that change. If one family member changes his or her behavior (e.g., no longer arguing with another family member), other members may resist this change to keep the family in balance. Members might also change their own behavior in response to the new behavior. One belief is that when one family member's "symptoms" improve, another member might become problematic. If the member does successfully change his or her behavior, other family members will be unable to behave as they had previously. Thus, change in one part of the system forces change in other parts of the system (Collins, Jordan, & Coleman, 1999).

Some suggest that this assumption provides a strong rationale for seeing the family as a unit. Some have observed, for example, that when one family member "gets better," another family member will develop symptoms. Therefore, by seeing the family as a whole, the worker will be in a good position to work with this "ripple effect."

Exercise 5.4

The Ripple Effect
(In Class)

Using the Stone family as a case example, discuss how to reinforce change of the family system. Keep in mind that if only one person in the system changes than pressure is put on that one person to revert to the old patterns.

Tenet # 3: The family as a whole is greater than the sum of its parts

A family is one of the most fundamental social systems that is more than the sum of the individual characteristics and behaviors of each member. No matter how well we know the individual personalities and backgrounds, it is impossible to comprehend behavior until we understand that person within the context of his or her family. This family context includes the relationships that members have with one another, the presence of subsystems, as well as the relationships of each subsystem both to individuals within the family and other subsystems.

Exercise 5.5

Counting the Possibilities
(In Class)

Consider the Stone family again - two children and a mother and father (throw in a dog if you would like!). Make a list of all of the possible relationships within this family. These include individual-to-individual relationships and subsystem-to-subsystem relationships. How many did you find? Describe these relationships and then compare your answer with your classmates' answers.

a.

b.

c.

d.

e.

f.

The intent of Exercise 5.5 is to uncover some of the possible configurations of relationships in this small, simple family. Based on the assumption that the family as a whole is greater than the sum of its parts, you can see that the family unit is greater than the mother plus the father plus the son plus the daughter. It consists of every family member's relationship to every other member (e.g., mother-to-son; mother-to-daughter; mother-to-father, etc.). It also consists of all of the subsystems and the relationship of these subsystems to every other subsystem in the family (e.g., mother-father subsystem to son-daughter subsystem; daughter-mother to father-son subsystem, etc.).

As well, *triangles* (mentioned in the first assumption) are vital subsystems to families (e.g., mother-daughter-son, father-mother-son, etc.). When you add up all of the possible configurations of relationships within this simple family unit, you certainly do get a system that is more than the sum of its parts. The number of possible relationships, subsystems, and triangles changes exponentially as more people enter (or leave as is the case of divorce and remarriage) the family unit. Therefore, the individual experience of each person in the family is unique and can never be experienced by anyone else.

Exercise 5.6

Family Subsystems
(In Class)

Identify the family subsystems in your family of origin. What were the triangles in your family? What were the predictable patterns? Describe the nature of the boundaries between these subsystems. For example, are people under involved or over involved with each other?

a.

b.

c.

d.

e.

f.

Tenet # 4: Families work toward a balance between change and stability

Family systems need stability, order, consistency, and predictability to function and survive. The tendency to hold onto stability is known as *homeostasis*. Implicit and explicit family rules regulate this homeostasis and determine which behaviors are allowed, creating order, predictability, stability, and consistency. For example, one family rule might exist that the whole family has dinner together during the weeknights. During the family dinner, people talk, patterns, or relationships are formed. Different people might assume different roles in preparing the dinner. This is a *predictable* feature of this family's life. Now imagine that the person who usually does the cooking is not present for dinner, either through another commitment or through some tragic event such as death. The homeostasis of this family is disrupted by the absence of that family member, this family will experience chaos until new rules, and behaviors are created to fill the void. Jackson (1972) was one of the first to use the metaphor of a thermostat used to keep the house temperature stable to describe homeostasis. This homeostasis keeps constant balance in the family. In families, the thermostat parallels family rules through which families try to function consistently and predictably.

Families struggle to keep things the same even if this status quo is harmful or destructive. At the same time, families face continuous urges to grow and develop in response to a changing external environment and the evolving needs of family members. In the process, families must find a balance in these two opposing pressures for consistency and change. Paradoxically, families must continually adapt and change in order to remain stable. In part, the need for stability occurs because destabilizing crises disrupt family patterns and make life unpredictable and stressful. Transitions and crises create family instability, during which time, rules, and patterns are disrupted. We point out in Chapter 8 on the family life cycle, that each transition brings with it family disruption and disorganization.

Exercise 5.7

Threats to Family Homeostasis
(In Class)

Reflect back on the previous chapters. Going chapter-by-chapter, pull out several events that can threaten family homeostasis. Compare your responses with your classmates.

a.

b.

c.

d.

The first response to a destabilizing family event is to fight change by holding onto balance and stability. Resistance can be forceful as family workers who have attempted to challenge rigidly maintained behavior patterns could verify. The tendency to hold onto familiar and often (but not always) comforting patterns is one reason why family work can be so challenging. After family work ends, family change may be difficult to hold onto unless steps are taken to ensure that families incorporate the changes permanently and these changes become important to family homeostasis. Remember the Transtheoretical Model and the *Maintenance Stage.* It is the tendency to move back to the familiar states that challenges families in the *Maintenance* Stage. Families might even experience distress or discomfort with new behaviors even when these changes are positive, such as when an alcoholic member stops drinking.

Positive family change demands that the family worker helps the family reset their thermostat and find a new point of homeostasis. To do so, the family must reorganize and develop new rules and patterns of behavior. For example, when a child is placed into foster care or residential treatment, families reorganize and develop new patterns to fill the space (Chapter 10). Family members are required to change interaction patterns, roles and behaviors to create a new family balance (homeostasis). The family becomes disorganized for awhile. Once a family has settled into a new state of homeostasis, based upon the absence of the child, returning of the child back into the home may be difficult. The family has reorganized such that the new rules, behaviors and interaction patterns exclude the child. Moreover, if the family does change back to older behaviors, the risk is that the reasons for the child's removal in the first place will remain the same. Thus, *crisis is opportunity on the tail of a dragon.* The tendency to re-establish stability and equilibrium and return to familiar patterns during periods of stress and change is a powerful force that must be reorganized and addressed to produce long lasting family change.

Change and stability occurring at the same time is a complex process. This arises out of polarized thinking that workers families are either stuck or entrenched (i.e., resistant) or that they are in total disequilibrium (i.e., chaotic). Workers need to understand that families have a blend of both. Perhaps this is what makes transition from one developmental stage to another so difficult.

Exercise 5.8

Homeostasis
(In Class)

Provide one example of a crisis that a family might face. Discuss what would motivate the family to change. What would be an example of why a family would not change in this particular instance?

What changes have you made in your life and how come? Do changes only occur when there is a crisis? What role does frustration, fear, and guilt play in the process of change? Do people start to change because of a simple desire to be better?

Example:

Exercise 5.9

Family Homeostasis
(In Class)

Reflect back on your family of origin and recall a couple of crises. Describe one situation where your family reverted to the way it was to keep homeostasis. Describe another crisis where the family did not revert to old patterns (homeostasis) very quickly. Compare the differences between the two. What are the differences? Compare your answers with your classmates.

Situation:

Second crisis situation:

Tenet # 5: Families function according to established rules

Families develop rules that regulate how they operate. Rules govern relationships and help decide what behavior is expected, allowed, or not allowed. Rules are crucial for the maintenance of family stability and homeostasis. However, family workers should not interchange stability with health. The payoff of stability is that it frees the energy of family members because they are not under continuous pressure to deal with demands, allowing members to function smoothly in daily routines. Family rules are understood at an unforeseen unconscious level and understanding interaction patterns in a family can help workers understand these unspoken rules. Families seldom discuss rules, but they are usually aware what they are. One worker task is to get family members to talk about what rules determine family functioning. "What rules does this family have, for example about homework time, curfew times, and household tasks?"

Family rules help keep the family "temperature" comfortable and predictable. Roles grow out of rules, such as how children will be disciplined, who does housework, who works outside the home, and who helps children with homework. Division of family labor evolves slowly and members might take on unique roles. Understanding family rules shows how members deal with one another. Family rules are made based on individual characteristics such as gender, age, culturally prescribed expectations, birth order and so on. What is important about rules is that they are habitual, and "habits do not invite change" (Minuchin, Colapinto, & Minuchin, 1998, p. 17). While rules can be changed once they are spelled out, changing them is not as simple as making a list because there are rules about rules, which determine how members interpret them as well as change them (Collins, Jordan, & Coleman, 1999).

Exercise 5.10

Family Rules
(In class)

Discuss what rules were in your family, (for example, phoning home if you are going to be late). How would you go about changing these rules? Can you think of a time when your family rules changed? How did this change come about?

Rules:

Exercise 5.11

Family Rules
(In class)

As mentioned in this chapter, all families are governed by a set of unspoken rules. Identify the rules of your family as you were growing up. You may want to break down the rules by key components such as age and gender.

Rules by Age and Gender:

Tenet # 6: Behaviors are circular

As mentioned, families function in predictable and patterned ways. Thus, family work includes an examination of *patterns*. Patterns of family relationships and patterns of interactions are important and are shown through communication patterns. Communication patterns in a family are reciprocal and mutually reinforcing (*circular*). Linear causality suggests that A causes B; the process does not affect A (Collins, Jordan, & Coleman, 1999).

By comparison, *circular causality* implies that A and B are both affected and are changed by the process such that their transaction is repeated as interactional sequences over time. That is, one person's behavior occurs in response to ongoing patterns of interaction with other family members that trigger and maintain this pattern. Circular patterns become the backdrop of ongoing communication patterns and relationships. Eventually, patterns of interaction solidify as family members repeat ongoing sequences of interactions. The following sections illustrate circular patterns and how to work with them.

These circular patterns are communication patterns consisting of thoughts, feelings, and behavior. Figure 5.2 shows the basic structure of a circular pattern. Cognitions, feelings, and behaviors are intricately connected. Consequently, it does not matter where you start. What matters is the connection that you make with an individual's thoughts, feelings, and behaviors, first, and then the transactions of thoughts, feelings, and behaviors of another person in response. Figure 5.3 shows a typical pattern wherein both people feel angry and their behavior, congruent with their feelings, is negative. It would be unusual for a person to have positive thoughts and feelings in the face of anger and negative and threatening behaviors. Alternatively, Figure 5.4 shows a circular pattern where positive feelings are evident. Similarly, negative behaviors, thoughts, and feelings would be unusual in this exchange.

Figures 5.4 and 5.5 provide more specific examples of possible circular patterns in a relationship. Remember, it is not important where you punctuate the pattern since the two people are in a repetitive and circular interaction. Let us examine Figure 5.4 in more detail. Let us say that two people (in this case husband and wife) have been involved in a negative exchange with one another over a period, and that this exchange is patterned, repetitive, and well established. Maybe the wife, in this situation is angry and frustrated (feelings) with her husband for failing to participate in household tasks. She believes (cognitions) that her partner does not respect her, does not care about her, and is taking her for granted. In response to these thoughts and feelings, she might criticize her husband for his lack of participation. The husband in this scenario believes that his wife does not care for him and is undermining his masculinity (thoughts). He also knows that he has failed as a husband and feels guilty and inadequate (feelings). In response, he withdraws from his wife, believing that he cannot please her. Part of this withdrawal may mean sitting in front of the television set for hours at a time, which means of course that he will not do any housework. His wife sees her husband's withdrawal and him not pulling his share in the household tasks and feels angry and frustrated....

Figure 5 shows a similar pattern between a parent and a child. The child, believing that s/he is not a good person and not accepted by his or her parent (thoughts), feels anxious, rejected, unwanted, and hurt (usually many negative emotions co-exist at the same time). When this child thinks these thoughts and feels these feelings, his or her typical response is to misbehave. There are many ways to "misbehave" depending on the age and particular disposition of the child. For example, younger children might throw a tantrum or be destructive. The child might lash out and hit a sibling or the parent. Older children might stomp out of the house or become involved in delinquent acts or abuse drugs. The parent, in response to the child's behavior, believes that the child is being vindictive, "bad," or selfish (cognitions). In response the parent feels angry and inadequate. (Remember, whenever anger exists, hurt is always a partner.) Anger is safer to express than hurt because hurt makes people vulnerable.) The parent expresses his or her anger through irritability, yelling, calling names, throwing things, or a whole host of other possible behaviors (again depending on the skills and the particular disposition of the parent). When the child sees the parent acting in this manner towards him or her, the child feels rejected, unwanted, like there is something the matter with him or her etc. These thoughts fuel the negative feelings and responses. As in Figure 4, this sequence of thoughts/feelings/behavior occurs over time, is repetitive, and becomes predictable patterns of interaction between the parent and the child.

In understanding circular causality, care must be taken to understand how power affects circular patterns. Up until the feminist critique of family systems theory, power was considered "too linear" to help in understanding patterns of interactions. Power was "owned" by the system rather than by individuals. The outcome of this reasoning was that women are battered as a product of circular causality, that they play a role in their own abuse. However, recalling the mobile metaphor - just as certain pieces of a mobile are heavier than others, different family members exert more or less influence over others, *depending on the power*. As feminists argue, power must be used to understand family relationships; otherwise an analysis of abuse in the family can blame the victim.

Figure 5.2

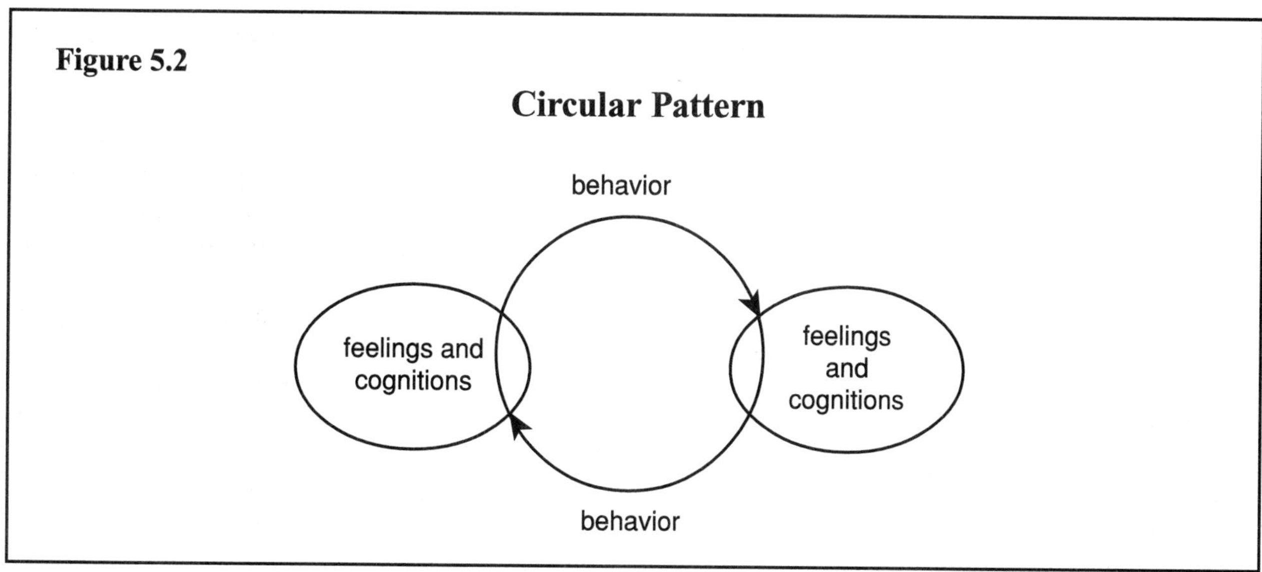

Figure 5.3

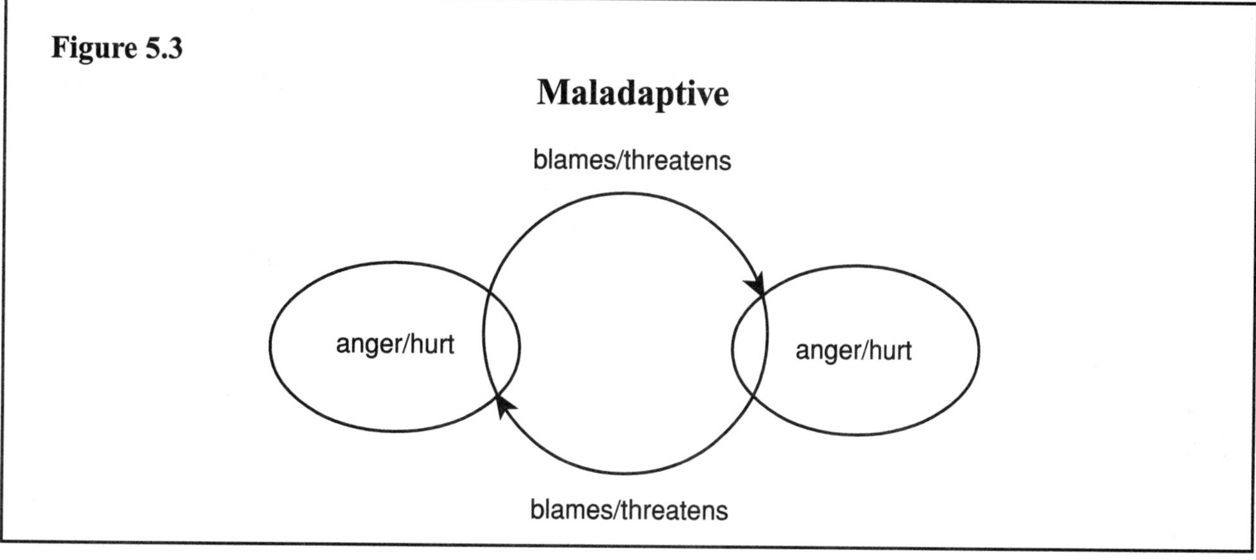

Figure 5.4

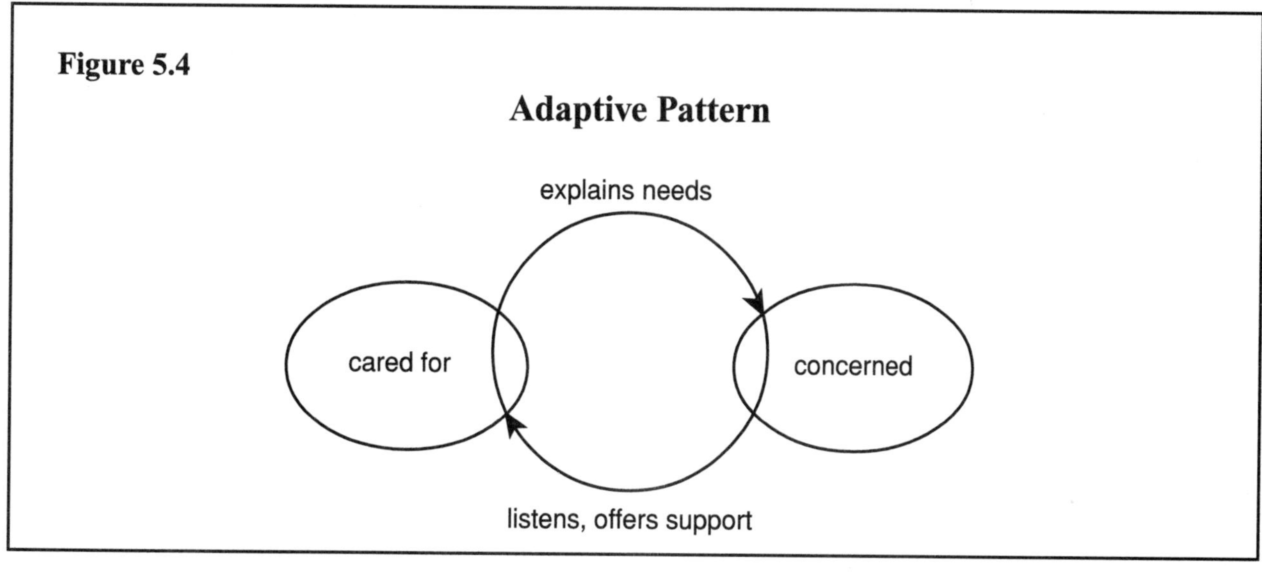

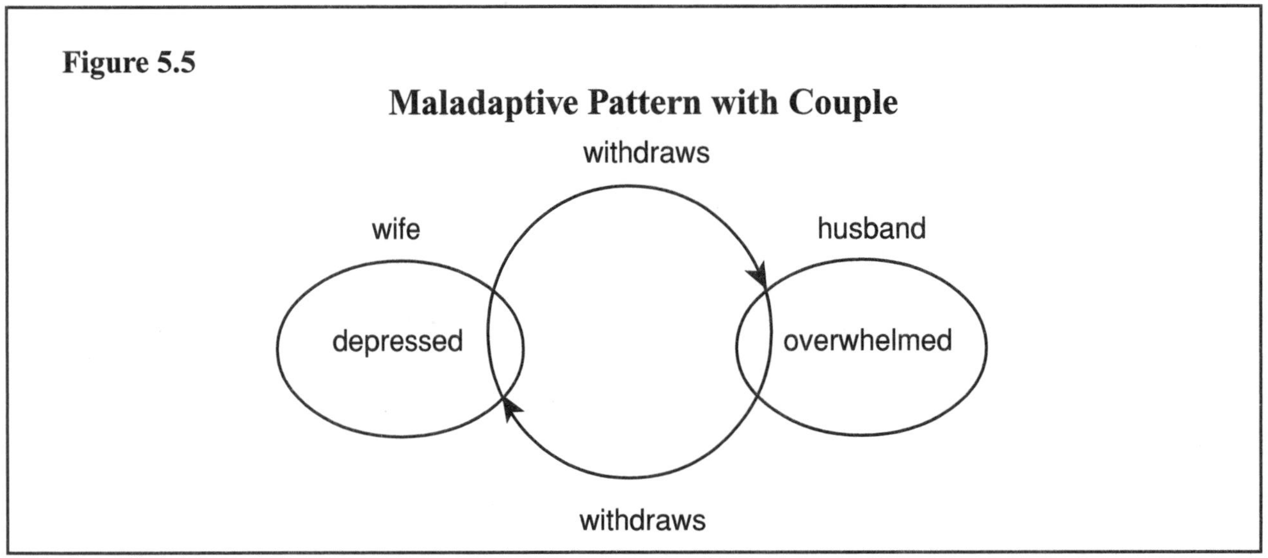
Figure 5.5
Maladaptive Pattern with Couple
withdraws
wife
husband
depressed
overwhelmed
withdraws

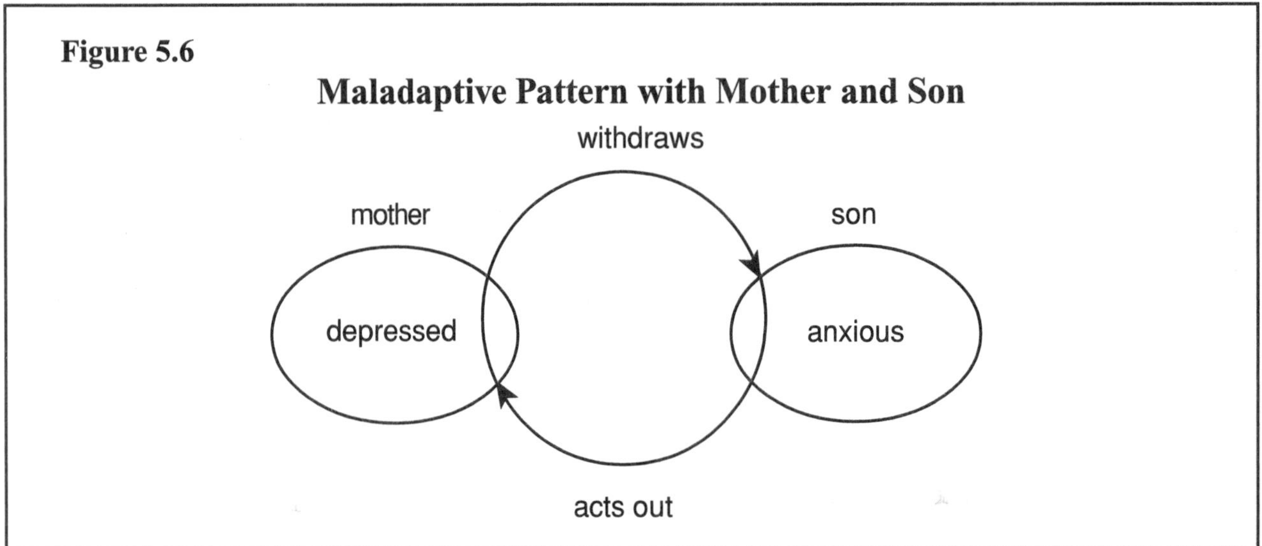
Figure 5.6
Maladaptive Pattern with Mother and Son
withdraws
mother
son
depressed
anxious
acts out

Exercise 5.12

The Stone Family
(In Class)

Figures 5.5 and 5.6 show two repetitive circular patterns within the Stone family. Write a narrative for each of these patterns describing the sequence of thoughts/feelings/behaviors within each pattern. Some of the detail is quite sketchy (e.g., no thoughts are provided, the feelings are basic, and the described behavior is vague. In your narrative of each Figure provide more detail on these three aspects of the circular exchange such that it draws a more complete picture. After you have completed this exercise, pair up with two other classmates and compare your responses. What did you miss? What are the differences and similarities?

Figure 5.5: Wife/husband pattern narrative

Figure 5.6: Mother/son pattern narrative

Exercise 5.13

Circular Causality
(In Class)

Examine one of your ongoing relationships. Recall an interactive pattern that is fairly predictable and identify an ongoing circular pattern of interaction with that significant other. It does not matter where you start to identify the pattern. (You might want to work together with this person). Start with one individual and identify, thoughts, feelings and behaviors, then moving to the second person and doing the same. Draw the pattern on a piece of paper, drawing the diagram one step at a time. How does circular causality work?

Pattern:

Understanding circular causality can be used both for assessment and intervention. Below, we discuss circular causality as an intervention tool.

Working with Circular Causality in a Family Interview: Stimulating Interaction

To work with circular causality, it is important to first identify problematic repetitive behavior and interactions patterns involving circular interaction patterns. Sometimes, circular patterns will spontaneously arise in a family session. Often patterns appear in the form of conflict. When the family worker sees the spontaneous expression of the pattern in the room, he or she has been given a gift in the form of a "teachable moment." When the worker witnesses this in a family session, we recommend sitting back for several moments until the pattern repeats itself several times. You might find it difficult to just sit back and allow yelling or other hurtful behavior unfold in front of you (of course you will have to stop physical violence). You might want to take notes (paying close attention to wording and nonverbal body language). Once the pattern has appeared several times, it is time for you to become a "traffic cop" and take charge of the process, to educate the family about circular causality and to help each person express his or her thought/feeling/behavior sequence. However, sometimes families do not offer a teachable moment when necessary. In this situation, you will have to create one.

You can create a teachable moment with the purpose of drawing out these repetitive circular patterns through "stimulating interaction" (similar to "enactment") with which to help families express typical family patterns. It means that workers do not have to wait for spontaneous family events to arise before working with patterns. Instead, the worker sets the stage to encourage family members to play out their usual family patterns. While observing typical family behavior is often useful, sometimes families appear "stuck" in family work or have difficulty expressing their usual patterns. In this case, the family worker tries to get the family to reveal their usual patterns. It is important that the worker learn balance without overtaking family interaction.

"Effective enactments empower the family, allowing them to express their usual ways of functioning and to explore new pathways on their own" (Minuchin, Colapinto, & Minuchin, 1998, p. 49). The worker through asking two people in the family to face each other and enter into a dialogue over a particular issue stimulates the enactment dialogue.

For example with the Stone family, the worker might introduce the enactments as follows:

> ***Worker***: *I would like to see how mom and dad resolve parenting differences. Mom and dad could you please face each other and discuss how you two can work better together as parents.*

The family worker now sits back and closely observes their communication for approximately five minutes (which is the usual length to observe a pattern of communication.) A practical definition of a pattern is a circular sequence of communication that occurs three times. The Stone couple will likely start talking and the family worker might notice Mrs. Stone looking more depressed, quiet, and withdrawn, and Mr. Stone looking uncertain, anxious and wanting to be quiet and withdraw. Working with one person at a time, the worker elicits from each member his or her thoughts/feelings/behaviors. It is important for the three to be connected.

> **Worker:** *Mr. and Mrs. Stone, I notice as you were both speaking, you went around and around, and how you responded to one another was repetitive. I would like to stop the action right now and take a closer look at what just went on between the two of you. Who would like to go first? (Be careful about you deciding the starting point, because as with the feminist critique, where you punctuate the exchange can subtly lay blame.)*

We recommend asking the couple who should go first. In our experience, we have never had anyone refuse to participate in this exercise. As one person is describing his or her thoughts/feelings/behavior, the other person must sit and listen without saying anything. The process might be proceeding as such (assuming that Mr. Stone has volunteered to go first):

> **Worker:** *Mr. Stone, when you and your wife were speaking, can you tell me what you saw your partner doing?*
> **Mr. Stone:** *I saw my wife's head look down, I saw a sad look on her face, I saw tears in her eyes.*
> **Worker:** *When you saw her head down, with a sad look on her face and tears in her eyes, what were you thinking?*
> **Mr. Stone:** *I started to think that I am a screw up as a husband. I don't think that I can do*

anything right and I don't know how much more I can take.
Worker: *Mr. Stone, when you have these thoughts, what kinds of feelings do you have.*
Mr. Stone: *Well, I usually feel overwhelmed and pretty worried. I am afraid of losing my wife and my family. I also feel lost because I am trying really hard to make everything work and nothing seems to be working. I just don't know what to do next.*
Worker: *Mr. Stone, when you are thinking that you are a failure and feeling worried and overwhelmed and sometimes lost, how do you respond ... what are your typical reactions?*
Mr. Stone: *Well I either watch TV by myself or putter in my workroom for a couple of hours.*
Worker: *It sounds like when you think and feel bad about what is going on, you withdraw. Is that right?*
Mr. Stone: *That sounds right.*
Worker: *Mr. Stone, I would like you to hold onto what we have just talked about for a moment while I speak with your wife. What you have to say is very, very important and I don't want to lose it. In a moment, we will be connecting what is going on for both of you.* (worker now turns to Mrs. Stone). *Mrs. Stone, I would like to explore the same things with you. Your husband has said that sometimes, when he is feeling badly, he withdraws by sitting in front of the television or puttering in his workroom, sometimes for hours at a time. When you see your husband withdrawing, what kinds of things go through your mind?*
Mrs. Stone: *Well, I start to think that I can't do anything right. I start to think that I am not a good wife and that no one is interested in me....*
Worker: (the worker will ask similar questions of husband and wife and elicit the details from each of the circular and repetitive pattern. We advise that the worker go around the circle at least three times so each member gets a sense of its repetitiveness). Once the pattern is made explicit (a flip chart is extremely useful here), the worker can say something like, *I can see a pattern here going on between you. Can each of you see the pattern? Could you please describe it?*
Complete a possible exchange with Mrs. Stone.

After the family worker has a cognitive understanding of the pattern (after it is repeated three times, or over five minute interval), it is important to stop the maladaptive pattern and work with the dyad. If, on the other hand, the couple is communicating in an adaptive way, let them continue! Adaptive communication is what they need to do and they should be encouraged in their efforts. For example, if the Stone couple is able to share their parenting concerns, listen to each other, and develop realistic plans, let them do so! After they complete an adaptive interchange, commend the efforts of the dyad and help them become aware of their adaptive circular communication. Unfortunately, most families who initially come to counseling are most likely to demonstrate maladaptive communication.

After stopping the maladaptive communication, the family worker has some choices about how to proceed:

- Create awareness of the basic circular pattern;
- Further clarification of this basic pattern;
- Awareness of complex pattern;
- Further clarification of complex pattern;
- Conceptualizing adaptive pattern;
- Dealing with affective blocks;
- Developing new awareness including new adaptive patterns;
- Assigning behavioral homework introducing new patterns.

Awareness of Basic Patterns

Drawing a family's circular patterns on a piece of paper is a useful exercise, especially patterns that involve a selected issue. A flipchart would be especially useful to allow everyone in the family to have the same visual picture of the circular pattern. Once family members understand the concept of circular causality, they can apply it to their own examples. The simplest patterns consist of thoughts-feelings-behavior-thoughts-feelings-behavior and around and around. The process of working with circular causality involves clarifying with the family these patterns, making the pattern explicit, and connecting the dots by pointing out the relationship between affect or feelings and behavior and the impact on the relationship. For example, father believes child is bad, gets annoyed, scolds child, child believes s/he is unwanted, feels hurt, child pouts, father feels frustrated, father scolds, and around and around the pattern goes. It is helpful for a family to see how they go around in these maladaptive patterns.

When the family becomes aware of the circular nature of their communication pattern, the worker can then clarify if there are any family *rules* or myths that keep these patterns going. One rule might be that the only way a child will listen to a parent is when the parent yells at the child.

Further Clarification of Basic Pattern

When clarifying a circular pattern with a family, it is necessary to explore underlying thoughts and feelings as well as increasing clarity of behaviors. In the process, the worker can point out evidence of emotional distress and help members label specific feelings. When feelings are in the open, they can be directly dealt with. When distress is especially high, the worker can encourage family members to provide others with reassurance and support. Bringing circular patterns out in the open and including underlying thoughts and feelings will help family members understand one another (Tomm & Wright, 1979). Through this exercise, family members learn to identify overt and covert patterns. When they are unable to do so, the worker might take the initiative and label them on behalf of the family. Helping the family explore affective, behavioral and cognitive consequences of their interaction directly with each other will help to eliminate blame and is the first step in changing the patterns. Confrontation works best within the context of support. Flushing out family rules and myths can also help members change the pattern.

Conceptualizing Adaptive Patterns

After the dysfunctional patterns have been identified, the worker should then get the family to think about helpful *adaptive* patterns to deal with problem situations. Often, replacement will start with eliciting what specific behaviors can be altered. For example, instead of Mr. Stone retreating to the front of the television set or work room, he can go hug Mrs. Stone. Family members will need help from the family negotiating simultaneous change since they might be reluctant to do so, perhaps because they do not feel safe or believe that making behavioral changes are a sign of failure. Each family member's constructive suggestions must be reinforced and then family members can be coached to try out new adaptive behaviors and assign realistic tasks explicitly as homework (Tomm & Wright, 1979). Practicing these new adaptive behaviors might be assigned as between-session homework.

Dealing with Affective Blocks

It is imperative that the family worker recognize persistent emotional distress (mood) as a block to problem solving and change. The first step in doing so is to differentiate specific affective states and recognize your own affective response to family members. Sitting in a unique spot, you can use your awareness to hypothesize the origin of affective blocks, paying close attention to the impact of your own interventions. You will want to point out evidence of emotional distress and label specific affect. The next step is to stimulate client self-reflection and encourage disclosure. During this phase, the empathic support of the family will create sufficient safety that will allow an exploration of related cognition. The worker acts as a model when these tasks become difficult. Once these tasks have been accomplished, the worker than relates affect to maladaptive interaction and ineffective problem solving.

Developing New Awareness and New Adaptive Patterns

Family members are more receptive to change when in some degree of crisis. After all, why change if everything is going well and you are feeling snug! Yet people will often not change unless the underlying affective blocks have been dealt with. As such, workers also need to understand learning theory and reinforcement principles because they are embedded in family patterns (See Chapter Nine). Once adaptive patterns emerge, the family can instill specific reinforcers in the new patterns to make certain that the new pattern continues. New circular patterns should have elements of positive reinforcement built in. The family worker can work with family members to identify new desired behaviors for themselves and help the family negotiate simultaneous change by reinforcing member's constructive suggestions. Then the worker can direct specific interactions verbally to initiate this change. Family members can be coached by family members in trying out new adaptive behaviors, with the worker relinquishing control when adaptive patterns appear. The next step is to stimulate hope in the family by pointing out probable consequences of the adaptive interaction.

Behavioral Homework Tasks

Homework assignments can then be given to the family. These tasks should be agreed upon by family members and should arise out of the work on circular causality done in the session. All behavioral homework needs to be debriefed in the next family session.

Exercise 5.14
(PBL Worksheet)

Working with Dyads

In the PBL groups practice having the family working in dyads. That is, instruct any two family members to sit together, facing each other and discussing any important issue they may have. The role of the family worker is to coach and support their clear, direct, problem solving communication process.

Exercise 5.15
(PBL Worksheet) [1]

Family Systems Thinking and Circular Causality

Today you are going to understand your family "as a social system." In doing so, you will begin to understand the ***patterns of relationships*** within the family. In the first part of your role-play, the family worker will start to examine ***circular causality*** between two family members. To do this, you will need to identify two people who display a problematic ***pattern*** of communication. Quite often this pattern is in the form of a conflict or a way of arguing. However, the pattern can also involve other problematic communication patterns within the family.

You have two choices in working with circular causality. The first choice is to wait for family patterns to arise naturally and then make use of this "teachable moment." The second choice is for family workers to work with a family dyad by stimulating interaction. That is, each group will pick a family dyad that has shown the best example of a circular pattern. The worker then instructs the dyad by saying, "I would like to see how the two of you resolve differences. Members of the dyad then turn and face each other and start to interact over an issue (select an issue relevant to the dyad).

For this role-play, the family worker will work with two members of the family, while the other family members look on with eager and intelligent curiosity. First, the worker, along with the family, will identify an ongoing pattern of communication between two people that is troublesome. The family worker will then engage the family in taking a closer look at this pattern. The first step is to get the two to exhibit their typical behavior. The next step is to help the dyad become aware of the sequence of activities in this circular pattern: thoughts-feelings-behavior-thoughts-feelings-behavior. They should get a good sense of their contribution to the pattern and their impact on the other person. Do not allow blaming and be very directive to members of the dyad as they are learning about their pattern. Have the two people work on the circular pattern for 20 minutes. You might want to have another student assume the role of the family worker and try this experience again for 20 minutes using a different family dyad.

It does not matter which part of the pattern the social worker starts at - this needs to be made clear to the family so members do not think that one member ***caused*** the problematic communication. Then, the family worker, focused on one part of the dyad, examines feelings, thoughts, and beliefs of the person in the circumstances under review. The worker then says "when you are feeling/thinking/believing ...., what do you do about it (or how do you express it, etc." This should take at least 5-10 minutes to explore this part of it. ***Write the comments on paper so the family can see them***. The worker then clarifies that the other person in the dyad agrees with and describes the behavior exhibited in the pattern. The worker then focuses on the second person's thoughts/beliefs/feelings, ending with a description of the behaviour of the second person.

The next step is to connect the behaviors to the thoughts/beliefs/feelings of the first person, and once this is done, the worker can start the pattern anew until people understand how they impact the other person. The next step is to ask, "Well, how is this ever going to change?" and let the individuals develop a concrete approach to what they are going to do to solve their difficulties. After this has occurred, you can bring in other family members to discuss their observations, learning and to see what they can do to help the proposed changes continue.

Hint: Remember to take about 10 minutes at the end of your role-play to process the major learning of the day. Include in this discussion how the exercises might be used in practice.

Chapter Summary

Family system theory is the foundation upon which most other family theories reside. The concept of patterns is the primary family systems theory idea. Family workers base their interventions based upon the six important assumptions of family systems theory. A family system is part of a larger social system and contains many other subsystems. A change in one family member affects the other family members and the family as a whole. The family as a whole is greater than the sum of its parts. Families strive toward homeostasis. Finally, family members' behavior is circular. Triangulation occurs in all families and deserve special attention when they become destructive.

[1] For exercise 5.15 on page 129, each group will need a flip chart, magic markers, and masking tape so they can stick their diagrams on the wall and then take them with them for later use.

Chapter 6 **Table of Contents**

FAMILY ASSESSMENT INSTRUMENTS
Family Categories Schema & Defining Problems

Chapter 6

Family Assessment Instruments:
Family Categories Schema & Defining Problems

Chapter Coverage

- Measuring Family Functioning
- Family Assessment Instruments
- Assessing Families Using the "Family Categories Schema"
- Summary of Other Assessment Tools
- Defining Problems
- Problem Solving Skills
- Communication Skill Training

Introduction

Numerous instruments are available to measure family functioning and we will discuss several of them.

Measuring Family Functioning

Apart from worker observations of interaction, or using a Genogram or Ecomap, workers have a number of assessment tools at their disposal. Many of these are pencil and paper measures that either the worker or family complete. Corcoran and Fisher (2000) have compiled an extensive collection of measurement tools for couples, families, and children in their two volumes on *Measures for clinical practice.* These instruments can help workers assess families on many dimensions as well as help them monitor and evaluate their practice.

At times, simple observations are insufficient to determine *what* and how *severe* the problem is. For example, sometimes two people can look at exactly the same thing, but see something entirely different. Many times, we can be quite confident about our observations and what they mean. However, when we compare them with other people, we are startled to discover just how different our impressions are. When two people (or an instrument that two people use) do not arrive at the same conclusions, we say that the observations or the instrument are *unreliable.* On the other hand, *validity* means that what you are describing or measuring is what you intended to measure. There are many approaches to determining reliability and validity, which we will not get into here. We encourage you to understand these concepts in more detail because instruments that are not valid or reliable are useless in practice and will not allow you to assess a family or understand the effectiveness of your practice.

Family Assessment Instruments

Using an instrument to measure family functioning is useful for a couple of reasons. First, you might want to use an instrument to pinpoint specific issues in family functioning. Doing so will help you sort out and classify the enormous amount of information that you have amassed on this particular family. A number of assessment devices are available to family workers and selecting one can help you narrow down the hypotheses you develop about a family. In this case, an instrument is an adjunct to your work. That is, it helps narrow down your hunches and observations.

The second reason for using a measurement device is to measure your practice effectiveness. For example, if you discover that the relationship between a parent and child is problematic at the outset of the work, you could select an instrument that measures this particular difficulty. You then use the instrument at the beginning of intervention, perhaps one or two times in the middle, once at the end of service, and if your agency allows, during a follow up period to determine if change persisted after you closed the file.

Many instruments are at your disposal. Some instruments measure marital or parent-child relationships. Others look at specific family issues such as sex roles, abuse, coping or cohesion. In reflecting back on your PBL family or family as you were growing up, what issues do you think should be measured?

Exercise 6.1

Measuring Family Change
(Out of Class)

Decide on a particular behavior, issue or relationship that you would like to measure in your PBL family or any other family. Then locate an instrument that is designed to measure this particular issue. Bring it to class and share it with your classmates.

Describe behavior/issue or relationship:

We mention several of the key instruments for families. Be aware that numerous instruments are available and you need to know what specific aspect of family functioning you would like to measure. For example, The Family Adaptability and Cohesion Scale (FACES III) measures two dimensions of family functioning: Adaptability and Cohesion. It is also known as the Circumplex Model. It is a 20-item measure that assesses ideal family functioning and what actually happens in these two areas. Adaptability measures how chaotic a family is while cohesion measures how enmeshed (Corcoran & Fischer, 2002).

The late Walter Hudson also developed a number of instruments pertaining to family functioning. These include the Index of Family Relations, The Index of Parental Attitudes, The Index of Sister Relations, and the

Index of Brother Relations. Each is designed to measure problems that family members might have in relationship to one another. The benefit of these various indexes is that they have Clinical Cutting scores in that scores above 30 suggest significant difficulties that warrant intervention.

One interesting scale is the Family Schema - Ethnic, constructed by McCubbin, Thompson, Elver, and Carpenter (Corcoran & Fischer, 2000). This instrument measures the extent to which a family has incorporated cultural and ethnic values into its identity.

Family Categories Schema

One popular method used to understand and assess family functioning is the Family Categories Schema based on the McMaster Family Model (Epstein, Baldwin, and Bishop, 1983). We include it here for a couple of reasons. The first is that it provides a conceptual awareness of many areas of family functioning. It provides a general outline with which family workers can conceptualize family functioning. It also measures categories in the model, using a pencil and paper measurement (Corcoran and Fischer, 2000). The theory is known as the Family Categories Schema while the paper and pencil instrument is called the Family Assessment Device. Both are based upon a holistic family perspective. The schema offers categories upon which to base observations. The instrument is filled in by family workers.

The Family Assessment Device has good reliability and validity. The instrument looks at family functioning, organization, and transactions, placing them into seven overlapping categories. This instrument, (and other family assessment tools), are presented in Measure for Clinical Practice (Corcoran & Fischer, 2000). Families can complete the instrument or workers might conduct an open-ended assessment using the outline and criteria covered by the different categories. In this chapter, we describe the seven categories, which will give you a framework with which to assess the family's holistic functioning. The Family Categories Schema and the Family Assessment Device is a well-recognized measurement instrument and is a well recognized tool for examining family functioning (see for example, Collins, Jordan, & Coleman 1999; Franklin, Hopson, & Ten Barge, 2003)

The outline of the categories in this Schema guides the conceptualization, observations, and questions as they work to understand the internal functioning of the family. Ordering information in each category will help structure a large amount of information that you collect from the family. Using the categories will also help you develop a coherent understanding of what issues need further attention in the family.

The Family Categories Schema assesses families in eight areas of functioning: (Corcoran & Fischer, 2000)

1. Problem Solving
2. Affective Responsiveness
3. Affective Involvement
4. Communication
5. Role Behavior
6. Autonomy
7. Modes of Behavioral Control
8. General Functioning

Assessment by Interviewing

In an assessment interview, the family worker uses basic interviewing skills. The following are a list of these basic skills:

A. "Joining" or engaging and assessment overlap.

Joining is a vital skill throughout family work. When clients feel heard and understood, they feel free to be open with you, permitting you to gather important information by observing how the client engages with the family worker during the helping process. Joining does not end at the beginning of family work, but continues throughout. At times of emotional distress or emotional disengagement, the worker can revisit the joining process, either by expressing empathy toward the client or by inviting a family member back into the process.

B. Listening carefully is a crucial skill throughout family work.

Without accurately tuning into thoughts, feelings, behaviors and family processes, you will miss critical pieces of information about the family and family members. Listening goes beyond merely hearing words with your ears - it also involves understanding the meaning behind the behavior and words. It is particularly important during engagement and assessment process and is critical to establishing rapport, building trust, and obtaining necessary information. However, we cannot imagine being effective in the work phase without carefully listening. It is the family worker's responsibility to ensure that the content of the client's communication, both verbal and nonverbal, is received, acknowledged, and understood. Therapeutic listening helps the clients become more self-aware, slow down, and respect their own wisdom. How do you know if you are listening attentively? Because attentive listening is hard work, we suggest that fatigue after an interview is one sign (not to be confused with staying up late the night before).

C. Appropriate use of questioning.

Questions are used to gather information and move clients to a deeper understanding of their issues. When used properly, questions convey an interest in the family and are useful engagement tools. Questions are not random. Rather, they are formulated based upon specific content. For example, when doing a Genogram with a family, your questions will be formulated to gather family tree information. Questions are the most abused but the most valuable tool at a worker's disposal. One common error in questioning is the use of closed ended questions (e.g., does your husband remind you of your father?). Instead, we encourage you to develop the "habit" of asking open-ended questions (e.g., who does your husband remind you of?). Questions should be formulated clearly before they pop out of your mouth. Otherwise, you risk asking double barreled or confusing questions (e.g., do you take the bus to school or your lunch?). In addition, improper use of questions can make people feel interrogated. The specific content of questions arises out of a theoretical framework. For example, based on a systems perspective, the family worker could ask, "What effect does your son's behavior have on your behavior toward him, and vice versa?"

1. Problem Solving

When assessing the family's problem solving behaviors, the worker focuses on the family's coping behaviors in the face of threats to its emotional and physical well being, and overall family survival. These threats are either instrumental (e.g., physical well-being) or affective (emotional well-being). Instrumental threats refer to the concrete aspects of family life (such as financial issues, food, health, or homelessness). Poverty or working in a minimum wage job, a family member's health problems, and car accidents are all examples of instrumental threats to a family. Affective threats undermine the emotional well being of families and their members. Examples include mental illness, stress, or ongoing marital conflict. Instrumental and affective difficulties are associated. For example, a parent may be depressed because of unemployment or health problems. Instrumental threats create stress for families. Families with well-developed problem solving abilities are able to use the problem-solving process effectively.

Exercise 6.2

Problem Solving in Your Family of Origin
(In Class)

Break into groups of two and discuss the following. Try to remember one outstanding problem from your family-of-origin. Was this problem resolved? How did your family address this particular problem? What was the style of problem solving? What were the strengths? Looking back on the problem now, what could have been done differently? Share with the class.

Examples of questions to ask about Problem Solving:

- What problems, both short term and long term, are family members experiencing?
- Do all family members experience the same problems or different ones?
- What are the problem solving behaviors in response to their problems?
- How severe are the problem(s)?
- How much is the family in crisis in response to the problems?
- How urgent are the family needs as a result of these problems?
- What is the history of the problem?
- What are the strengths and resources of the family and its members that can be mobilized to resolve the problem?
- What is the history of problem-solving in this particular family? How has the family approached outstanding problems within the family?

2. Affective Responsiveness

In well functioning families, family members should be allowed the opportunity to express a range of feelings and be accepted and supported in doing so. Possible emotions include: (1) Welfare emotions (happiness, joy tenderness, love, and sympathy), and (2) Emergency emotions (rage, fear, anger, and depression). In assessing affective responsiveness, it is important to assess whether family members express feelings in a congruent way. The emotion and its intensity must match what they are responding to. The *pattern* of emotional expression is especially important - that is, is emotional responsiveness predictable within the family. It also entails how emotions are expressed and whether they are clear, direct, open and honest, or indirect, masked or dishonest. The extent to which all family members express feelings is also noteworthy.

Exercise 6.3

Affective Responsiveness
(In Class)

Break into groups of two or three students. Each student will take a turn describing how their family-of-origin shared feelings with one another. Note the range of feelings and whether one feeling was expressed most often. What impact does this style have on you at this moment in time? How is this style recreated in current relationships?

Examples of questions to ask about Affective Responsiveness

- How does the family express a range of feelings?
- What is the range of feelings that are expressed?
- How do individual members let you know when they are happy, sad, angry, etc.?
- Is one type of feeling more acceptable than others?
- How does this family convey support and caring?
- Who expresses what feelings to whom?
- Is one set of feelings (e.g., anger) preferred over an opposite set (e.g., caring)?

3. Affective Involvement

Affective involvement entails the frequency and depth to which family members are emotionally involved, through shared activities and interests, in addition to involvement needed for daily family operations. Affective involvement captures the amount and quality of emotional involvement of family members with each other and is demonstrated through the quality and expression of relationships. For example, does the parent drop off a child at a baseball game or does s/he stay around watch and then talk about the game with the child afterwards. In Chapter 7, we discuss the importance of parents being connected to important people in children's lives, such as school and friends. Thus, parents need to be continually and actively involved in their children's lives without being overbearing and controlling. Recent surveys of adolescents suggest that they would like their parents more involved in their lives; they are referring to their parents' affective involvement.

It is important that parents feel close to their children by feeling emotionally attached to them and by becoming involved in their daily activities. Without *Affective Involvement,* problems can become worse and parents will lose the influence they have over children. However, for many reasons some parents have a difficult time being involved with their children. As mentioned, they may be buried under an enormous level of stress. They may be exhausted from parenting a child with behavior problems. They may be working at low paying, time-consuming, stressful or dissatisfying jobs. They might have other children with special needs. They may be single parents, overwhelmed with all that they have to juggle. Being a parent is not easy. It is probably one of the most difficult jobs demanded of anyone.

Exercise 6.4

Increasing Affective Involvement
(In Class)

Imagine that you are the parent of a child with very difficult behavior. Because of the child's behavior you are inclined to avoid contact from that child, although you recognize that your reactions are unfair to the child. You would like to change this pattern. For each of the ages below, prepare a list of enjoyable activities that you can do with your child to help improve the relationship. Also, decide how frequently this activity should occur

	Activity	Frequency
Toddler		
Preschooler		
Elementary school age		
Pre-teen		
Young adolescent		
Older adolescent		

Examples of questions to ask about Affective Involvement

- Who is involved with whom? What activities are family members involved with each other?
- Who takes care of family members when they are ill? Who attends the parent-teacher interviews?
- Who do the children turn to when having relationship problems?
- How empathic are family members with one another?
- Do parents monitor and supervise their children's activities? Do parents know their children's friends?
- Do they know where their children are at all times, and what they are doing?

4. Communication

We know that "you cannot not communicate," making understanding verbal and nonverbal communication essential. Communication concerns both "*what*" and "*how*" messages are conveyed. The *what* of communication is the content, whereas the *how* involves the process of what was said, and the nature of the relationship. Listening carefully to *how* communication occurs provides clues about family relationships. For example, a message based on concern has a different underlying message than one out of impatience. This is true regardless of the content.

As mentioned, healthy communication is clear, direct, open, and honest (see Chapter 3 for a description and examples). Communication can convey either emotional or instrumental messages. Affective messages contain feelings whereas instrumental messages concern behaviors and activities about tasks of daily life and routines. Communication is both verbal and nonverbal. Most communication is nonverbal (e.g., selection of words, body language, and tone of voice). Words might communicate, "I care," conveyed through eye contact, attentive body language, matching words and gestures and a soft tone of voice. However, the same words delivered when the speaker is watching television, eyes averted, and in an impatient tone of voice, conveys an opposite message. Verbal and nonverbal communication should match. Additionally, communication should go two ways rather than have one person "speak at" another.

Exercise 6.5

Communication
(In Class)

Break into groups of two or three students. Allow students 5-10 minutes each to share their members of communication within their family-of-origin. What were the nonverbal modes of communication? How were messages conveyed verbally? Were messages open, honest, and direct? If you were to change the communication style of your family, what would you like to see changed? How would you go about changing the communication?

Examples of questions to ask about Communication

- How do individual family members communicate to other members?
- Are there repetitive patterns of communication, for example, angry exchanges over household tasks?
- Is communication direct, open, and honest?
- Can family members have pleasant conversations with each other?
- What are the circular patterns of communication evident in this family (Chapter 5)?
- Do some family members communicate regularly? Are some left out of the conversation?
- Is communication delivered congruently?
- What are the patterns of interaction between family members?
- What interaction patterns seem to maintain the problem?
- What are the ongoing patterns and themes in the client's family?
- How is the client functioning in their informal and formal roles?

***Helping family members communicate*:** As mentioned, open, direct, honest, clear, and congruent communication is the foundation of family work. Communication without these qualities interferes with every aspect of family life. Family workers can identify communication blocks and identify possible sources of family problems. Communication improves when family members acquire better communication skills. Workers can teach these skills by direct instruction or through modeling them to family members.

Altering problematic communication occurs over three steps:

1. Family members discuss communication and develop a beginning awareness of what they are doing. Sometimes family members can play back to the speaker what they hear the person saying;
2. They then analyze their behaviors and emotional responses; This can occur with feedback and by the speaker responding to the feedback received, and
3. The final step is to examine the impact of the interaction on relationships. Here two people can give their response to what was said to them. For example, members can say, "When you said x, I felt hurt, etc. (Watzlawick, Beavin, & Jackson, 1967).

Family members spend most of their waking moments together, but often fail to communicate clearly. Because communication is habitual, we seldom stop and reflect on the underlying meaning of what we hear or what we are saying. Beneath the surface of most communication is metacommunication, defined as "communication about communication" or a "message about a message." Moreover, most communication is a request (Satir, 1967). In correcting communication, it is useful to check out *in the moment*, the meaning of what another has just said. It requires that the worker pay close attention to interactions, stop the process, and engage the family in a discussion of the events that just occurred. If videotaping equipment is available, the recordings can be played back to the family to bring the patterns to conscious awareness. Doing so will help members replace dysfunctional patterns of communication with healthier patterns.

***Listening and Empathizing*:** One common method of improving communication is teaching the use of paraphrasing. Through paraphrasing, family members develop skills of active listening, so they do not jump to conclusions and misinterpret what was said. Paraphrasing shows that a message was heard. For instance, a woman says to her partner, "I am upset because you are never around to help with the housework." Her husband echoes her, saying, "You are mad because I do not help around the house." Rather than arguing, the listener restates the message, including both content and feelings, and communicates to his partner that he heard what she said. If the paraphrase is incorrect, the wife has an opportunity to clarify the message.

***Using "I" Statements"*:** When people speak with one another, they often say something like, "You make me feel so mad." This message conveys blame. And the use of "I" statements can clarify "who owns what." Using "I" statements to communicate a message, can decrease family conflicts. The angry partner in the previous paragraph can say, "You are a lazy idiot! You are self centered and never raise a finger to help out!" Blaming puts the other party on the defensive and starts a round of arguing. Alternatively, she can use an "I" statement to express how her partner's behavior affects her. For example, "When you sit around all day and I am working hard, I feel angry and used, because I am doing all the work by myself." The general format for making I statements is "I feel *(speaker's feeling),* when you *(family member's behavior),* because (*rationale*)."

This opens the door to negotiation and possible solutions, such as, "Could we make a deal that I will not get on you case if you agree to sit down with me so we can make a list of chores for both of us to do" The listener could offer alternative solutions and the two can negotiate and they both agree. Family members can practice active listening and "I" statements with the family worker coach them.

5. Role Behavior

Family members must work together to ensure that family tasks and responsibilities are met. Each member plays a range of roles in the family that eventually become well engrained and predictable. Roles, therefore, are predictable behaviors and can take many forms, including those that follow traditional family patterns based on gender, age and marital relationship. Some roles are more unique. Roles are either instrumental or affective. Regardless of whether roles are traditional or nontraditional, they are effective when they fulfill the following criteria: When all family tasks are covered, all family members are satisfied with their roles, and where there is a fair balance. In addition, the roles of adults and children must be clearly differentiated, be flexible enough to respond to different situations, and be performed competently.

Roles are performed both inside and outside the family. Common internal family roles include, family relationships, childcare activities, health practices, and household activities. External family roles include; use of external resources, social activities, and behaviors related to financial issues and the relationship of the family to the worker (Geismar & Ayres, 1959).

We have discussed the traditional family elsewhere in this book. In the traditional family, members assume gender stereotypical roles. While gender roles are changing, women still fill them disproportionately and many still consider childcare to be primarily the mother's responsibility. Some roles fuel family conflict such who is responsible for child management and other instrumental tasks, especially housework. Unique roles can emerge that depart from traditional prescriptions. These unique roles can be reverse of expected social roles such as a father staying home to raise children. Other idiosyncratic roles may relate to family problems, such as the scapegoat, the parentified child, the clown, the black sheep, or the sick one.

Exercise 6.6

Roles
(In Class)

Again, break into groups of two or three students. Based on your family-of-origin or on a current relationship, describe the roles that various members play. How did these roles come about? Were members satisfied with these roles? How would you go about changing these roles?

Examples of questions to ask about Behavior

- What are the roles that individual family members assume?
- Are the needs of the household and family fulfilled by the performance of these roles?
- Do people understand and agree with the roles they have been assigned?
- Do parents and children have different roles, according to their age and individual abilities?
- How satisfied are family members with the roles they assume in the family?
- How balanced is the assignment of roles?
- What are the conflicts pertaining to the assignment and assumption of individual roles?
- How does the client describe their family responsibilities and how they fulfill them?
- What is the nature of the relationships within the family?
- Who makes decisions for the family about things like meals, family activities, and family holidays?

6. Autonomy

Autonomy occurs when family members have permission to function independently and make decisions based on age and ability. It is demonstrated through members being allowed to act as individuals. They are permitted to make independent decisions and the flip side is that they are capable of accepting responsibility for their decisions. When individuals are not allowed to make independent decisions, we see a power imbalance in the family. For example, when women are not permitted to handle money in the family, when children are overly restricted in their activities (e.g., not allowed to play sports out of fear for their well-being), or when members' behavior is so tightly regulated, they are not given space for individual expression. Autonomy is a particularly salient issue of adolescence, within certain sensible parameters of course.

Examples of questions to ask about Autonomy

- What activities do family members do on their own? Are these activities accepted by others?
- What rules exist in terms of how long family members can be away from home?
- Are family members allowed to disagree with one another and have their opinions accepted?
- Do family members have permission to make their own choices in areas that are important to them or do they have to abide by the opinions of the parents?
- Do family members accept responsibility for the choices they make?

7. Behavioral Control

When we refer to behavioral control, we are describing how the family deals with impulses and threatening situations. We are also referring to how behavior is managed within the family, ranging from rigid to chaotic. We are particularly interested in how the behavior of children is controlled. The four categories for behavior control of children are generally accepted in family work literature (Collins, Jordan, & Coleman, 1999).

1. *Rigid* behavior control is a firmly established pattern that fails to accommodate behavioral individual variation (e.g., a family where children always have to go to bed at 9:30 regardless of the circumstances. We recall one situation with visiting friends who had children the same age as ours. The parents insisted on the children going to bed very early, making no allowance for the fact that the children had not seen each other in a long time and despite the protestations of the children).
2. *Flexible* behavior control occurs when standard behavior is clearly spelled out and firmly enforced but remains flexible depending on the circumstances. Exceptions to the rules can occur in appropriate circumstances (e.g., a family where agreed upon family rules exist, but may be bent under special conditions. A family rule may be that children usually have to go to bed at 9:30 but can stay up later when friends come to visit).
3. *Laissez-faire* behavior control occurs when enforcing rules are ineffective or when no rules exist at all. Parents allow children to do what they wish with no guidelines. The rules are not predictable (e.g., a family where there are no rules about going to bed - the children go whenever they please).
4. *Chaotic* behavior control exists when behavior control is inconsistent and when rules change from one circumstance to another with no apparent reason. Rules are therefore completely unpredictable (e.g., a family where children go to bed at midnight one night and the next night go to bed at 7:00, without any apparent rationale or differing context).

These four modes of behavior control need to be evaluated whether they are consistent or inconsistent, and whether they are predictable or unpredictable. Family workers need to understand whether rules are made in the family, what the expectations for behavior are, and if the rules about behavior are enforced consistently.

Examples of questions to ask about Behavioral Control:

- What are rules about specific behavior in the family?
- How are the rules enforced? Is enforcement consistent?
- Do family members know what is acceptable and what are unacceptable behaviors?
- Is enforcement of the rules fair and predictable?
- Are the consequences for breaking rules reasonable and do they match "the crime?"
- What is the parenting disciplinary style?
- Do your rules change depending on the circumstance?

8. General Functioning

General functioning is the sum of all of these categories. What problems have you identified and agreed to work on? What are the strengths and weaknesses of the family system? What are areas of competence? What are the psychological and social resources used for daily living as well as dealing with crises as they appear?

Examples of questions about General Functioning:

- How would you describe how this family gets along overall?
- What would you see as the weaknesses in your family?
- What would you see as the strengths in your family?
- What are areas of strength in this particular family in any of the six categories identified above?
- What are areas that need to be worked on?
- Does the family agree with the difficulties that were discovered?

Exercise 6.7

Formulating Clear Questions
(In Class)

Split into dyads and role play alternating between family worker and client. You will practice the effective use of questioning. Formulate questions for the client about what family work has been like for him or her thus far. In the first ten minutes, the worker questions will be clear and open ended. After ten minutes, the worker switches to use poorly formulated questions (closed, garbled, asking multiple questions quickly in a row, why questions). Compare the first part of the role play minutes with the last part. What were the differences? Which segment did the client prefer and how come?

Exercise 6.8

Assessing a Family: The Family Categories Schema
(In Class)

Select a family portrayed on television (e.g., the Simpsons, Seventh Heaven, etc.). Break into small groups and assess this particular family using the categories from the Family Categories Schema. Provide concrete examples to back up your conclusions. Re-convene in the larger class and compare your responses.

Answer the following questions:

1. What are the problems that the Simpsons face? How do the Simpsons solve these problems?

2. How do the various members of the Simpson family respond to each other emotionally?

3. What is the range of emotions that family members express? How do they show caring toward one another? What are the feelings that are expressed when the family is facing a crisis?

4. How involved are family members with each other? In what activities do the children participate? To what extent are Marge and Homer involved in their children's activities? In what activities do the parents participate? Are the parents involved in any activity with one another?

(continued)

5. Describe the roles in this family. What are the traditional roles? What are the idiosyncratic roles in the family? Which family member would you think would be the impetus for the family coming to a social service agency?

6. To what extent are family members allowed autonomy? Is there a difference in the amount of autonomy allowed for males and females? Is the amount of autonomy permitted for the different ages and abilities appropriate?

7. How are the children disciplined? How would you describe the behavior control: rigid, flexible, laissez faire or chaotic?

8. Given the issues that you identified in the previous seven questions, how you would assess the overall functioning of the family?

Think of the Family Categories Schema presented above. This form provides a useful framework to carry around with you to structure family assessment. After your family interviews, use this form for your record keeping. The form is straightforward to complete if you keep in mind the form with the categories and blank paragraph spaces (see Figure 6.1 and Figure 6.2). Blank items will alert you to the need to ask further questions in this area to fill in the gap.

Figure 6.1

Family Categories Schema

Problem Solving

Affective Responsiveness

Affective Involvement

Communication

Role Behavior

Autonomy

Modes of Behavioral Control

General Functioning

Figure 6.2

Thumbnail Sketch of the Stone Family
Family Categories Schema

Problem Solving

The family has some ability to solve instrumental problems yet members avoid affective problem solving. For example they have difficulty keeping on a manageable budget.

Affective Responsiveness

Family members express some feelings, primarily those of depression or anger. Members offer little expression of support and caring for each other as family members are withdrawn and express few feelings toward one another.

Affective Involvement

Very little involvement in each other's lives. Each family member goes his or her own way and shows little interest in the activities of others.

Communication

Family members avoid having any meaningful communication with each other. Communication is not clear and is expressed indirectly.

Role Behavior

Father fills the role of stepfather yet this has not been defined or agreed upon by the family. Mrs. Stone feels primarily responsible for family problems in her role as wife and mother but fills the sick role. Michael pays an acting out teenager role and assumes little responsibility for completing family tasks. He plays the role of scapegoat and black sheep. Daughter, Mary, withdrawn yet excelling as a good student. She is labeled as the good child.

Autonomy

Both teenagers are allowed a lot of autonomy, as parents are rather uninvolved with children and overwhelmed by parenting and marital issues.

Modes of Behavioral Control

Rather laissez faire methods of behavior control due to mother's withdrawal and uninvolvement. Stepfather is the main disciplinarian yet somewhat inconsistent in enforcing rules.

General Functioning

The Stone family, other than the daughter, is isolated from social contacts and sources of social support. The family has poor and ineffective affective problem solving skills with little affective communication shown in the family. The family copes on a day-to-day basis but is overwhelmed by its issues. Communication, roles, and affective are targets of change.

Exercise 6.9

Family Categories Assessment
(PBL Worksheet)

Today, in your PBL groups, you will continue to formally conduct an assessment on your practice family, using the family categories schema as a framework.

The family worker will ask questions related to the eight categories in this schema, while helping the family understand how they are functioning in these areas. We suggest that that you begin by talking about Roles and leave discussion of Affective Involvement to the end. You will be able to gather a picture of how all the individual family members perceive the family. Take about five minutes to debrief the results with the family.

Then move onto debriefing the process of assessment using this guideline. What was the process like for you? What would be the best way to integrate this into your practice with families? Would you do anything differently next time when assessing families?

Assessment Tools

So far in the book we have covered the *Genogram*, Family Systems theory (including circular causality), and the Family Categories Schema. In the next chapter, we present the Ecomap, which includes a person-in-environment assessment. In Chapter 8, we present an assessment framework based on the Family Life Cycle. Each of these frameworks will help you assess families from unique angles and help you zero in on areas that need change in the family. We now move onto discuss four different perspectives available to you to further your understanding of the family: the biological, analytic, learning and social interactional perspectives.

Four Perspectives: Biological; Analytic; Learning; and, Social Interactional

One premise of generalist family work is that we understand families from many different angles including the person-in-environment perspective. Another interesting way to look at family problems is by using four perspectives, which allows the worker to view and assess family problems from four quite different angles. These four perspectives include:

1. Biological
2. Analytic
3. Learning
4. Social Interactional

The easiest way to understand the four perspectives is for family workers to imagine themselves wearing four different hats: a medical doctor's hat for the biological perspective; a traditional psychiatrist's hat for the analytic perspective; a psychologist's hat for the learning perspective; and a social workers hat for the social interactional perspective.

1. Biological

In the biological perspective, problems are viewed with an understanding of the biological connection to the problem. For example, an encopretic child (a child who soils his or her pants) might be assessed for lack of sphincter muscle control possibly due to a recent bowel infection. Treatment, using a biological understanding, would first include referring the child for a medical assessment and then developing an intervention if a biological cause is discovered, to clear up the infection and assign sphincter muscle exercises to restore these muscles to a normal state. In the case of the Stone family, the mother's depression might be viewed as a chemical imbalance and pharmacological drug treatment would be initiated.

The biological perspective looks at the interconnection between physical health and emotional well being and it is premised on the belief that the mind and the body are connected. People, who eat well, sleep well, and exercise, thereby maintaining a healthy physical state, are more likely to feel emotionally healthy. It is thus important for the family worker to ask each family member what they do to take care of themselves physically, including eating, sleeping and physical activities. Workers must also be open to the possibility of behaviors having a physical connection. For example, a child who is misbehaving and throwing tantrums might be tired, hungry, or thirsty.

2. Analytic

In the analytic perspective we put on a traditional psychiatric hat and view problems as individual internal struggles accompanied with unresolved feelings. At its most basic level, we want to know how people deal with their feelings. Using our example of an encopretic child, we might hypothesize that the behavior may be related to unresolved feelings of anger that are bottled up inside the child, yet leak out through encoprecis. (Of course, before you jump to any conclusion, you will have explored what the literature and research suggests about this particular condition.) You might explore this hypothesis by asking the family how they express their feelings such as happiness, sadness and finally anger, noticing that when you raise the issue of anger with the family, the mother withdraws, the child appears anxious, and the father says, "No one gets anger in this house!" From this, you get a clear, yet indirect message that the expression of anger is not permissible in this family. The treatment plan would be for family counseling to help family members learn to express a wider range of feelings, including anger, in appropriate ways. With the Stone family, a similar treatment plan would involve teaching the family how to not only express depression and sadness appropriately but also learn to show appropriate listening, support and caring to each other.

3. Learning

Using this perspective, problems are thought to occur as a result of faulty learning. In the example of the encopretic child, a standard procedure is to take a base line measure of the encopretic occurrences. This is accomplished by asking the family to keep a daily log of when they notice that the child has soiled his pants. It may be that the family records that the child soils his pants every weekday around 4:30 pm. However, the baseline measure also helps point out that the child does not soil his pants on the weekends. After investigating this pattern deeper, it becomes readily apparent that the child is at school until 4 o'clock and soils his pants regularly on the way home. Clearly, a family behavioral approach is put into place whereby the family works with the school to ensure the child goes to the bathroom prior to leaving the school, and when he returns home the family reinforces clean pants using praise. With the Stone family, Mrs. Stone may have learned to show depression by withdrawing. Instead a family approach would teach Mrs. Stone to reach out to others in her family for emotional support and teach her other alternative behaviors to replace withdrawal. In response, the family would respond to her reaching out by providing her with support and appreciation. Another alternative would be that when she feels depressed, she would get involved in an active physical activity. It is difficult to remain depressed when jogging!

4. Social Interactional

In this perspective, problems are thought to stem from problems embedded in relationships. In family work, the belief is that problems are produced by maladaptive family interaction and relationships. For example, a classic family pattern is that of scapegoating. In our encropesis example, we might hypothesize that the child is the scapegoat for marital problems. That is, instead of the husband and wife dealing directly with each other about marital discord, the child is triangulated into the relationship and becomes the repository of their negative feelings (Chapter 5). The child is thus blamed for marital and family problems. "If it was not for you, mom and dad would get along." "We would have money if it were not for the kids." By being concerned about the child, mother and father can more easily avoid problems in their relationship.

Being the family scapegoat is overwhelming for children and comes with costs that are emotional, and in our example, physical. Checking out this hypothesis requires some tact on part of the family worker. However usually it goes something like this: "I imagine it has been difficult for both of you as parents to deal with your child's soiling. I wonder how the two of you work together as parents?" A typical response might be mother responding, "My husband is never around to help me out." Then you could say, "I sense that there is not only parenting issues but also some marital conflict present in your family." Families who feel connected with you as the family worker will feel comfortable enough admitting that they do indeed have marital issues and these issues affect their parenting and their relationship with their child. Thus, intervention might also include marital counseling. In the Stone family, depression would be viewed as maladaptive patterns of communication in the family, particularly between husband and wife, and thus marital counseling would occur. (See Chapter 5 on family systems and circular causality for a fuller understanding of the social interactional perspective as it is based on systems theory.)

Exercise 6.10

Four Perspectives
(PBL Worksheet)

In your PBL groups, identify one main problem your PBL family is experiencing. Now as a group, explore the problem to see if you can uncover issues that arise from a biological, analytical, learning, and social interactional perspective (20-30 minutes). For each of these perspectives, write down a possible intervention plan. Share your assessment and intervention plans with the large class.

Biological Assessment	Intervention Plan
Analytical Assessment	Intervention Plan
Learning Assessment	Intervention Plan
Social Interactional Assessment	Intervention Plan

Table 6.1

List of Assessment Tools

Genogram
Circular Causality
Family Systems Theory
Family Categories Schema
Ecomap
Family Life Cycle Assessment
Four Perspectives
  Biological
  Analytical
  Learning
  Social Interactional

Definition of Problems

At this point, we broaden our understanding of family problems even further. It is important to realize that the way that workers and family members define a problem influences the intervention and the actions that are taken to resolve the problem. We then present three practical skill sets to helping families: problem solving skills, communication skill training, and loss counseling skills.

Contrasting Assumptions Regarding Problems

How we view and understand a problem is fundamental to any helping process and family work is no exception. The particular viewpoint or definition that is assumed directs the course of intervention. Most problem definitions within a family follow a systemic perspective. Yet a number of systemic views exist apart from basic systems theory and each is radically different from the other. In the following discussion, we present six different ways to view problems with related intervention models, most of which are discussed in more detail in future chapters. The way you define a problem often depends on many things:

- How the family initially defines the problem;
- How the worker prefers to define problems, that is, the theoretical perspective you are most comfortable and familiar with as well as the mandate of your agency and how the agency views problems. For example, some agencies are heavily oriented towards solution focused counseling and would expect workers to define problems to fit this view;
- Finally, and hopefully ultimately, the problem is defined jointly between the family and yourself in a way that both you and the family believe provides best opportunities to create positive change.

6 Different Ways to Define Problems

1. A traditional analytic view is that the Symptomatic Person is the Problem.

We start with the most common way traditionally educated counselors define problems. This traditional view places problems within an individual's personality. This perspective is rooted in individual psychopathology. Individuals are believed to have internal struggles with unresolved conflicts, ego problems, lack of motivation, poor impulse control, lack of moral fiber, attachment difficulties, etc. Nearly all workers involved in individual counseling subscribe to this view at least somewhat. However, the influence of a more generalist, ecological view has re-routed the exclusive focus on individual psychopathology to take the effect of larger social systems on an individual's well being more into account.

The traditional analytic view might hypothesize, for example, that Mrs. Stone is depressed because of unresolved self-esteem issues. Stemming from this individually oriented assessment of the problem, the treatment approach would be individual counseling for Mrs. Stone and might include pharmaceutical support.

Exercise 6.11

The Individual is the Problem
(PBL Worksheet)

Interview your PBL family and define the main problem from this individual perspective. Develop your understanding of the problem by obtaining a history of the problem and attempts to resolve it. Debrief in larger class.

2. The Social Systems perspective is that the Family is the Problem (the basic systems view).

Family systems theory helped change the way problems are understood. Instead of seeing problems as an individual issue, problems were recast as systemic problems that are embedded within relationships. Thus, the primary system of concern and the one that exerts the most influence on an individual is the family. Thus the social systems assumption that the family is the problem, involving the patterned ways family members relate to each, could be considered problematic. Major family therapy models, which ascribe to this view, include the communicative model and structural family therapy models.

For example, the Stone family has difficulties relating to each other in ways that members receive sufficient affective support in order to deal with a member's depression. By defining the depression as a family systems problem, the treatment approach would involve family counseling, focusing on how the family as a whole supports members to deal with depression.

Exercise 6.12

The Family Is the Problem
(PBL Worksheet)

Interview your PBL family and define the main problem from a family systems perspective. Develop your understanding of the problem by obtaining a history of the problem and attempts to resolve it. Debrief in larger class.

3. The Mental Research Institute in Palo Alto perspective is that the attempted solution is the problem (an interactional view).

The following saying captures a rather interesting view: "If what you are doing does not work, stop doing it, and try something different!" If yelling at your children to do their homework is not working, try something different. If nagging to get your partner to help with household chores is not working, try something different. Thus, what you previously considered a solution to a problem, such as yelling to get a family member to do something, is not working. These so-called solutions have now become the problem that needs to be changed. As an example, instead of yelling to get children to do homework, give them a time out (Chapter 8). In terms of household chores, replace the nagging with sitting down with a person and developing a task chart assigning household chores that is then posted on the fridge. Behavioral family therapy becomes a helpful model to look at alternative behaviors (solutions) to help to achieve desired family changes (See Chapter 8).

In the Stone family, the mother's *withdrawal* (their attempted solution) from each other increases family member's feelings of being overwhelmed, isolated, and depressed. Family counseling could be offered by focusing on changing the family behavioral pattern of withdrawal to more adaptive behaviors such as activities that increase involvement with each other.

Exercise 6.13

The Attempted Solution Is the Problem
(PBL Worksheet)

Interview your PBL family and define the main problem, as the attempted solution is the problem. Develop your understanding of the problem by obtaining a history of the problem and attempts to resolve it. Debrief in larger class.

4. The Milan group says the problem is the solution (a functional cybernetic view).

The Milan group is a major school of Strategic family therapy. Problems are seen as playing a function or role for the family system. Thus, within family relationships or the family system a functional reason exists for the problem. In other words, the problem serves an important role in family functioning. It is therefore important to assess and hypothesis what function the problem is having and then turn this function around, thus making "the problem the solution."

For example, by being depressed the Stone family will learn the value of affective closeness (i.e. family depression will force the family to become affectively close).

Again, given this definition of the problem, family counseling would occur. The family would be made aware of the "payoff" or the function that depression serves for the family, thereby attempting to force the family to become more affectively close. The family would be supported in becoming routinely affectively close without the need for depression to force them.

Exercise 6.14

The Problem Is the Solution
(PBL Worksheet)

Interview your PBL family and define the main problem from this problem is the solution perspective. Develop your understanding of the problem by obtaining a history of the problem and attempts to resolve it. Debrief in larger class.

5. **Michael White, a social worker from Australia, offers a unique way of understanding problems.**

The Narrative Model perspective views **the symptom (problem) as a restraint** (evolutionary cybernetic view; i.e. the direction of interaction between the problem and solution is important). The problem separated from the individual, rather than as part of the individual. The family worker maps the influence of the problem on family members and also maps how family members have at times overcome the problem (see Chapter 11).

For example, the Stone family, at times, allows **depression** to take control of the family and members will need to become more vigilant as a family unit to keep **depression** away. (Depression is conceptualized verbally as an external entity). The focus in family work would be to help the family become aware of the power or influence that depression has at times on the family. The family would be encouraged to make greater efforts in doing behaviors that have been successful in minimizing the impact depression has on them (for example, family recreational activities, family talk times, etc.)

Exercise 6.15

The Problem as a Restraint
(PBL Worksheet)

Interview your PBL family and define the main problem as a restraint. Hint: externalize the problem, that is make the problem an entity that is external to the family. Develop your understanding of the problem by obtaining a history of the problem and attempts to resolve it. Debrief in larger class.

6. Maturana sees the distinction as the problem (the structured determined view).

Depression can be viewed as either overwhelming or as a challenge. Seeing whether the family defines depression as a negative (i.e. overwhelming) or as a positive challenge opens up different opportunities for change. It parallels the view of whether a person views him or herself as an optimist or a pessimist. Do you make the distinction that the glass is half-empty or half full? When you wake up in the morning do you say to yourself "I do not want to get out of bed — I hate going to work," which may lead to a more negative attitude and approach to the day, compared with getting up in the morning and saying, "What a beautiful morning, I am going to have a great day!" leading to positive experiences over the day.

In a family interview, the family is encouraged to redefine the problem, depression, in a way that opens up opportunities for members. For example, depression can help people better appreciate the times in the family when depression is not present. The depressed mother could be defined differently (restoried), to reflect that she is a very sensitive, caring parent, deeply involved and moved by what is happening in her family. It is hoped that by not viewing her as a depressed person but as a very sensitive, caring parent deeply involved and moved by what is happening in her family, she will receive the support she needs to continue to try to be a good parent without self-doubt and self-blame.

The Stone family, the mother, in particular, may see life as depressing with little hope of getting out of their troubles. She may see her husband as distant, uninvolved, and uncaring. As well, she may view the children as overwhelming and her son as a bad child. All these views sap energy and limit possibilities for change. Instead, the family worker would help the family create new views that open up opportunities for change. For example, the husband can be framed as being so caring that he himself is overwhelmed of what to do differently, but by coming to family work he is willing to change. Adolescents would be understood as challenges instead of problems. The son Michael would be redefined, not as a bad child, but as a hurting youngster who is in need of support and guidance. Finally, the mother's depression could be redescribed as a very sensitive caring mother who wants to do a good job yet requiring more support.

Exercise 6.16

The Distinction as the Problem
(PBL Worksheet)

Interview your PBL family and define the main problem in a way that opens up possibilities for the family, that is, reframe the problem with words that allow for creative change. Develop your understanding of the problem by obtaining a history of the problem and attempts to resolve it. Debrief in larger class.

Exercise 6.17

Different Problem Definitions
(PBL Worksheet)

Putting together exercises 6.3 to 6.9, in your PBL groups, identify one key problem facing the PBL family and redefine that problem from six different ways. Have all the PBL groups members engaged in these problem definitions (20-30 minutes). Write down the six definitions and report to the large class the different definitions.

Six Different Problems Definitions

1.

2.

3.

4.

5.

6.

A Systemic Perspective Utilizing Problem-Solving and Communication Skills Training

Teaching problem-solving is a core approach of Generalist Family Practice. Teaching problem solving skills to clients requires a shift in thinking for the family worker who becomes a facilitator rather than an expert. As a facilitator and a consultant, the family worker teaches the family to find their own solutions and learn problem-solving skills rather than relying on outside help or waiting for someone else to solve their problems for them. Families range in their problem-solving abilities. Some are completely incapable of solving problems, while others are willing to engage in problem-solving activities and are quite successful in doing so. Somewhere in the middle are those families that would like to solve problems and are occasionally able to do so. These families usually arrange special times during which they meet, discuss problems, and generate solutions (Franklin, Hopson, & Ten Barge, 2003).

Many vulnerable and high-risk families cannot solve daily problems or severe crises very well. Perhaps they are vulnerable because of the lack of problem solving skills and the lack of these skills makes them vulnerable. Disorganized and unskilled families often lack skills to solve problems adequately. To function effectively families need to have skills to face day to day and future problems. As we saw in the Family Categories Schema, how a family problem-solves is a central aspect of their function. Jahoda (1958, cited in Wasik, Bryant, & Lyon, 1990) pointed out that problem-solving skills and mental health status are related. Through effective problem solving, people are better equipped to deal with life and personal problems as they arise. Problems do not accumulate. Teaching people how to problem-solve is one of the most fundamental intervention skills that can be used in working with people. Competent problem solving goes a long way in contributing to the individual well being of family members, family functioning and enhancing parenting skills. Learning problem-solving skills can benefit a family enormously, by teaching conflict resolution and dealing with life and personal problems that occur on a daily basis. Thus, teaching problem-solving and communicative interventions strengthens the effectiveness of family work. The problem-solving approach teaches members to negotiate solutions to their problems that are acceptable to all.

The problem solving approach first teaches families skills to manage current difficulties. These skills can be used to address many life difficulties. Thus, one goal of the problem solving approach is to help families to become more competent by developing greater independence and self-reliance in managing life difficulties.

In the process of teaching problem-solving skills, the family worker is a teacher and a coach, walking families through the problem solving process from beginning to end. In some other models, workers help clients define problems and then provide solutions. Conversely, the problem-solving model described here is designed to empower families to take an active role in identifying their needs and goals. When a family has difficulty navigating the problem solving process, the family worker simplifies the tasks for them by breaking them down into discrete steps. For example, if a family can only vaguely define a difficult situation, the family worker might start by taking a more active role in identifying and defining a problem, but involving the family in whatever capacity they are able. However, the long-term goal is for the family to assume this responsibility as they develop the skills.

Because family workers often have more theoretical knowledge and practice about issues than the family, they can provide a unique vantage by offering pertinent information. However, the source of the solutions should come from the family, giving them a sense of power and competence. The family worker can offer opinions yet recognize that the final decision comes from the family. Allowing families freedom to make decision conveys a special message to them about their competence to problem solve (Collins, Jordan, & Coleman, 1999; Wasik, Bryant, & Lyon, 1990).

The general problem-solving approach is a seven-step process. These seven steps include:

1) *Defining the problem.* At this point, family members or an individual identify a problem that is troubling them for which they have been unable to find a resolution. Problem definition describes the problem and details. A situation becomes a problem when it is not easily resolved and when it distresses at least one person. Problem definition also involves uncovering how family members contribute to the development and maintenance of the problem. When more than one problem exists, the client prioritizes them and decides which one to tackle first.
2) *Selecting a goal.* In families, goal selection describes what each person would like to see happen differently. Individuals might have personal goals about the problem and they should feel free to share them. The worker can help family members see the complete family picture in selecting a goal and take individuals past individual wishes. A problem might have a number of possible solutions, not just a single right answer. The goal gives a direction.

(continued)

3) *Generating solutions.* At this stage, family members can brainstorm, without censure, to produce a number of different possibilities for solving the problem. We are often surprised when we ask people to do this...they are able to generate a number of creative solutions. Generation of solutions, through brainstorming, will lead to the identification of a number of alternative responses that may resolve the specific problem.
4) *Listing consequences.* Each possible solution posed is examined with regard to potential positive and negative consequences that might occur as a result of instituting them. Consequences involve the impact and on other people, possible reactions, and the effort needed to carry through on it. This can be accomplished by mapping the possible consequences on a piece of paper.
5) *Making the decision.* Once the possible consequences are flushed out, the person makes a decision based on the best fit in terms of the goal and potential consequences. Decisions are thus based on estimating the effect of proposed solutions and possible consequences, and then deciding which one is best. Decision-making includes consideration of priorities and values and then contracting a solution.
6) *Implementation.* Here, the family takes action based on the best solution that was selected.
7) *Evaluation.* In this final stage, the family evaluates the outcome as to whether the intervention was effective and whether it sufficiently addressed the selected goals. If the solution is unsatisfactory, the family starts at Step 3 and looks at other possible solutions. The final step in evaluation is a review of the results of the problem solving exercise and deciding whether it addressed the goals. If changes are necessary, another option must be selected

Exercise 6.18

Beliefs and Problems

(In Class)

Think about some type of clients or problems that might pose difficulty for you to work with. List five of these and devise a plan of what you might do with each problem.

Problem	Plan
1.	
2.	
3.	
4.	
5.	

Exercise 6.19

Teaching Problem Solving
(PBL Worksheet)

In your PBL group, have the family select a problem to be solved. Walking through the stages of the Problem-Solving model, teach them skills necessary to solve their problem. Then help the family transfer their skills to other problems.

Chapter Summary

This chapter focuses on different ways to assess a family. First we discussed several measurement instruments. Instruments can help you confirm hypotheses about your assessment and they can also help you measure the effectiveness of your practice. We then talked about the Family Categories Schema, which is a model used to evaluated holistic family functioning. The accompanying instrument is the Family Assessment Device. How you define a problem will determine what you do about it. A problem can be defined in six possible ways.

Chapter 7 **Table of Contents**

THE ECOMAP

Chapter 7

The Ecomap

Chapter Coverage

- Ecological Theory
- Ecomap
- Ecomap Questions
- Case Management

Introduction

In this chapter, we broaden your assessment skills by incorporating ecological theory and the use of the *Ecomap* into understanding the family. Generalist practice involves work where problems are not just viewed coming from an individual, or even a family context, but is also mindful of the effect of larger social systems upon the functioning of a family and its well-being. The *Ecomap,* presented in this chapter, is an extremely useful tool to understand the influence of larger systems on a family.

While Ecomaps are indispensable with which to understand the interaction of a family with its environment, it is particularly useful in working with diversity. Many of the difficulties of minority families, regardless of whether they have achieved minority status through cultural or ethnic diversity or through characteristics that set them apart from the stereotype of what is "normal," reside within a social environment that is often inhospitable. *Ecomaps* help identify what the issues are for these families in a focused and structured way.

Exercise 7.1

Family Needs Through the Life Cycle
(In Class)

Using the basic human needs of physical, safety, belonging, esteem, and actualization, give examples of these needs for individuals within the family, ways of getting these needs met, who meets these needs within the family and the community, and how the needs might be threatened (adapted fronm Collins, Jordan, & Coleman. 1999).

Individual	Needs	How Needs Get Met	Threats to the Needs
Infant/toddler	1. physical 2. safety 3. belonging 4. esteem 5. actualization		
School Child	1. physical 2. safety 3. belonging 4. esteem 5. actualization		
Adolescent	1. physical 2. safety 3. belonging 4. esteem 5. actualization		
Mother	1. physical 2. safety 3. belonging 4. esteem 5. actualization		
Father	1. physical 2. safety 3. belonging 4. esteem 5. actualization		
Grandparent	1. phsical 2. safety 3. belonging 4. esteem 5. actualization		

Ecological Theory

All forms of life strive to reach a favorable fit with the environment so needs are met and survival is ensured.
Rothman, 1994

All families have connections with the larger outside world. Family boundaries determine how open families are. Some families may be very involved with formal agencies and have less of a connection with informal supports. Families that are involved with many community agencies may have a variety of helpers working with individuals or the family as a whole. While independence is one strong American social value, it overlooks the simple fact that no one can exist without interdependence with significant others. Some troubled families face enormous odds in terms of the balance of resources and stresses and have been labeled "multiproblem," "disadvantaged," "vulnerable," "crisis prone," or, "multicrisis." In such families, workers have difficulty seeing below the surface to locate family strengths. Living in any society carries with it both risks and opportunities and unfortunately, many families we work with face more risk than opportunity. One shortcoming of focusing exclusively on families is that workers often believe that only clinical services are needed for a particular family, forgetting that other options for helping often exist outside the family.

By wearing an ecological lens, workers begin to understand the interrelated social systems that affect day-to-day living. A family is in constant interaction with its social environment. An infant starts life in constant communication, usually with one key person, who nurtures that child and meets that child's basic needs as he or she grows and develops.

At the smallest level is the *microsystem.* It is with this system that the individual has day-to-day, face-to-face contact. The first microsystem is a dyad - nurturer and child - but as the child becomes more capable and independent, his or her social life expands, interacting with a growing number of significant other people. The older the child, the wider and more varied the environment and the interaction. "We measure the social riches of a child by enduring, reciprocal, multifaceted relationships that emphasize playing, working, and loving" (Garbarino, 1982, p. 22). Microsystems form the bedrock of family life and the nature of the microsystem also affects the quality of life. "A *microsystem* should be a gateway to the world, not a locked room" (p. 35).

Interaction within the microsystem needs to be reciprocal, not one-way. McGoldrick and Gerson (1985) suggest that the intensity of relationships within a family and the family's relationships with outsiders are related. When relationships are especially close (enmeshed) within the family, the relationship with outsiders might be distant, suggesting closed family boundaries. We see families where relationships are so close that boundaries around the family are impermeable. We are unwelcome intruders. Family members seem to be very involved with one another and have little time or investment with others outside the family. On the other end of the continuum are families where members are so invested in friends and activities outside that they seem to neglect family members. Other families fall somewhere in between.

Exercise 7.2

Microsystem
(In Class)

Break into groups of two. Describe your microsystem. Identify the nature of your relationships with these people. To what extent does your microsystem meet your needs? What is missing for you?

The next level is the *mesosystem*. The mesosystem is neither a concrete nor tangible entity, but rather consists of the *relationships* between microsystems. Thus, parents need to be connected to important people in their children's life. They need to know and be involved with children's friends, teachers, friends' parents, sports team coaches and so on. Important people in children's lives must also work toward the same goals on behalf of the child. For example, teachers and parents should act as a team and one should not undermine the other. How well a child welfare agency gets along with important supports in a child's life (such as grandparents and extended kin) is vital to the case plan. Yet, when parents believe that teachers are being unfair to their child, they should be willing to advocate on behalf of him or her. Mesosystems should be strong as well as diverse.

Exercise 7.3

Mesosytem

(In Class)

Break into groups of two. Describe your mesosystem. How well do the different parts of your mesosystem get along? What are potential sources of conflict? What needs to happen to deal with this conflict?

Exosystems are systems that play a role in a person's life but the role is indirect. Decisions made about school policy, conflicts at the parents' place of employment, and decisions to build or not build a playground in the neighborhood are all examples of exosystem-level decisions that affect children. Other examples include the type of service an agency offers (e.g., family preservation program or enhanced foster care services).

Exercise 7.4

Exosystem

(In Class)

Break into groups of two. Describe your exosystem. What decisions made in your exosystem make your life easier and what decisions make your life more difficult?

The largest system, the *macrosystem*, embraces the social values and institutional patterns of life within a certain culture, much of which is ideology and values. For example, in the 1950s, children underwent mock nuclear bomb attacks and did drills by hiding under their desks. The ideology of the cold war affected children on every level every day. While some adults may look back on these times with amusement, for children at the time, the experience was terrifying. Racial or religious intolerance has a stilting effect on members of groups that are not part of "mainstream" society. Sexism hurts everyone, not just females because it impoverishes roles and limits opportunities for both sexes. The macrosystem acts as a cultural blueprint and contains both risk and opportunity as well. Geographical mobility and poverty threatens families. Privacy is another risk factor that isolates people from useful information and support and allows abuse to continue.

Exercise 7.5

Macrosystems
(In Class)

Break into groups of two. Describe your macrosystem. How does your macrosystem provide risks and opportunities for you?

Ecological theory recognizes that families are nested within a set of wider social structures, similar to Russian nesting dolls. The saying that "no man (person) is an island" captures the essence of social living. However, two of the blueprints of Western culture are individualism and independence. Just as individual therapy was once considered too limiting because it failed to recognize the enormous family context, we now know that a single focus on families is too narrow because it fails to recognize the impact of the social environment on families.

The quality of a family's relationship with its environment has an enormous impact on family functioning. For example, the risk of physical abuse within the family increases when parents have negative relationships with those outside the family. During transitions, such as when a child goes to school for the first time, the quality of the new and ongoing school connection plays a role in school adjustment. Positive social connections fare well within a developmental context. For example, discouraging children from going to a friend's home or discouraging them from bringing friends home, especially as they get older, inhibits a child's social development. Connections that are too closed or too open undermine child development and well being. Sometimes, the support network is invisible to workers and they treat families as though they are islands and workers need to find ways of flushing out a family's relationship with its environment.

People navigate life with a toolbox of strengths and deficits. We are just starting to understand resilience, the ability of people to overcome overwhelming odds and function well in their lives. For some families, resilience and strength have yet to be tapped. For others, their difficulties, combined with lack of environmental support, can be devastating. However, deficits originating within a family or individual can be offset by strong external supports (Rothman, 1994). An enormous social service machine, originally designed to support vulnerable populations, has become fragmented, complex, and continuously shifting.

Social support is an invaluable social resource that plays a huge role in individual and family well being. *Informal* social supports are particularly valuable and preferred. Many families, however, are involved extensively with *formal* helping systems, social agencies in particular. Formal helpers are sometimes intrusive and uncoordinated to the extent that services work at cross-purposes and fragment families (Minuchin, Colapinto, & Minuchin, 1998). For example, children may enter foster care or residential treatment and unless the family is an integral part of the treatment team, workers might find returning the child to the family difficult. When families have difficulty responding to the 'supports" that are provided to them, they are labeled resistant or dysfunctional. Workers need to use their authority with sensitivity to avoid undermining existing strengths and resources within a family.

We must remember that when working with families, understanding family strengths such as mutual caring, is necessary in order to obtain a balanced view of the family (Minuchin, Colapinto, & Minuchin, 1998). Without understanding family strengths, plugging in resources will probably be a mismatch for family needs. In addition, when outsiders make decisions over family members, families are in a powerless position in relation to the authority figures running their lives. Minuchin and colleagues capture this point well:

> Many poor families have difficulty focusing on their own internal processes, precisely because the intervention of social agencies is a chronic fixture in their lives. A family may be involved simultaneously with multiple agencies, each with its own agenda, and all of them regularly penetrating the family's boundaries (p. 63).

Ecomap

The *Ecomap* flows from ecological theory, capturing the external family relationships. Similar to the *Genogram*, the *Ecomap* tells a story about the micro and meso-level relationships between the family and the outside world (ecosystem). It pinpoints to whom family members family relate, available resources, and potential points of intervention. The depiction also captures the strength and quality of external connections, including stressful contacts between the environment and the family. It will also help identify opportunities and risks in the environment to children and their families. One particularly important focus is movement of resources to and from the family, such as sources of social support, unmet needs, and family contributions to the community. Understanding transactions with the environment helps assess and conceptualize families holistically and contextually.

A major benefit of an *Ecomap* is how it captures an extensive amount of information on a single page, revealing the strength and quality of external connections. It is particularly useful for understanding key figures to whom the family relates. Family work relies heavily on the information portrayed by an *Ecomap* because fulfilling needs and working with community resources are key elements.

Creating an *Ecomap* with a family during the assessment and goal setting phases of work focuses on important systems characteristics such as boundary issues and the direction, rate, and mutuality of social relationships. Similar to the *Genogram,* there are tradeoffs between the amount of detail required and the time it takes to complete an *Ecomap*. Completing an *Ecomap* with a family opens the door to "teachable moments," as family members present and evaluate how they relate to important people in the community. It can also be a starting point for problem identification, identification of strengths, and goal setting. An additional benefit is that it is also a wonderful tool for establishing rapport.

When used and revised as a family changes over time, *Ecomaps* capture changes in family resources and rather than a snapshot, "videotapes" how well the work has progressed in terms of connecting with the community and developing more sources of social support. They are standard fare in many case files, particularly in agencies. Developing an *Ecomap* with the family can benefit the entire family, since *Ecomaps* tell a story about the distinct challenges that a family faces because every family's connection its social environment is unique. For example, ethnically diverse families who have experienced discrimination or oppression will see the discrimination mapped out for them in the diagram.

Ecomaps and *Genograms* can be used in combination to create a comprehensive and integrated picture of a family's situation. Concrete and diagrammatic depictions of abstract concepts contained in *Genograms* and *Ecomaps* produce greater understanding and retention of material.

Exercise 7.6

Ecological Roles
(In Class)

List some roles in specific situations that the family worker might perform in implementing an ecological intervention. Alongside the worker list, make a list of some roles that you might expect the family to play.

Roles of Family Worker	Roles of Family
a.	
b.	
c.	
d.	

Drawing an Ecomap

The *Ecomap* consists of a cluster of circles placed outside the family. Each circle represents a different system with which the family is connected. Each circle represents a system that affects the family (at any level). The first step in creating an *Ecomap* is educating the family about it and the rationale for using one. While some families feel disconnected or otherwise treated unfairly by elements in their environment, the *Ecomap* helps families focus on what may be troubling them. Bringing issues out into the open in a structured way helps the family articulate what its issues are, understand the impact of social isolation and oppression on their well-being, and set goals for changing their situation.

Once family members understand the purpose of an *Ecomap*, members need to create meaning from the *Ecomap*. In doing so, the family has the opportunity to understand that some of its problems reside outside the family and members might feel less blamed for their difficulties. They can then assemble plans to improve their situation. The next step is to place the previously constructed Genogram in a center circle labeled as the family or household. However, not all *Ecomaps* contain a *Genogram* since including both on one page may be too overwhelming. Depending upon the level of detail required, the family might be merely represented as one large circle in the middle of the page and the *Genogram* can be put on another page.

Family members identify and describe their connection with significant others outside the family. Usually, while each member is giving information, other members of the family listen and gain a better understanding about the life of each family member. Circles include details such as significant people, agencies, or organizations. Any other descriptive information can also be included. Examples of a community connection include, friends, recreation clubs, religious organization affiliation, education, employment, and social agency connection. The size of the circles is irrelevant. The connection with social agencies can very revealing as some vulnerable families have relationships with a range of social agencies that might be working at competing purposes.

Exercise 7.7

Community Connections
(In Class)

Make an individual list of all your community connections. How many do you have? Combine your list with those of your classmates. This master list will give you an idea of many the possible community connections.

a.

b.

c.

d.

e.

f.

g.

Others.

Lines describe specific relationships. Straight lines [—] depict strong positive or strong connections; dotted lines [.......] indicate tenuous or weak relationships, and slashed lines [-/-/-/-]) show conflictual relationships. If a relationship is especially positive or negative, the width of the line can be adjusted accordingly. Thick lines show more positive connections. Arrows, drawn alongside the lines (_), depict the flow of energy and resources to and from the family. Arrows can point to outside the circle showing that the flow of resources is from the family to the outside world. Conversely, arrows going from the environment to inside the family show resources moving from the environment to the family. If the arrow goes in both directions, the relationship is mutual. The *Ecomap* can be expanded as more information is uncovered or as the family makes improvement in connecting with its environment. Additional circles can be drawn as necessary, depending upon the number of significant contacts identified by members. The *Ecomap* can be modified as the family changes or as the family shares further information with the family worker. An example of an Ecomap is shown in Figure 7.1.

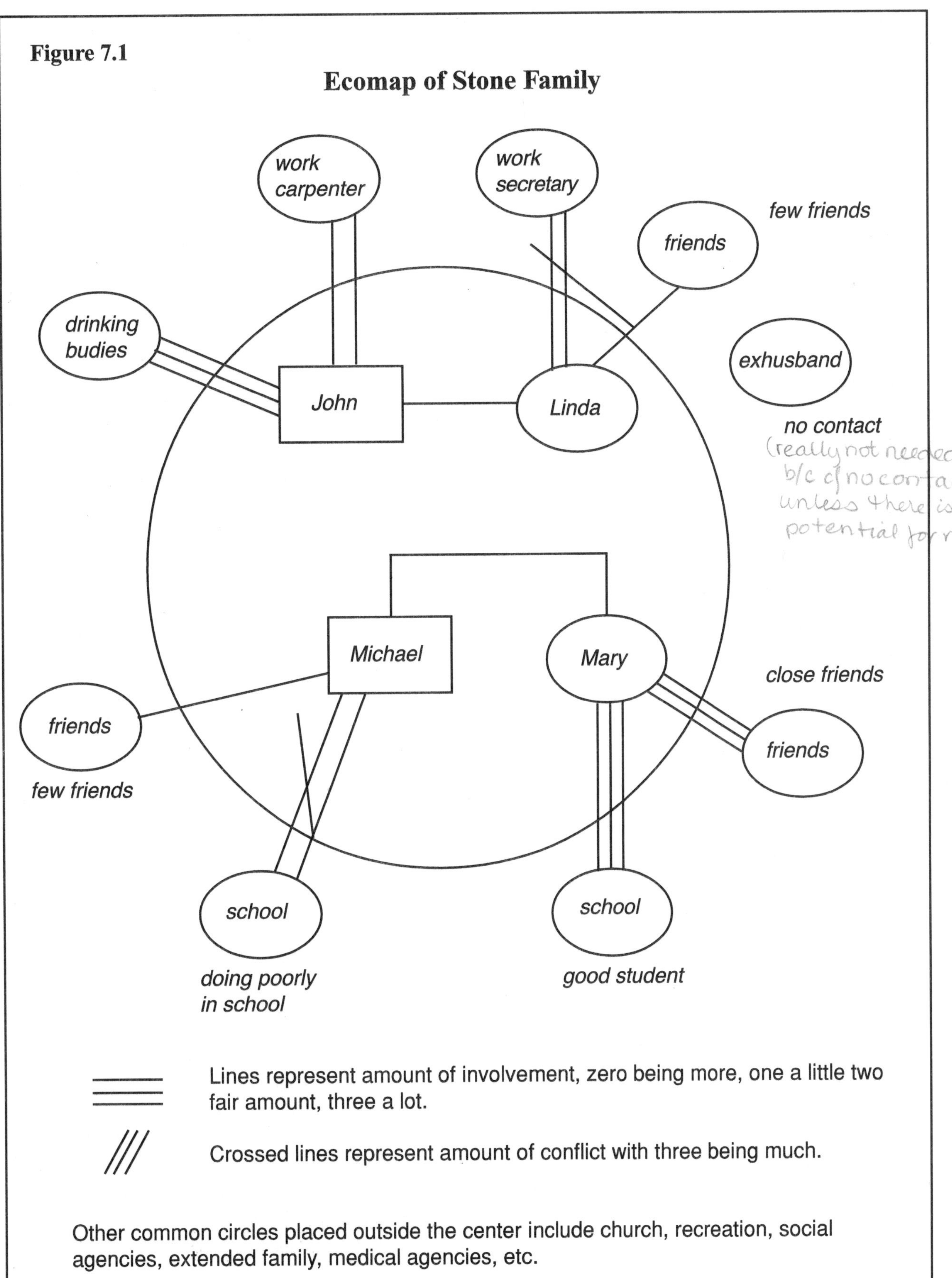

Figure 7.1

Ecomap of Stone Family

Lines represent amount of involvement, zero being more, one a little two fair amount, three a lot.

Crossed lines represent amount of conflict with three being much.

Other common circles placed outside the center include church, recreation, social agencies, extended family, medical agencies, etc.

Process of Ecomap Creation

Construction of the *Ecomap* unfolds in the following five steps:

1. Introducing the Ecomap:

In this fist step, the worker educates the family about the *Ecomap* by describing the rationale for its use. The worker might tell the family that it is important to explore what it is like for them to live in a particular community.

2. Whom to start with:

Similar to issues relating to introductions, deciding where to start the *Ecomap* construction is important. You could start by asking the family as a whole who would like to go first. Alternatively, you could start with the parents who probably (and hopefully) have greater community connections and who can model responses to the children. Children might want to listen to the answers of other family members first, because through their experience, their interest has been piqued and they will be motivated to hear others' stories and generate responses for themselves later.

3. Examples of questions to ask:

The formulation of questions is important, and after asking several questions, the process will become easier. No set of questions exist might and you will develop your own style with experience. After deciding where to start, you could say, "*Joe, 'let's start by making a list of the important people and groups in your life that you are in contact with outside the family*." As each person compiles his or her list, the family worker draws circles outside the family unit near to where that particular individual is situated. After each list, go back to each item on the list and ask, "*Now that we have a list of the important people and groups that you are in contact with, let's go back to each one and see what your connection with them are like*." [Explain the meaning of the different lines]. "*I see that you mentioned your work as an important connection for you outside the family. How would you describe this connection? What is going on for you that you see this connections as [positive, stressful, distant? [using the client's own words]*." As the family member describes this connection with each contact on the list, the family worker will draw the connection, using the most appropriate line to represent the quality of the particular relationship. It is important to verbally articulate, as each line is being drawn, what the lines mean. Remember to check the accuracy of how the relationship is depicted after each line is drawn. Once the *Ecomap* is depicted for one family member, move onto the next person in the family.

4. Helping the family synthesize the information:

The completion of a family *Ecomap* might take one session or longer, depending on the size of the family and the level of detail needed. By the end of the descriptive phase of *Ecomap* construction, you will have considerable detail on the paper. There are several possibilities with what you do with this information. One option would be to say, "*I see that we have lots of information about this family here. Is there anything else that any one would like to add or comment on?*" At this point, family members might want to give their impressions about the connections that other family members have with the outside world. Family members might disagree about the connections that others have described themselves. However, what is important is perceptions of these connections and each family member will have unique and individual perceptions. If major disagreement exists, you might want to record the disagreement, remembering that individuals have the right to describe their individual connectedness as they experience them. Another approach would be to get the members to describe their overall impressions about the *Ecomap.* For example, you might make a comment similar to the following, "*Now that we have the connections of each family member down on this Ecomap, what kinds of things do you see going on for members of this family? Alternatively, "I notice that x has very good connections with friends, but less satisfying connections with school, [or employment, social agencies, etc.]. What does this mean to you?"*

5. Setting goals from the Ecomap:

Family members will be able to decide how well they are connected to their environment and their level of satisfaction or dissatisfaction with the various components of it. Based on the level of satisfaction with these elements, family members might want to set goals for strengthening the relationships, eliminating them, or forging new ones. Each member should be asked to set goals in this regard.

Examples of Eco-Map Questions

The eco-map assessment can be complicated because the family worker is interested in both individual family members' relationship with their social environment, and the complete family unit's relationship with the social environment. However, the focus of *Ecomap* construction can be based on the following considerations.

1. What is the number of connections of family members with the outside world?
2. What are the formal and informal sources of support?
3. What is the nature of the individual, as well as family as a whole, relationships with the social environment? Do community connections nurture or hinder individual client or family functioning?
4. What is the quality of the client' and family's interactions with significant others outside the family, including the breadth and depth of outside relationships and the impact of external factors on the client and the family?
5 How do individuals and the family get basic needs met? Which needs are being met and which are not?
6. Who can the client and the family as a whole rely on in time of need? What is the nature of contact with support people in terms of quantity and quality?
7. How dependent or self-sufficient is the client and the family in terms of external resources?
8. How do individuals and the family unit relate to key people, including, family, friends, relatives, teachers, coworkers, church members, and health care workers?
9. What are individuals and the family unit's relationships to other members of their ethno-cultural group?
10. What are the impacts and influences of religious beliefs and values? Do family members have differing levels of connection with religious institutions and if so, what impact does this have on the family?
11. What aspects of cultural heritage provide strengths or barriers?
12. What are the formal and informal support systems?
13. Who is most vulnerable in the family in terms of negative or nonexistent relationships with the environment?
14. What are the strengths within this particular family with regard to how members relate to the environment?
15. How does this family contribute to the community?

(Author unknown, n.d.)

Exercise 7.8

Developing Questions for Ecomap Construction

(In Class)

For each of the twelve items presented below, devise two questions that can be asked of family members.

1. Overall view of the social environment and its impact:
   a.
   b.
2. Quality of interactions with outside world:
   a.
   b.
3. Meeting of basic needs:
   a.
   b.
4. People to rely on; quantity and quality of supports:
   a.
   b.
5. Self-sufficiency and dependency:
   a.
   b.
6. Relationship with key people:
   a.
   b.
7. Ethnocultural connections:
   a.
   b.
8. Impact of religious beliefs:
   a.
   b.
9. Strengths and barriers of cultural heritage:
   a.
   b.
10. Formal and informal support systems:
    a.
    b.
11. Vulnerability:
    a.
    b.
12. Strengths:
    a.
    b.

Exercise 7.9

Drawing Your Ecomap
(In Class)

Create an Ecomap of your family. Identify what systems outside your family were significant in the life of your family as you were growing up. Make an Ecomap of your life three years ago and one of your present age. Compare the Ecomaps from the two different times in your life. What differences do you see? How do the Ecomaps change from one time to another? How do these changes reflect your different developmental and social circumstances at each point in time?

Present Ecomap

Ecomap when growing up

Ecomap of three years ago

Exercise 7.10

Ecomap of PBL Family
(PBL Worksheet)

Today the family worker will complete an Ecomap interview with the PBL family. The content from this chapter will serve as a guide for these family depictions. It is important for the family worker to get a picture of the family from every family member, without letting the parents dominate the discussion. The family worker should start out by introducing one of the family depictions at a time by addressing the purpose of the Ecomap, the rules around its construction (e.g. no interruptions, everyone will get a chance for input, etc.).

Nevertheless, it is important that the parents provide the initial input into the Ecomap. It is also important not to "lose" the children while this is happening. Thus, the family worker can briefly ask the child(ren) what s/he thinks about what s/he has just heard…then move onto the parents. Allow each member to tell about their particular part of the family tree uninterrupted. Use a flip chart or blackboard to show the family what you are doing while you are doing it. The family worker might point out or ask about patterns while the Ecomap is being constructed.

The Ecomap will be the same for each PBL family group. However, the analysis of them can be different for individual members of the PBL group.

Ecomap of PBL Family

Exercise 7.11

Meeting Family Needs
(In Class)

The following list includes needs of families. Provide examples of needs in each category and beside each example indicate the ecological resources that can meet these needs. Provide examples of a variety of formal and informal sources of support as well as whether they are developmental or basic. Compare the list of formal and informal connections. What needs do each of them meet? Are there any formal relationships in terms of needs that can be met by informal sources?

Needs	Formal Connections	Informal Connections
Physical Needs		
Safety Needs		
Belonging Needs		
Esteem Needs		
Self-Actualization Needs		

Exercise 7.12

Ecological Intervention
(In Class)

Design an ecological intervention for the Stone family. The intervention should flow logically from an Ecomap.

Intervention:

Case Management

Understanding that different agencies are interactive forces within the network encompassing a family is a cornerstone of collaborative work, and is essential for handing interventions at cross-purposes
(Minuchin, Colapinto, & Minuchin, 1998)

Balancing need with parsimony is a tall order....
(Minuchin, Colapinto, & Minuchin, 1998)

Workers might be surprised, after completing the *Ecomap,* to discover the number of formal and informal services involved with the family. They might have been previously aware of one or two agencies, but when the entire network of formal services jumps off the page, concerns might arise about the goals, focus, and impact of these services on the family. Case management is one worker role that intersects a family and its environment.

Vulnerable families do not manage their contacts with agencies, workers, and institutions very well (Minuchin, Colapinto, & Minuchin, 1998, p. 59). Their contact with these systems places agencies in positions of authority and because the intervention of external agencies is a chronic fixture of their lives, many poor families have difficulty focusing on their own internal processes.

Thus, intervention has two components - the direct services provided by the family worker and the management of indirect services provided by other resource systems. Both interventions help reach family goals, but through different methods. Direct services are services that the worker provides face-to-face with the family. Indirect services occur when the worker intervenes behind the scenes, often without the family present, to orchestrate the many services that a family receives. As with any other intervention, case management must be culturally sensitive. For example, family groups from a number of cultural groups prefer informal networks of support to formal agencies. When the services of formal agencies are required, some agencies have workers fluent in a particular language or come from a particular cultural group. Family members must give input into whether they would like to see a worker from their own culture, because there are both advantages and disadvantages of coming from the same cultural group as that of the client.

Services, particularly those to vulnerable families, are complex but plentiful. The downside is that these services are often fragmented, ever changing, and not well coordinated. Because these services often fail to link well, they enter a family's space with a unique agenda, and often work at cross-purposes. Some services may serve the same needs, while others are concerned with an individual and fail to consider the entire family system. Yet some agencies enter the family in a "policing" capacity. Finally, the sole reason for another cluster of services might be supportive. When services are uncoordinated and have different goals, the result can be devastating for the family. Members might see other family members as the problem, particularly when they receive individual treatment.

Moreover, services have their own unique challenges when working with one another, not the least of which involves turf battles. Turf issues can erupt over philosophy (e.g., a policing versus a supportive role), professional qualifications (e.g., social workers versus psychologists), power issues (I have the final decision), or agency mandates (e.g., child welfare versus family therapy). Agreeing upon the focus and procedures can be problematic for home-based workers who are in a relatively powerless position (Minuchin, Colapinto, & Minuchin, 1998, p. 232). Turf battles echo other issues

> ...when workers make contradictory diagnoses of the family's needs and spend time arguing diverse views, their behavior may mirror the conflicts and unsuccessful coping patterns of family life" (p. 40).

The various agencies might be working at cross-purposes, or alternatively, provide overlapping or redundant services. When multiple agencies are involved with a single family, the impact can be chaotic and undermining. The family worker thus needs to direct work with families and take charge to ensure that the overall agency involvement is managed effectively to serve the best interests of the family. For example, family members might be involved with services that apply specifically to them, such as substance abuse counseling, mental health services, probation, a school counselor, etc. Family servicing agencies might also be involved. Child welfare is one such example. Unless a worker in one of these agencies takes the time to sort out the role and focus of all the various agencies, a chaotic service network will bombard the family and undermine overall effectiveness. Even one or two agencies can rupture a coherent service package to the family.

Just as collaboration with a family contributes to improved service provision, so should collaboration among the various agencies. Case management is the process of assisting families with multiple service needs. The family worker, as case manager, organizes, coordinates, and sustains the network of formal and informal supports and activities designed to optimize family functioning and well-being of the family with multiple needs (Moxley, 1989, p. 21).

Thus the family worker, acting on behalf of the best interests of the family, coordinates services provided by a quilt work patch of agencies, organizations, and facilities. The goals of family case management are to mobilize a family's strengths, to marshal resources, and maximize functioning (Green & Kropf, 2003, p. 85). The family case manager is responsible for linking the family with outside resources and ensuring that these links are positive and coherent. Through assessment, the family worker determines the suitability of the resources that the family is receiving.

In order to develop an appropriate service network, the worker starts with setting goals with the family. Goal setting helps families envision what they are hoping to achieve. Setting goals within the context of a service network also helps families think about their problems and evaluate progress. The family worker brings to this network a unique family perspective and helps maintain a whole family focus.

Principles of Case Management

Gerhart (1990) and Rothman (1994) identify several principles of case management:

- **Services should be individualized**: This means developing or designing services specifically to meet the identified needs of the family. Thus, the family worker assesses what services the family needs and helps the family obtain these services specific to their unique needs and to the goals it wishes to meet. The worker needs to determine whether the support system is supportive. For example, how well does the family relate with their extended family, friends, and neighbours?

  One of the first steps in doing an assessment is to decide what the primary issues are and then what the goals are. The next step involves assessing whether or not the family has the appropriate kinds of supports. As a result, the case manager makes community connections to help families achieve change, keeping in mind that families sometime try to blame one person in the family. Instead, it is important to help the family find and change the destructive patterns that keep the family as a whole stuck.

- **Services should be comprehensive:** Services should be comprehensive such that they wrap around all areas of the family's needs including housing, recreation, employment, education, social, financial, medical care, mental health care, etc. This principle helps ensure that no family need will go unfulfilled.

- **Services should be parsimonious**: Duplication of services should be avoided and the costs will be contained. Uncoordinated services results in some needs being met by duplicate agencies while other needs go unmet. The lack of coordination might also mean that the services of some agencies might work against the family.

- **Services should foster autonomy**: Another focus of case management is on helping families become as self-sufficient as possible. It also means ensuring maximum client self-determination so the family makes as many decisions regarding their own care as possible. Case management is a means to assist families locate resources that help them become more autonomous. Services should not overpower families, especially when families can do for themselves.

- **Services should ensure continuity of care**: Continuity of care means that as the family moves through its life and members negotiate changes, shifts, and alterations in their relationships with one another. (Life cycle issues are discussed in more detail in Chapter 8). These life cycle changes require a wide range of social and health care services over the lifetime of a family. Through case management activities, the family is assured of continuous monitoring of its needs. We also expect that all families require assistance throughout their lives and should not be stigmatized because of their needs.

- **Services should link clients with necessary services**: Case managers have the responsibility of ensuring that *formal* services adequately to family needs. This may entail referring a client to an agency based on an assessed client need. Given that the system of social agencies is often confusing and complex, even for the most experienced worker, this responsibility can be daunting. It requires that workers advocate on behalf of clients when waiting lists are too long, when they are being denied legitimate service, and when families become lost under a pile of paperwork. To fulfill this role, workers must nurture relationships with community agencies and their workers. The worker

(continued)

helps families develop skills to identify and use different agencies. It also means knowing about available programs and how they fit client needs. Rothman (1994) suggests that in order for workers to fulfill this function, they must have organization skills (who to contact) and community-oriented skills (knowing what policies and agency mandates fit and knowing about the development of new services). Another facet of this role is to help strengthen and build bridges with *informal* support services in the family's life - friends, families, and neighbors. These are the natural helping networks in a family's life (Rothman, 1994). Members of many ethnic groups turn to these natural helping networks first. In performing any of these roles, the worker should never do for the family what it can do for itself.

- **Assuring service:** This role involves taking steps to ensure that difficulties encountered with agencies are addressed. Case managers can work behind the scene. Alternatively, they can coach families to overcome service-related difficulties. At other times, the worker and family can collaborate to address problems. When clients encounter barricades in accessing these services, the worker acts as an advocate.

- **Coordinating services:** At this level, workers from various *formal* agencies must coordinate their work. It could also involve bringing in *informal* supports to help in the treatment plan. Through service coordination, the worker coordinates the various services and people providing these services to ensure that they are working toward a common goal. Case coordination occurs through case conferences with all the helpers at one time to discuss mutual concerns and establish plans to meet the family's issues. Depending upon the goal and philosophy, family members might attend these conferences.

Assessment of Family's Ability to Meet Environmental Challenges

Not all families are able to adapt easily to changes in their environment. While some may appear stubborn and unwilling to change (recall the issues related to stages of change and family systems theory pertaining to family homeostasis), it is important for the case manager to remember that change is often scary because it means facing the unknown. People like to stay within their comfort zone.

Case management is distinguished from other direct services by its use of both formal and informal community resources as a source of intervention (Hardcastle, Wenour & Powers, 1997). The case manager role often involves building these support systems for the family.

Case-management uses a problem-solving process. The family's difficulties are often multiple, requiring the assistance of many agencies and organizations. Case management starts with the identification of services required by the clients and finishes with the case manager obtaining them. For example, the Stone family may have a mental health worker, family doctor, school counselor, and probation officer involved. Family case managers provide a seamless link between families and the human services system. The case manager may advocate for the family in situations when the services or resources to which a family is entitled are not forthcoming. In this case, the family worker takes the required steps to remedy the problem. All available resources are used to the maximum extent possible. If services or resources do not exist, the family worker has an obligation to work toward development of such resources.

Exercise 7.13

Case Conference
(PBL Worksheet)

For this role-play, it will be necessary for "family members" to step out of their family role and instead assume the role of an agency representative with whom one family member or the entire family unit is involved. Ideally, identification of the specific agencies will flow from the *Ecomap* that you did on the client family. (If the agencies were not identified, you might want to include them now). You are going to have a case conference designed to make certain all the family needs are met. As well, the family worker will coordinate the services that the various agency representatives provide to your PBL family. The family worker will be armed with the family's *Ecomap* and form it, can create strategic goals on behalf of the family. For example, is there a particular agency with which the family is in conflict? Do the agencies agree upon common goals? Are any of the services redundant? What are the unmet needs within this family and how can services work to meet these unmet needs? How best can the various agencies work together to met this particular family's needs.

After your role-play, the members can debrief their experience, using the above questions as a guideline.

Chapter Summary

Ecological theory reveals how family members are embedded within a set of larger social systems. Families rely on their environment to get most of their needs met. However, at times they lack the skills to access important resources. On other occasions, the environment is inhospitable for families. An Ecomap is a standard recording tool that is used in many agencies. An Ecomap graphs a family's relationship with its social environment, pointing out resources, risks, and opportunities. When many formal agencies are involved with a single family, the worker assumes a case management role, coordinating services so the family's needs are adequately met.

Chapter 8

Table of Contents

FAMILY LIFE CYCLE ASSESSMENT

Chapter 8

Family Life Cycle Assessment

It is time for us professionals to give up our attachments to the old ideals and to put a more positive conceptual frame around what is: two-paycheck marriages, permanent single-parent households; unmarried, remarried; and gay and lesbian couples and families; single parent adoptions; and women of all ages alone.
- (Carter & McGoldrick, 1999)

Chapter Coverage

- Family Life Cycle
- Family Developmental Assessment Questions
- Diversity in the Family Life Cycle

Introduction

The following discussion builds upon information obtained from the Genogram. In this chapter, we discuss the family life cycle, influences upon it, and how it might diverge from the traditional family. In addition to collecting information about the family structure with a Genogram, it is also useful to make sense of family issues from a developmental life cycle perspective. A family life cycle assessment sheds light on family functioning and needs and family workers can incorporate this perspective in family assessment and intervention.

Families share a common history (Carter & McGoldrick, 1999) and understanding this history in the form of family development deepens a family assessment. Looking at families from this angle helps workers understand family issues that appear at specific points in family's history and subsequent transitions. The historical period affects the family life cycle. For example, the percentage of households headed by a single parent mother has increased (Moore Hines, 1999). Families are also affected by racism and poverty. Other factors that affect the family life cycle include substance use, violence, and disability.

One criticism of the family life cycle theory is that it captures developmental stages based of middle class, nuclear, and traditional families, creating the illusion that most families remain together. Family life cycle theory, it is argued, fails to acknowledge family diversity, including single-parent never-married families, gay and lesbian families and multicultural family forms. It also does not recognize such as divorce, adoption, and remarriage. In addition, sexual orientation, social class, culture, and family forms make the course of family development unique. The family life cycle is not as clear-cut as once believed and numerous factors enter into the life course of each family.

One of the first transitions is the movement of a family from one without children to a family with children. One possible worker intervention is to educate parents about what is "normal" or expected at each stage, without trivializing the pain, fears, or distress that family members might feel (Patterson, Williams, Grauf-Grounds, & Chamow, 1998). Knowledge about the family life cycle help a family create a new family structure that "cultivates a place for each member to be included and respected' (p. 126).

Culture also gives a unique flavor to family life cycle issues (Carter & McGoldrick, 1999). For example, African American families have an accelerated movement through the family life cycle. Variations in the life cycle occur with shorter adolescence and longer courtship (as in Mexican American families). In other cultures, the involvement of the extended family exerts a unique influence on each stage. We have had students in our classes from polygamous families. Nowhere have we read about polygamous families and the family life cycle although we expect that the family life cycle would be quite complex in these families.

Each transition requires a new family response and poses a new set of stressors and every crisis contains both a threat and an opportunity. Indeed, many difficulties echo family development transitions and, assessing a family using a development framework, sheds light on how a family meets social expectations (Holman, 1983). For example, families with young children must use different disciplinary methods than families with adolescents. Few families move seamlessly from one stage to another and stress is especially likely to emerge during critical family transitions. In the dominant culture, young people leave the family in late adolescence (or in the early twenties), while other cultures expect young people to remain more closely connected to the family-of-origin. Moreover, when members of different cultures form a partnership, the different families and individuals experience greater stress than would otherwise be expected. *My Big Fat Greek Wedding* shows the beliefs of two cultures about the family life cycle and the stresses involved in resolving these differences. It also demonstrates how the tasks associated with each stage vary according to culture - some cultures expect departing members to remain tightly connected with the family-of-origin, while other cultures expect distance.

Social Class:

Social class affects health status and quality of life, the resources available to a family and the institutional responses to family crises. For example, in poor and working class families, there are compressed intervals between stages (Kliman & Madsen, 1999). Grandchildren may arrive earlier and grandparents might become more involved in the family. Middle class families often expect that children to continue in school, keeping children in the family home longer. Misunderstanding can arise when workers come from a different social class than the families with whom they are working. This is understandable since many professionals are educated middle-class individuals while the focus of services is often on poor and lower class families.

Exercise 8.1

Class Differences
(In class)

What kinds of differences might an educated therapist from a middle class family experience in working with a poor or lower class family? How might beliefs, expectations, and behaviors be different? What would the impact of family life cycle be on family work?

Differences and Impact:

Gender:

Women's life cycle roles are changing (McGoldrick, 1999). The ethnicity and culture of a woman also affects the life cycle. Women with young children are now more educated than their foremothers and more women are in the paid workforce. In response, couple relationships are also changing and women are assuming an even greater range of roles than before. Nevertheless, women usually work for lower wages, on average, and their careers are often interrupted for childbirth. Because families are more mobile, they are also removed from the support of the extended family, making them more vulnerable to life cycle stresses (p. 113). Men are also undergoing rapid changes (Rosen, 1999). New social expectations about fathering can create anxiety and confusion for men. New social expectations about fathering also create anxiety and confusion and divorced men may be cut off from contact with their children. Once children leave home, the couple's roles must once again be redefined.

Exercise 8.2

Gender and the Family Life Cycle
(In class)

Provide five examples of how the changes in women's and men's social roles might influence the family life cycle.

1.

2.

3.

4.

5.

Culture:

It is easy to be "color blind" and "culture blind," even with good intentions. We might feel uncomfortable with the discrimination clients have experienced because of their race or culture, and ignore their experiences. Culture has an enormous impact on the family life cycle, interacting with social class and gender to create some interesting family life cycle patterns. Culture also affects family organization, migration, the family life cycle, and transitional markers and rituals (Falicov, 1999). First generation cultural groups are likely to maintain close contact with their cultural heritage and children might experience a clash of cultures especially when start school. Rituals surrounding dating, childbirth, and establishing separate households are unique to each culture as is the role of extended family in the life of new families. Migration is an especially important feature because through it, families are caught between two worlds. The reason for migration and the age at which migration occurs is an important factor that family workers cannot overlook. Having young children who blend into the new culture easily contributes to both the ease with which acculturation occurs as well as the sense of disjointedness between generations.

Exercise 8.3

Culture and the Family Life Cycle

(In class)

What is your ethnic and cultural heritage? How has your heritage affected the course of your family life development in terms of the following issues:

When your family immigrated

Reasons for immigration

Experience of young children if newly immigrated

Dating

Relationships with extended kin

Living arrangements

Multigenerational relationships

Family rituals

Old age

Compare your answers with that of your classmates.

Sibling Relationships:

"Sibling relationships are the longest that most of us have in life" (McGoldrick, Watson, & Benson, 1999, p.153) and theories fail to pay sufficient attention to their role. Families may contain full sibling relationships as well as stepsiblings and half siblings. Some children may be close in age, while others have greater age distance from one another. With the increase in multiple births others siblings are twins, triplets, or even quadruplets. The gender of siblings is also important and many siblings report being closest to their sisters (p.155). Sibling relationships, both in terms of gender, number of children in a family and birth order, determine the different roles. Sibling roles also take on a different tone when one sibling is disabled (p.157). As with other factors, sibling relationships interact with gender, culture, and social class.

Exercise 8.4

Sibling Relationships
(In class)

Compare your family's sibling configuration with those of your classmates. Can you identify any trend (e.g., birth order and occupation, coupling patterns, or ...)? What role did your siblings play in your life? How might your life be different without your particular siblings?

Family Life Cycle

As mentioned, one suggestion about traditional family life is that it unfolds in predictable and linear stages. Understanding the "normal" evolution of family life can shed light on family issues at each stage, recognizing that "normal" is probably the exception. Each stage demands emotional responses and related tasks within the family. Based on a cautious awareness, workers are able to place family lifespan crises within a meaningful context and incorporate family life cycle issues into a Genogram.

Despite the unique events faced by individual families and different family forms, families face similar developmental issues such as leaving home, aging, and death and in the process, they deal with similar developmental tasks. Each stage starts with a marker event such as the start of a relationship, the birth of the first child, children as teenagers, or the death of a member. Every development stage poses a new challenge as families encounter unfamiliar issues, tasks, emotional demands, and potential crises. When a family fails to meet these challenges, it is unable to adapt and becomes stuck. Understanding family development pinpoints the changes required so the family can resolve the crisis and move onto the next stage.

By being aware of the family life cycle issues and tasks, family members alter their unproductive attitudes and relationships to adapt to the new demands (Holman, 1983). Since family life cycle stressors are predictable, they can consider crises as normal but understand the stress in a new light. Seeing a crisis as something to be expected can help families rally their resources to deal with it. They will also be less inclined to blame the errant family member. When a crisis arises in the family, it is safe to assume that it is encountering some difficulty dealing with a particular stage. While developmental stressors are common to all families, each family is unique in how it experiences them. Some have well-developed problem solving skills bolstered by strong support networks, making them respond quite smoothly to challenges. Family workers, when identifying family development issues, can help families access the tools necessary to cope with them by strengthening the knowledge, skills, and strategies of families.

As more resources are required to meet family needs, some vulnerable families become more disorganized and stressed as they move through the family cycle (Geismar & Krisberg, 1966). Families face an increasing demand for resources, both social and economic, as they move through the cycle and these increasing demands strains impoverished families' abilities to respond. Such families experience incongruence between the *need* for service and resources and the *availability* of services and resources. They also might be unskilled in their ability to *use* the resources.

As mentioned, the family faces common and predictable tasks in each stage. Movement to a new stage unfolds slowly. Every new demand requires adjustment in roles and family boundaries, for example, both of which must adapt. As children get older, family boundaries must become more open and flexible as they widen their social network and move to greater independence. Boundaries that are too rigid stifle the social development of family members and prohibit growing skills aimed at independence. If boundaries do not change in the course of a family's existence, children could fail to get their individual developmental needs met. Boundaries that are too flexible in early childhood places children at risk through lack of supervision and exposure to greater risks. When boundaries are too open during adolescence, there may be lack of adequate supervision.

Carter and McGoldrick (1999) are key theorists of the family life cycle. While several proposed family life cycle models exist, generally the family life cycle involves:

- Leaving home
- Partnering
- Birth of first child
- Families with preschool children
- Families with school-aged children
- Families with teenagers
- Families with young people leaving home (launching, referred to as the "Empty Nest") (notice where one family ends, another begins)
- Middle age
- Aging
- Families in later life

Exercise 8.5

Variations in Family Development
(In Class)

Identify a family in which the family life cycle differs from the model proposed by Carter and McGoldrick (1999). How does this family differ? Develop a model of the family life cycle based upon this particular family. Beside each stage, write down the associated the tasks. What are the implications for intervention?

Stage	Tasks	Intervention Implications

Again, we remind you that the model best captures the white, middle-class family (i.e., traditional family). However, even in middle class families, the cycle often does not follow a clear-cut course. Also, note how the model emphasizes development based on the issues of one family member (often the oldest child). Some families have young children in addition to adolescents or even adult children. Other variations could include a family from another culture, a never-married single parent family, a blended family, or a family where children remain in the home for the duration of their adult life. Families may move back and forth between stages rather than experience a linear path.

The types of "non-traditional" family forms are varied and can be quite complex. Families break up because of separation, divorce, or death. Others are "blended" and approximately half of all children will live in a single parent household. Variation also occurs based on the work experience of parents (e.g., commuter relationships, dual income wage earners, stay-at-home dads, etc.), requiring distinct childcare arrangements. Many couples remain childless, whether through intent or for biological reasons, while others delay childbirth until their bioloical clocks start ticking and careers are well established. Roles are also changing and we hear about some fathers who have decided to raise children while the mothers work, a decision that was unheard of a generation ago. Other families struggle with both parents being unemployed. In yet other families, children are adopted, skipping the childbirth phase. Finally, grandparents or extended kin may be primary caretakers, again making the family life cycle unique. These are only a few of the basic differences in family forms. We have heard of many other complex family forms that would be hard to capture in a single paragraph.

Other family life cycle patterns are rooted in cultural patterns not encapsulated by the "traditional" family life cycle. Families in some cultures are based on an extensive kin network that can include multiple households or generations. In recently immigrated families, the older generation often leads the family. Families function as collective units, demanding that the worker understand the intergenerational relationships of parents, children, grandparents, relatives, and extended kin. In these families, decisions might depend upon how the complete family unit is affected.

Figure 8.1

"Normative" Stages of the Family Life Cycle[1]

Stage	*Family Tasks*
1. Partnering[2]	• Committing to another person • Creating new roles, rules, and responsibilities • Becoming a distinct unit • Disengaging from family-of- origin and incorporating a new family unit (in-laws) • Making compromises and negotiating concrete and personal needs
2. Birth of first child and families with young children	• Reestablishing the marital unit based upon a new member • Accepting and integrating child(ren) into the family • Developing new roles based on childrearing, household tasks and employment
3. Families with school-aged children	• Reworking the couple relationship and relationship to work • Making family boundaries more flexible to allow for greater child independence and to accommodate outside relationships • Changing roles
4. Families with teenagers	• Changing rules, limit setting, role negotiation, and discipline • Allowing for independence while maintaining a relationship and child monitoring • Preparing to care for older generation • Young adults formulating a new self definition • Children assuming personal responsibility • Recreating the marital relationship
5. Launching	• Making career and relationship decisions • Accepting old age • Involvement with grandchildren and partners of the children • Dealing with loss
6. Families in later life	

[1]Adapted from Collins, Jordan, & Coleman, 1999; Carter & McGoldrick, 1988; Patterson, Williams, Grauf-Grounds, & Chamow, 1998).

[2]We use the word partnering to respect all types of unions, not just state sanctioned ones.

Exercise 8.6

Life Cycle and Culture
(In Class)

Based on your particular culture, outline your family life cycle. Compare your outline with your classmates. How typical is your family life cycle and to what extent are the differences due to culture?

Exercise 8.7

Family Stages and Crisis
(In Class)

Think about the historical progression of your own family. What specific family stages can you demarcate? What were examples of the associated crises during each stage? What other issues did you family face during each transition and how did they affect your family's life cycle?

Your Age	Family Members' Ages	Family Stage	Family Task	Crisis

Partnering

> *...couples come in many varieties: gay and straight; married and unmarried; tall, ambitious wives and short nurturing homebody husbands.*
>
> McGoldrick (1999b)

As with other stages, partnering is affected by culture, social class, and sexual orientation. Nevertheless, society has romanticized marriage and we now know that the new relationship benefits men more than women, in terms of mental and physical health and income (Bernard, 1982, cited in McGoldrick, 1999b). Yet, the stereotype is one in which women cast elaborate nets with which to snare a partner.

People are marrying at an older age than thirty years ago. Many also live in a series of monogamous relationships until they settle down with one person. Relationships initiated at younger ages are usually more unstable than those in which people marry later. In addition, relationships where children arrive on the scene early leave little time for adjustment. Usually, young people leave their family before marrying. Changes in coupling patterns have occurred over the past four decades in that marriage is no longer necessary for a sexual relationship. Gay and lesbian couples still feel social stigma, but at the same time are less bound by rigid social rules (McGoldrick, 1999b). In the coupling stage, members must separate from their family of origin, develop intimate relationships, and start work. People also differ on the extent to which they separate from their family-of -origin, some of which is influenced by culture.

The process of coupling involves making many decisions. These decisions concern issues pertaining to: economic; emotional, power arrangements; boundaries; sexuality; child rearing; chores; and, leisure activities (Almeida, Woods, Messineo, & Font, 1998, cited in McGoldrick, 1999b). Thus, at the partnering stage, the couple must negotiate roles and tasks that were once within the domain of individuals. In new relationships, people must blend their unique lifestyles and differentiate themselves from their family-of-origin. The couple must create new ground rules about their life together (housework, having children, money management, and friends) and at the same time re-configure relationships with their families. The couple must learn to deal with interpersonal conflict to minimize stress, and freeing energies for daily tasks.

Forming such a relationship (whether legally recognized or common law) places a lot of demands on people who must sacrifice some of their own needs and make compromises. The adjustment period is stressful, and the couple must manage stress successfully so that that the relationship can survive. The family worker can focus on satisfaction with the relationship, relationship issues with extended family, and decisions surrounding parenthood. A marital satisfaction scale is one tool that the family worker can use to assess marital satisfaction (For example, see Corcoran and Fischer, 2000, pp.119-128). Assessment of the couple's relationship can also include issues of commitment, issues of control and responsibility, the couple's interactions, and conflict resolution (Patterson, Williams, Grauf-Grounds & Chamow, 1998). Since the couple is the "architect" of the family, unsuccessful resolution of these issues can seep into other stages of the family life cycle.

Exercise 8.8

Crises in this First Stage
(In Class)

Problems may appear on different fronts during this first phase of the family life cycle. List five potential pitfalls related to the tasks of forming a relationship that might produce a crisis for the couple. Compare your list with that of your classmates.

1.

2.

3.

4.

5.

Becoming Parents

Parenthood is another transition demanding additional adjustments. The couple must shift from focusing on the individual and couple needs, to focusing on the needs of a dependent and vulnerable human being. Many times, the decision to have children is not rational and it is not common for people to ask why they want to have children and all that it entails.

Exercise 8.9

Reasons for Having Children
(In class)

Make a list of five reasons why people have children. Compare this list with that of your classmates. How many reasons for having children do you think are "rational" and how many reasons are based on the couple's personal needs? Which reasons may lead to disappointment or crisis in the future?

1.

2.

3.

4.

5.

As with coupling, having children has been romanticized and people often have children equipped with many unrealistic expectations and misconceptions (Carter, 1999). The birth of a child is one of the first triangles through which couple must navigate (see Chapter 5, Family Systems Theory). The arrival of a first child is a crisis that is pleasant for some, but also a time of tremendous family stresses. Having children demands lifetime of responsibility for which some new parents are inadequately prepared. Parents must juggle multiple commitments to the children and to the partner, stressing the relationship and contributing to decreased satisfaction. The first task of this stage is preparing for and adapting to the birth. The couple must also deal with the anxiety of being a parent. Those who have children to fulfill personal needs are startled to find out that children have greater needs than they do. A host of issues complicates the birth of many children, including, but not limited to poor teenaged mothers, homelessness, disability, child abuse, and infertility (Carter, 1999). Growing awareness about Fetal Alcohol Syndrome and babies born to drug-addicted mothers, make the pregnancy period a particularly vital time for early intervention. Couples who are unable to conceive might choose to adopt, although the number of available children for adoption is less than several decades ago. We also hear a lot about international or interracial adoptions. With the development of new reproductive technologies, infertile couples and gay and lesbian people are more able to conceive.

With children on the scene, new roles are required. Parents must grieve their lost lifestyle, especially losses in leisure, money, and sleep. The couple devotes less time for personal and interpersonal needs, which comes as a shock. It is also a time when many families experience financial difficulties and are on the bottom of the rung in their careers. Parents discover that the needs of children are more pressing than their personal needs and those who have difficulty meeting their personal needs often experience difficulty meeting the needs of a young child. Parents can no longer sleep in and the changing focus can result feelings of neglect or misunderstanding. While gender roles are changing and men are assuming more responsibility for housework and childcare, it is not yet equal.

It comes as a surprise to many to discover just how dependent young children are on their parents . Young parents must develop healthy attachment with their children, and understand and respond to the child's needs. Mothers usually assume primary childcare responsibilities, although this pattern might be shifting somewhat. During this time, family power shifts to become more traditional (Carter, 1999). Working parents might experience angst about childcare arrangements and theories of child development now focus on the importance of early attachment between a child and a significant other. These theories have infiltrated mainstream thinking, adding to guilt and anxiety about leaving children with caretakers other than the parents. New parents whose own parents are available to care for young children are fortunate, although extended family dynamics are also intensified. Worksite daycare available to working parents can ease the burden. Other worksites are less supportive. For example, one of the authors had to leave work early one day when her five-year old daughter broke her foot at school. She was deducted an afternoon's salary for her efforts.

Adjusting to parenthood is complicated by the fact that few people are equipped with the knowledge and skills to meet the needs of children. Many are naïve about parenting and child development. Here, the Genogram could be useful, because under stress, people often revert to what was familiar to them - and in this case, it is probably their own upbringing. New parents who are socially isolated lack supports in terms of information and concrete assistance. An *Ecomap* (Chapter 6) will help assess the couple's social network because having an infant poses emotional and material challenges and a lack of resources can result in neglect (Patterson, Williams, Grauf-Grounds & Chamow, 1998). A child born into an economically disadvantaged or socially isolated family produces additional stress. Stress is also expressed by parents who must come to terms with work around the house and financial issues (Patterson, Williams, Grauf-Grounds & Chamow, 1998). The economy has adjusted to dual wage earner families and parents must decide whether both will work outside the home. This stage and the next stage of the family cycle can be emotionally and physically exhausting. In fact, we believe that sleeping is a skill that is unlearned once children arrive on the scene.

Many events can derail the "typical" course, placing more stress and intensify a family life stage crisis. We have a niece who recently gave birth to a Downs Syndrome child. The parents were totally unprepared and the child also had heart troubles and had to travel to another city for medical treatment. The health difficulties of this child intensified their adjustment to a new baby. Thus, children born with special needs stress even the most resourceful family and make the tasks of this stage out of the ordinary. Other issues might include infertility, disagreement about whether to even have children, work and careers plans, and unexpected pregnancies. Can you think of more issues?

As the child becomes more mobile and independent, he or she needs a wise balance of supervision and independence. Children's demand for independence can tax the energy of the parents. Children also need a balance of cognitive stimulation, play, and instrumental attention from their parents, and some parents have little energy for any. Poor supervision places children at risk and having more children only intensifies the exhaustion. We believe that one child is a lot of work, while the work of two, three, or more children increases the work exponentially! Parents who are unprepared for the demands of parenthood and those who are under stress - due to relationship issues, financial pressures, or social isolation, may have little energy left over to meet the child's needs. As the child gets older, social relationships must grow larger (Garbarino, 1982; Patterson, Williams, Grauf-Grounds & Chamow, 1998). Lack of external social contact hampers a child's social development. If both parents work, safe and stimulating childcare arrangements need to be made.

Exercise 8.10

Stressful Events in the Life Cycle
(In Class)

Families can often experience a lot of stress. When events occur that are out of the ordinary, the family experiences even more stress. Make a list of possible events than can increase family stress. What are the implications for family work? Compare this list with those of your classmates.

Events	Implications for Family Work
a.	
b.	
c.	
d.	

Exercise 8.11

Social Relationships of Children
(In Class)

Imagine that you are the parent of a child. Select a theory of child development (e.g. cognitive psycho-sexual, social); make a list of the various social relationships and activities that enhance the child's development. What do you notice about the size and complexity as the child gets older?

	Developmental Stage and Task	Social Needs
Newborn		
Toddler		
Pre-school		
School-aged		
Adolescent		

Families with Children Aged 5-12

Families face a new set of challenges when the oldest child begins school. Time, or lack of it, is a family's greatest enemy. New and hectic schedules intensify the burden on the family, particularly if parents work shifts or if younger children are in the home. Increasing needs for child independence (at times culturally prescribed), places greater even more demands upon the family as they shuffle their children back and forth from visits with friends, school activities and music or sports practices. In some families, transportation is unavailable, threatening opportunities for out-of-school contact.

While school success is associated with success in later life, sometimes parents lack the time, energy, or resources to support their children in this stage. Homework, purchasing school supplies, allowing time to play, doing household chores, having family time and supporting outside activities pose new challenges. While creating structure and routines for homework will help children achieve in school; however many disorganized, stressed, or chaotic families have difficulty. Some children experience stress adjusting to going to school because of difficulties separating from parents. Rallying daily routines to get children to school can be a monumental challenge. For those children who resist going to school, the daily routine can be strenuous. Academic success requires that children learn to function in a structured school environment. The job of parents is to help children develop necessary skills and attitudes for survival in a school environment. This might be difficult in families that have no daily routine and little predictable structure. While some children adapt easily to school, others have difficulty sitting still, focusing on tasks, and developing harmonious relationships with peers.

As children develop friendships and participate in structured activities outside of school, time and resources, such as transportation are required. Children are exposed to commercialism through commercials and their friends' possessions and differences in family resources become glaringly visible now. School lunch programs are especially important for children growing up in disadvantaged families. Again, working parents must make appropriate out-of-school care arrangements, before and after school as well during summer vacation. Lack of financial resources and social support challenge disadvantaged families in particular and children from poor families can suffer unless they have adequate social support and provided their parents are not overburdened. As the child's social network expands, parents then need to develop strong connections with the child's outside life.

Exercise 8.12

Supporting School
(In Class)

Children need the support of parents in education and social development. Make a list of a child needs, how parents can support these needs, and the blocks to getting these needs achieved. What can you do as a family worker to help parents better support children in school?

Child Needs	How to Help	Blocks to these Needs	Possible Intervention
a.			
b.			
c.			
d.			

Families with Teenagers

Most parents dread adolescence because of its conflict-ridden and anxiety provoking reputation. To survive families need flexibility, a new set of parenting skills, and above all, a sense of humor. Indeed, in today's dangerous world, on all fronts, many parents feel anxious about their adolescents' bids for independence (Garcia-Preto, 1999b). However, in most families, adolescence is merely a seamless continuation of previous stages of family development. Yet previous unresolved family issues might catch now, increasing stress and contributing to child behavior difficulties. The most glaring issue concerns family boundaries, rules, and quests for autonomy. We recommend "firm flexibility!" Adolescence is also a period of increased family breakup (Patterson, Williams, Grauf-Grounds & Chamow, 1998).

Parents struggle with what to expect and knowing which rules are reasonable. Families in which independence and autonomy invokes anxiety may struggle with rules related to independence. Conversely, disengaged families (loosely connected) might have difficulty providing sufficient guidance and structure for their young people. New "rules of engagement" need to be established around the parent-child relationship, the amount of freedom that is appropriate, and the limits of acceptable behavior. Above all, parents need a sense of humor during their children's teenage years.

Other events can impinge on parenting and divert the parents' energy from setting appropriate limits. When crises appear, the parent-child relationship becomes more strained and less enjoyable. Other family events can make the situation worse. For example, grandparents might be experiencing health difficulties, marital tensions might surface, and poverty and discrimination may become particularly salient. A concern of every parent is the increasingly toxic forces outside the home - drug abuse, violence, eating disorders, depression, teen pregnancy, illegal activities, and other high-risk behavior might emerge.

Exercise 8.13

Family Stressors
(In Class)

Make a list of possible family stressors that might arise during adolescence. Next to the stressor, make a list of what impact this might have on the family.

Stressors	Possible Impact
e.g. Money	Increased parent-child conflict Decreased child and parent self-esteem
a.	
b.	
c.	
d.	

Adolescence coincides with parents confronting new personal issues. Middle age, career issues, and a looming time together all must be faced. As children mature sexually, parents face a new set of values and some find that their child's sexual maturation and demands for more privileges and freedom unnerving. Teens shift their focus to outside the as peers take on special importance and family relationships weaken. As teens become more independent, they still must learn new behaviors within the sheltered confines of the family and parents are challenged to find a wise balance of appropriate independence versus overprotection or under protection.

Some parents become distraught with their teenagers' behavior and bring their adolescents to counseling to be "fixed." (Not like the fix we have for dogs and cats, although some parents might wish this!). The challenge to workers is to help parents understand the behavior within the context of family development, for without such awareness, parents will have difficulty adapting their behavior to address the issues. A starting point might be to identify how family members are worried and stressed at what is happening, without scapegoating the teen. However, substance use, risky sexual behavior, criminal activity, and other high-risk behavior warrant immediate attention.

Exercise 8.14

Your Own Adolescence
(In Class)

Reflect back to your own adolescence and describe what was going on in your family and how you and/or your siblings' teen years stressed the family system and/or created conflict in the family?

Your Behavior	Parent Reaction	Family Response

Launching Children

The family survived adolescent only to face the next hurdle - children leaving home. Once known as the "Empty Nest" stage, we are now aware that children leaving home can be a liberating time. Many women embrace this stage with vigor as they set new sights on the rest of their lives, while men might not be impacted as greatly (Blacker, 1999). However, relief might be mixed with concern and worry about how their children will fare on their own. Culture, social class, sexual orientation, and gender affect the manner in which a child leaves home. In economically disadvantaged families, for example, the young adult might face a time of decreasing job opportunities (Blacker, 1999). In addition, families in some cultures and socioeconomic groups offer greater assistance to their children's independence than others. Relationships become redefined and power differences in the couple's relationships begin to shift once again. Some couples decide to separate after the departure of their children,

When young people leave home, tasks again change. Today, it is commonplace for children to leave home and return before leaving permanently. They are referred to as "boomerang children." Other young people remain longer within the family because of difficulty supporting them and parents might assist the young person creating additional financial burdens. Parents thus delay their financial security for several more years. Parents may feel ambivalence at this time, combining elation and grief. At the same time, parents re-negotiate their relationship without children while facing personal issues such as growing older and possible health problems. If the young person who has left home is the oldest child, parents are can focus more fully on the younger children.

Young people must balance independence while maintaining family ties. Some will start their own families and if young people leave home before being adequately equipped, the process can be stressful. Young people in middle class families are less likely to leave their family-of-origin prematurely because of educational expectations and high rates of unemployment. In other families, young people leave home too early, run away, drop out of school, or work in low-paying unskilled positions. How a young person leaves the family home affects the remainder of their life. While people can return to school later, this is difficult if they are responsible for a family. Thus, there is a relationship between how people leave home and the educational attainment and careers they bring to later life.

The state of the economy challenges many young people in their quest for independence. Young people may prepare to leave by first taking on menial or low paying work. During this phase, they learn how to handle money as well as how to balance a personal life and a working life. In the process, they struggle to find personally meaningful work. Some succeed while others do not. In middle class families, their family obligations are put on hold. We see talk shows where families become stuck in this stage - adult children hang on for too long while neglecting adult responsibilities (such as paying room and board or not being responsible for household tasks). It is also a time when young people might be searching for a mate. Fulmer (1999) suggests that at this stage, love interests might be an attempt to address issues from the family-of-origin, such as moving from someone who was taken care of to someone who takes care of another. When children leave home for real, they must learn to set up a place of their own

Exercise 8.15

Launching
(Out of Class)

Talk to your parents about their feelings and experiences when you left home. Report to the class. What commonalities do the parents share? What are the differences?

Family Developmental Assessment Questions

Below are questions the family worker can ask a family to gain an understanding of developmental issues faced by the family.

- At what stage in the family life cycle is this family? How adequately does the family meeting the developmental needs of members?
- How well are family members fulfilling their developmental roles and tasks?
- What are the family's usual ways of resolving developmental crises?
- At what point, if any, is this family stuck with regard to life cycle issues?
- What are the expectations and beliefs of the parents at this stage?
- What developmental issues does the family need to address that it isn't?
- What are the demands on family resources at this stage? What resources does the family have?
- What are the unresolved family issues?
- How does culture affect the development of this particular family?

Exercise 8.16

Family Development Assessment
(In Class)

Using your family-of-origin or your PBL family, do a family developmental assessment. If you use your own family, select a specific phase. Describe the ages of family members and outline key family developmental issues at one particular time. Pay particular attention to periods when your family appeared to be stuck or overwhelmed by unexpected events. What would you recommend that the family do differently to overcome its developmental blocks?

Family Development Assessment:

Later Family Life Stages

We provide a short overview of the final stages of the family life cycle. The primary task of middle-aged parents who no longer have their children living at home is to reinvent their relationship. The relationship will be different than when they first got together or when children were at home. Some couples decide they no longer want to be a couple and have waited for the children to leave before separating.

The final stage - the aging family - lasts until the death of one of the partners. As they face issues aging and their own mortality becomes apparent. Social isolation is a threat as friends die or they are institutionalized. Inadequate resources are a burden to many older adults and some move into their children's homes. Some grandparents may step in and become the primary caretakers for their grandchildren.

Diversity in the Family Life Cycle

As mentioned several times, the developmental stages presented above make sweeping generalizations about the family life cycle. These generalizations are premised on the belief that all families have children, parents stay together, the partners are heterosexual, and they are part of on the dominant culture. Clearly, this is probably the exception rather than the rule. Cross cultural families, those who have divorced, never married, or blended, couples who marry late in life, gay/lesbian couples with or without children, and families with extended kin living within one household are not represented by the "typical family life cycle" model. In some families, one or more children never leave home. The decline in fertility in Western countries has also affected the family life cycle. This diversity of family styles brings with it variations in family cycle development.

Separation and Divorce

Divorce is a common feature of the family landscape such that over half of all marriages end in divorce. In some, single parenthood, and remarriage can occur more than once. Divorce rates are affected by many factors: age at marriage, religious affiliation, cultural and socioeconomic issues, education, and even geographical location (Ahrons, 1999). Despite the fact that it is most often women who make the initial decision to divorce (Ahrons, 1999), divorce often erodes their economic and emotional resources, especially when there are children. It is also a major life loss. Separation and divorce is stressful, even when the relationship was unpleasant, in part because it requires practical and emotional readjustment (Carter & McGoldrick, 1999b). Divorce seems to affect men and women differently.

Divorce carries with it phases that differ from those of intact families. The *ideal* is that even though the relationship ends, parents will cooperate in their parenting. We recognize that people often have too much emotional baggage that interferes with their ability or willingness to cooperate. The process of divorce unfolds over several stages. However, the process is often not linear (Ahrons, 1999; Carter & McGoldrick, 1999b):

1. Making the decision to divorce
2. Making concrete plans to end the relationship
3. Announcing the decision to the world
4. The physical and emotional separation (sometimes the emotional separation is the most difficult)
5. The legal divorce through the courts
6. Deciding on issues related to custodial and noncustodial arrangements
7. Making the decision to move on

Every family member must deal with personal issues during a divorce but adjustment is complicated when one partner is often more reluctant to divorce. No two people are in the same point of readiness or acceptance when divorce occurs. The couple, now each as an individual, must redefine relationships with extended family and friends, and mourn their losses. After divorce, both must reinvent their lives as single people. Divorce does not happen for everyone at the same stage of family development and the point at which divorce happens in family life determines the nature of the family cycle (Ahrons, 1999).

Divorce affects every family member and children in particular need special consideration during the process. Unfortunately, their needs are often overshadowed by the needs of their parents who are busy nursing wounds and planning counterattacks. Critical decisions about custody must be made and children suffer when parents use them as pawns in their ongoing conflict, making divorce mediation especially important. We know of one judge who awards custody to both parents when appropriate, but to lessen the impact on children, the children remain in the family home while the parents move back and forth. Unless there are factors that prevent both parents from parenting equally (such as abuse, substance abuse, or mental illness), the ideal arrangement for children is for parents to share custody. However, they must be capable of putting the needs of the children before their personal injuries. Visitation for noncustodial parents must also be negotiated with *the best interest of the children in mind* and the effects of the divorce on children must be kept to a minimum (Ahrons, 1999).

Custodial parents often experience role-strain and face challenges on multiple fronts - home responsibilities, childcare, worked-related issues and re-establishing a personal life (Burden, 1986; Carter & McGoldrick, 1999b). Single parents who fail to get respite from childcare face increased stress that affects their parenting and social isolation contributes to depression and poor parenting, making social support particularly important.

Exercise 8.17

Using Children as Pawns
(In Class)

Provide five examples of how children can be used as pawns in parental conflict and/or divorce. With each example, give a family worker response. Compare your findings with other members of the class.

Example	Worker Response
1.	
2.	
3.	
4.	
5.	

Children of all ages feel distress and responsible for their parents' divorce. As well, they must deal with their own personal challenges before moving on. Concentrating on school may be difficult. They might be overwhelmed with conflicting emotions in the process of coming to terms with this major life event. Because parents are often consumed by their own crises, they risk marginalizing the children's needs and it may take several years for children's lives to stabilize.

Divorce deprives children of needed resources - psychological, material, and social. Additional stress is placed on children when parents demand loyalty from the children. Custody and access arrangements become a focal point of an ongoing battle between parents who have yet to divorce emotionally. Other parents may cut off ties completely. We are also hearing more about noncustodial parents who disappear with the children. Finally, if parents establish new relationships they may include partners with children of their own, a new set of adjustments emerge.

Divorce affects each child differently, depending on their relationship with the parents, the amount of conflict in the marriage and the divorce, and the extent to which they are resilient. Divorce does not doom a child to a lifetime of dysfunction, but they do have issues to deal with in order to get on with their lives. These include:

- Feelings of self-blame and guilt, denial, worry, anxiety, abandonment, anger, and resentment.
- Being caught in the middle of a bitter and ongoing parental conflict, while needing to have a positive relationship with both parents.
- Establishing a "normal life" and a predictable routine.
- Grieving their losses.
- Reaching closure.
- Learning to establish and maintain healthy interpersonal relationships.

(Collins, Jordan & Coleman, 1999)

Exercise 8.18

Death in the Family
(PBL Worksheet)

In your PBL groups, imagine one of the parents had died one year before your family work. Interview the family members, exploring their feelings and issues around the loss of this parent (20-30 minutes). Debrief in large class.

Single Parent Families

Before we discuss single parent families, we need to say that we do not believe single parent families are defective and that being raised in single parent families does not doom children to a life of misery and dysfunction. The number of single people and single parent families is increasing (Berliner, Jacob, & Schwartzberg, 1999) and nearly half of all children will live in a single parent home. In most cases, the mother becomes the custodial parent, even these days. Despite stigmatization evident in a conservative social climate, single parent families and blended family structures are neither problematic nor inferior. The attitude toward single parenthood is also determined by ethnicity and culture (p. 363). Most single parent families function quite well. However, others vulnerable families have difficulty navigating common landmines. It is not necessarily the functioning of single parents that creates difficulties but other factors such as social support, poverty, and education play a huge role in their well being. Children also react to whether the divorce was amiable, the extent of conflict, and whether they were used as pawns in ongoing resentments. Single parenting can occur through death, divorce, desertion, and never being married.

This being said, workers need to be cognizant of some of the most salient issues that single parents face:

Single Parent Issues

- Social isolation and feelings of loneliness. It is imperative that single parents develop adequate social support systems. Without support they are poorly buffered against the impact of stress.
- Deciding whether to cooperate with contact with the ex-spouse in his or her bids for child contact. We arguer that it is usually in the best interests of the children to cooperate. In many instances where children experience difficulties, they have irregular contact with the noncustodial parent (Ahrons, 1999).
- Children need support to help with school performance, emotional needs and behavioral guidance.
- Economic difficulties compounding personal issues
- Fatigue and role overload. The danger is that role overload will contribute to family disorganization, increase social isolation, and create problems in the parent-child relationship. Again, shared parenting can relieve much of this fatigue.
- With adequate income and support, single parent families are as viable as two parent families.
- Childcare arrangements to ensure constant and adequate supervision of the children. Again, this issue speaks to the importance of divorced parents cooperating.
- Development of child management and time management skills.
- Recognize and mobilize strengths and resources.

Death of a Parent

While in some ways, death parallels issues related to divorce, there are some differences for children. Family workers can help by recognizing that:

- Death is a traumatic event and people need space to grieve.
- Is final for children.
- Widowed parents are not likely to remarry.
- Contact with the deceased partner's family is important.
- Socioeconomic stress is less of a burden, but still produces stress.
- Parents experience role overload.

Based on the issues identified above, it would be easy to conclude that we should avoid divorce and separation at all costs. Such a view is not helpful. Instead, looking for family friendly and solution focused approaches are best. Interventions should be ecologically based, and include working with concrete resources and formal and informal social support networks.

Exercise 8.19

Single Parent Families
(PBL Worksheet)

In your PBL groups imagine your family is a single parent family. Explore the issues facing this family (20-30 minutes). Debrief in large class.

Remarriage, Step-Parenting, and Blended Families

After a difficult divorce, it is natural for to have fears and anxieties about entering into new relationships. Nevertheless, once the fears about entering into a new relationship are faced, stepfamilies have a number of issues need to be dealt with. Family workers can help:

- Reach closure on their losses;
- Develop new rules about family patterns, childcare, and discipline.
- Define new relationships;
- Support connections with the children's biological parent, when appropriate, by allowing children ongoing and healthy relationships with the noncustodial parent. This includes negotiating visitation, custody, and child support arrangements. Children who have ongoing relationships with their noncustodial parent and are permitted loyalty to their other parent fare best (McGoldrick & Carter, 1999).
- Establish new households roles and routines;
- Come to terms with the new parent (children);
- Manage sibling rivalry;
- Create a satisfactory step-parenting role;
- Form new attachments in the family;
- Establish new boundaries.

Exercise 8.20

Blended Families
(PBL Worksheet)

In your PBL groups imagine your family is a blended family. Explore the issues due to being a blended family (20-30 minutes). Debrief in large class.

Parenting by Grandparents

A common saying is that grandparents and grandchildren get along so well because they have a common enemy (Walsh, 1999, p.311).

While most grandparents expect to be involved in the lives of their grandchildren, many are relieved not to have primary caretaking responsibilities (Walsh, 1999). Yet, grandparents as primary caretakers, is common in some cultures and is becoming more common in the mainstream when parents become incapacitated for a variety of reasons. Some grandparents prefer to take on the primary child care of their grandchildren rather than lose them completely. We recall our friendship with Bob a man in his late 70s. Bob's daughter was an alcoholic, out of concern for his grandchildren, Bob, a widower, took custody of the young children, and raised them. However, this necessitated him putting aside their life issues. Upon his death, his granddaughter told us that Bob was mother, father, and grandfather to her so she lost three people.

The parenting style of grandparents is often based on what was normal when they were raising children and these strategies might conflict with modern parenting approaches. They also must plan for what will happen with their grandchildren in the case of their illness or death. Even when they do not assume custody of grandchildren, grandparents can play an important role in the lives of their grandchildren and it is not unusual to see children developing closer bonds with grandparents when parent-child strain is experienced (Collins, Jordan, & Coleman, 1999).

Exercise 8.21

Parenting by Grandparents
(PBL Worksheet)

In your PBL groups imagine your families primary parents are the grandparents. Explore the issues facing this family (20-30 minutes). Debrief in large class.

Exercise 8.22

Developmental Challenges in Different Family Structures
(In Class)

Make a list of the challenges you believe a family experiences at the point of divorce, loss through death, extended family units, and single parent families. Compare the items in each column. What role can a family worker play during and after these critical periods?

	Divorce	Single Parent	Death	Extended Family
a.				
b.				
c.				
d.				

Exercise 8.23

Cultural Variations
(PBL Worksheet)

In your PBL groups, explore cultural issues with this family as it relates to family life cycle issues (20-30 minutes). Debrief in large class.

Gay and Lesbian Families

The life cycle model does not fit well with gay and lesbian families in part because the concept of family among members of this group places greater emphasis on friends and does not always include children (Johnson & Colucci, 1999). While time will tell, at the time of this writing, gay and lesbian marriages are generally not legally sanctioned. Relationships with the family-of-origin do not generally follow the prescribed issues. If and how a person comes out to his or her own family also creates stress on individuals, particularly if the process occurs with the formation of the first gay or lesbian relationship. Social discrimination also places tensions and stresses upon gay and lesbian relationships. As mentioned, with new reproductive technologies, it is possible for more gay and lesbian people to have children. The decision to have children in gay and lesbian relationships is mediated by the values of the medical system. Others may decide to adopt, but again, state laws determine the process. We discuss gay and lesbian families in more detail in Chapter 2.

Example 8.1: Developmental Assessment with the Stone Family

The Stone family is encountering some normal developmental issues faced by families with teenagers. For example, a new set of values is being formed. Thirteen year-old Mary realizes the importance of school in her life, yet Michael does not. Michael needs to learn to control his anger outbursts and seek the support of family members. The influence of peers takes center stage for Michael and his sister. Mary has developed a strong supportive peer group. Michael is isolated from peers and will need to be connected to age appropriate peer group, for example, becoming involved in a peer sport or hobby group. As teens become more independent, they still must learn new behaviors within the protective confines of the family. Clear rules concerning right and wrong behaviors need to be established. Appropriate consequences for inappropriate behavior need to be put into place as well as support for appropriate behaviors. Parents are challenged to find the wisdom of allowing appropriate independence-seeking behavior versus over protecting or allowing their children free rein.

Complicating the issues of a family with teenagers is that this is a blended family. The two teenagers are from Mrs. Stone's first marriage and the present father is a stepfather of six years. There has been, and continues to be, struggles related to the stepfather being integrated into the family. In particular, he tends to withdraw from parenting conflicts, leaving most of parenting to his wife. Family discussions need to occur around the stepfather's role in disciplining the adolescents as well as role of support person in the family. Rules need to be created around "who does what with whom." Who helps the teens with their homework? Who gets involved in sports or other activities with the teens? What arrangements are made for the teens, individually and together to spend quality time with each, and both parents?

Chapter Summary

The traditional family life cycle model helps clarify expectations about family events and tasks as families move through life. The family life cycle is affected by many issues including divorce, death, cultural nuance, and remarriage. While laying out the life cycle as stages of predictable family experiences, we must be aware that each family experiences its life cycle in different ways. Family workers can educate families about what to expect at each stage and interpret family events in such a way that perceived abnormal behavior becomes more understandable.

Exercise 8.24

Family Life Cycle
(PBL Worksheet)

Today, you will continue to conduct an assessment on your PBL family. For starters, you can examine issues related to the Family Life Cycle. To do this, the family worker should lead a discussion about the areas covered by the Schema. Try to develop questions related to each of the areas. Questions can also be developed related to the Family Life Cycle as well. You will also be able to retrieve information about the family related to your previous exposure to the family.

Outside of class, take a moment to reflect on your family as to how the issues covered in class are replicated in real life with "real families." Some family members do not show up. What is the impact on the sessions as a result? What are some ways to minimize these kinds of problems? How is your role-play family similar or different from families portrayed by the family life cycle? Family members also have different levels of motivation. What is the impact of these differing levels on the family work that is being done?

By now, you will have some sense of the family problem and are starting to get a glimpse of family patterns and roles. The task of the family social worker is to:

- Examine, discuss, and summarize the family's history and the present day implications. How did the family get to where it is now?
- Re-formulate concerns and problems within the context of the family life cycle.
- Check out any losses or feelings of grief with the changes the family has gone through developmentally.
- Explore if there is (are) member(s) who are not sensitive to the growth and development of other family members
- Determine the degree to which members feel they can make an impact within the family (Can they help with decisions? Do they get enough attention? Can they be themselves? Is there respect for them in the family?)

Tips for family workers

- ➢ Encourage continual family interactions. Do not allow all communication to go through you. Encourage active listening, looking at each other, and speaking from self or "I."
- ➢ Work to ensure family members speak for themselves.
- ➢ Encourage each to take responsibility for thoughts, feelings, and actions (no blaming others).
- ➢ Encourage the family to make discoveries about their own process.
- ➢ Go from facts to feelings and from actions to process.
- ➢ Use an example from your own family's development in order to increase awareness within this family.

Chapter 9 **Table of Contents**

BEHAVIORAL FAMILY WORK

Chapter 9

Behavioral Family Work

Chapter Coverage

- The Behavioral Approach
- Social Learning Theory
- Teaching Parenting Skills

Introduction: The Behavioral Approach

One influential belief about families is that problems develop because of deficits in skills, particularly parenting skills. What is learned can also be unlearned and replaced with more effective parenting skills. New tasks demanded of the family in the various different stages of family development require that members develop new skills based on evolving needs. When parents develop consistent skills, children know what to expect and behave accordingly. Socializing children to be responsible and competent adults requires that parents take an active role in teaching children to be prosocial in their behavior and skills as they navigate issues throughout their lives. Parents are the guiding force behind the acquisition of social skills and children them learn through subtle family interactions. We know that these interactions either reinforce behavior, thus encouraging it, or punish behavior, thus eliminating it. The focus of behavioral work is on educating parents to use consequences to shape behavior effectively.

Children behave differently in various settings, suggesting that their behavior is dependent on the reactions of people around them. Children with behavior problems learn to expend a lot of energy trying to gain control their environment. Behavioral interventions are effective in dealing with a number of problem behaviors such as temper tantrums, disobedience, homework refusal, bed-wetting, delinquency, and aggression (Collins, Jordan, & Coleman, 1999). Similarly, abusive parents can learn parenting skills, self-control and more effective child management skills. Research has shown that parents of children with behavior problems have ineffective parenting skills although they can correct their deficits skills by learning new strategies.

Children with behavior problems have usually experienced few rules and negative reinforcement (discussed in more detail in this chapter) leading to problem behaviors. Aversive behavior responses such as spanking or yelling do not encourage positive child social behavior and instead produce undesirable child behavior such as whining and tantrums. Negative reinforcement increases the likelihood of negative responses.

To change a child's behavior, parents together with the family worker must do a careful and detailed assessment and develop strategic interventions aimed at eliminating problem behaviors and producing ones that are more acceptable. Before embarking on a behavioral program, parents first need to understand demands that will be placed on them in terms of time and energy. They should also be aware that change will not happen immediately and persistence and perseverance is required. With the family worker's guidance, parents learn to understand and use behavioral principles consistently with their children, reinforcing desirable behavior and eliminating problematic behavior.

Behavioral work with families is founded on the principle that behavior is maintained or extinguished by its consequences. Rewards are used to reinforce and strengthen a desired response. (Rewards occur using a positive reinforcement or the removal of a negative behavior). This means that parents learn to reinforce positive behavior, rather than negative behavior.

Teaching reinforcement and learning new skills are most effective when children are young, before behavioral patterns are well established and difficult to change (Kadzin, 2004). Thus, early intervention is very important. Research suggests that children with behavior problems can be identified early. Their behavior is often formed through "coercive family processes" in which children and parents have discovered that they can use negative behaviors to control each another. Parenting behaviors become ineffective when children receive attention for negative behavior instead of positive behavior. Parents do not often pay attention to a child's behavior until it is negative. They also have difficulty being on top of (i.e., continuous awareness and monitoring) their children's behavior in an ongoing and consistent way. This tracking also applies to activities outside the home when parents do not know where the children are or what they are doing.

Because of limited funding and legislation based on "least intrusive measures," appropriate resources might not be available for early intervention. Then, as children get older, they encounter stronger influences, many outside the home, that weaken a family's ability to reinforce positive child behavior. This is particularly true for teenagers who are out of the home more often than they are in the family. However, the basic principles of behavioral family work can be used in the early and later stages of child development. By learning effective ways to manage and shape their children's behavior, parents can exert a more positive influence on their children and in the process establish a more positive parent-child relationship. Recall one of the assumptions of systems thinking — a change in one part of the system has a ripple effect will happen with the rest of the family. Therefore, a change in a parent's behavior would have a ripple effect of the rest of the family.

Exercise 9.1

Early Intervention
(In Class)

Examine various family service agencies in your community and see what age group the agency primarily serves? How many agencies serve young families versus adolescents? Of the agencies serving adolescents, can you develop a picture of the length of time the adolescents have been in receipt of the attention of social agencies in your communities? For the agencies that serve young children, what are the parameters around service delivery? For example, are the services voluntary? How long is the service to young people compared with services for adolescents? Can you identify any agencies that practice early intervention? What is the policy concerning "least intrusive measures?"

Agency and Age Group Served

a.

b.

c.

d.

e.

f.

Many misconceptions exist about behavioral work. One is that behavioral work it is too technical or mechanical. In fact, teaching parents to work with their children is highly engaging and creative as family workers, parents and children embark on a journey that can greatly improve family functioning. Another misconception is that the therapeutic relationship is unimportant in behavioral work. Again, few parents or children would actively participate in a program unless they believed in and trusted the worker. Behavioral work, such as teaching parenting skills, demands much in terms of knowledge, observation skills, relationship skills, teaching skills, and evaluation skills. It also gives structure and focus and provides parents with practical parenting strategies. Often, behavior work occurs in the children's natural environment - their home - using "teachable moments" to modify behavior. It is also easier for people to use skills in the same environment in which they learned them (remember the discussion on transfer of learning). Conversely, techniques taught in office-based work seem removed from a family's day-to-day experiences.

Foundations of Behavioral Intervention

Behavioral interventions revolve around family relationships and how interactions encourage or discourage behavior. However, the family worker's relationship with the family, particularly he parents, is integral in that it opens the door to the use of teaching, modeling and coaching. Strategic changes in a parent's behavior will spillover to changes in children's behavior. Behavior problems are learned responses that become behavior habits over time with continuous reinforcement. Family members are usually unaware of how they reinforce behavior. Therefore becoming aware of interactions is one of the first steps in producing behavior change. Self-awareness and tracking child behavior is challenging for parents who must free up energy to learn new behaviors with their children. In some situations, for example, negative attention may keep behavior going since it is better than no attention at all. At other times, parents might reinforce unacceptable behavior directly, making it difficult to eliminate the behavior (e.g., giving into the child when s/he is disobedient).

Often parents do not know how to use consequences effectively, thinking that discipline only entails the use of punishment for unacceptable behavior. Sometimes they fail to implement threats or rules and instead use consequences ineffectively. They may believe that effective parenting is only about punishment, forgetting that their relationship with their children is crucial. On the other hand, we have had parents in our office who believe that *any* type of discipline is abusive and they therefore refrain from setting any limits on their children. For others, consequences might not be imposed immediately. On other occasions, the consequence does not match the severity of the problematic behavior. Negative parent behavior is apt to produce negative child behavior. Sometimes the danger is that negative behavior will receive more attention than positive child behavior. All these errors erode parental effectiveness. The most effective approach is to reward positive behaviors, getting into the "habit" when children are young. Positive behavioral changes by either the parent or the child will instigate a spiral of positive family interactions. (Recall Chapter 5, *A change in one part of the system will lead to a change in other parts of the system).* The challenge is to keep the momentum going and not sliding into negative "habits." With effective parenting techniques, the parent-child relationship becomes positive and the use of coercive and aversive methods of behavior control are discarded.

The foundation of behavioral work is that behaviors are shaped and maintained through interactions with influential people. When you reflect upon your many life experiences, you might recall that your experiences with positive reinforcement made you more determined to continue your behavior and punishment probably made you want to stop a particular behavior (or at least not be caught). In addition to teaching parents effective skills, the worker is also in a position to coach parents to reconnect with their children, and forge closer bonds with schools and peers. Because parents can control many parts of their children's environment, particularly when children are young, they are in an excellent position to produce behavioral change.

Behavior change occurs *first* with the parent and later with the child. Parents become their child's "therapists." If we believe, as is the philosophy of family work, that problems arise out of relationships, then changing the nature of relationships can help people deal with their problems. Putting parents in the therapist role has multiple advantages, not the least of which is the empowerment they feel when they learn that the worker will not be "fixing" their child or blaming. Moreover, parents will have acquired the necessary skills for effective parenting once the worker has left.

Exercise 9.2

Learning New Skills
(In Class)

Reflect on a time when you learned to do something for yourself. What were the circumstances of this time? How did you learn these new skills? Was there an opportunity for someone else to do this particular thing for you? What was it like to do this new behavior for yourself? How well has this skill stuck with you?

Now think back to a time when you could have learned something for yourself, but someone else did it for you. What were the circumstances? How did you feel about someone taking over this responsibility from you?

In behavioral work, the family worker teaches parents to understand their children's behavior through paying close attention, understanding, and taking action *directly* and *immediately*. Because parents live with children, they exert a continuous influence over them. If parents learn to manage their child consistently, even when the family worker is not present, behavior change can continue after the worker closes the case. Cognitive techniques are increasingly being blended with behavioral techniques. In Chapter 5 on Family Systems theory and circular causality, we learned about the thoughts-feelings-behavior sequence. Behavioral work helps parents disassemble and then reassemble this sequence more specifically to produce behavior change.

Learning new skills is least effective when "noise" detracts the learner from the work at hand. Noise can include parental stress (e.g., marital problems or financial difficulties), lifestyle issues (e.g., a hectic schedule or exhaustion), or conditions that interfere with effective work (e.g., my child is behaving this way to get back at me; my child is the cause of my family's problems). Therefore, before new skills can be learned, the family worker should help parents address these distractions so they can be freed to pay full attention to their child.

Social Learning Theory

The techniques of behavioral family work come from social learning theory. A variety of behavioral techniques are available, some of which can be used in combination. Many are based on operant conditioning through which behavior is shaped by its consequences (Bloomquist, 1996; Kadzin, 2004). Because consequences determine a behavior, when consequences are changed, the behavior will also change. The primary mechanisms of operant conditioning are positive and negative reinforcement and punishment.

Positive Reinforcement

Positive reinforcement strengthens a behavior and increases the probability of a behavior happening in the future, because the consequence feels good. It is most effective when parents have a close emotional tie with their children, although paradoxically, a close emotional connection happens most often when the relationship is on an even keel. Lack of involvement and emotional distance can make the problems worse and water down the impact of the reinforcer (Bloomquist, 1996). Thus, one of the first steps is to increase parent-child involvement and decrease emotional distance by scheduling parent-child activities. The activities should be mutually enjoyable such as playing a game. While positive reinforcement is a vital component of creating new positive behaviors, parents are sometimes too tired to notice these positive behaviors and instead only notice annoying or troublesome behavior. Parents get in the "habit" of only noticing behaviors that bother them and ignoring the child the rest of the time. They therefore need to develop the habit of focusing on their children regularly and be able to identify positive child behaviors they want to reinforce.

Parents usually start out using positive reinforcement with young children as they are learning new skills. Gradually the glow of the novelty wears off and as children get older, parents start to rely more frequently on punishment. Some even develop "habits" of negative reinforcement. Punishment is quick and takes less time and effort than ongoing positive reinforcement. Parents might need assistance in knowing which behaviors require positive attention and which behaviors should be ignored or punished. Because of the subtlety of many interactions, many parents slide into a pattern of negative interaction and need help to develop most positive parenting habits.

We all appreciate positive reinforcers, which can be either social or material. For example, people generally respond well to praise, if the praise is sincere and not manipulative. A monetary bonus for a job well done at work will make people attempt the same level of performance in the future. The same is true for children. Children generally respond well to such social reinforcers such as praise or special privileges. They will also respond to material reinforcers such as earning stars for a new bike or a monetary reward for acceptable behavior. However, we encourage the use of social rather than material reinforcers. Social reinforcers are readily available, through them children learn to value relationships over material things, and they strengthen the parent-child bond.

Parents often reinforce a child's behavior accidentally rather than intentionally necessitating that they understand the connection between their responses and the child's behavior. They need to connect the child's response with the role that *positive reinforcement* plays. They also should also understand how to *extinguish* behavior (getting rid of behavior through inattention).

Teaching parents effective reinforcement methods involves getting them to first track and evaluate the child's behavior. Parents should have some understanding of child development so they know their child's needs and can recognize what is normal. The family worker should be attuned to the needs of parents and children. For example, in the process, the family worker may discover that parental stress is interfering with an ability to parent. The family worker must also be tuned into the reaction and influence of significant others to coordinate their efforts.

> *Positive consequences are preferable to punishment. The guiding rule should be: whenever possible, use positive reinforcement.*

Negative Reinforcement

Negative reinforcement is a consequence that strengthens or maintains a behavior through its removal. When a negative behavior is removed, it also produces good feelings. For example, a parent receives negative reinforcement when the child gives into the inappropriate behavior of the parent (e.g. yelling) and the child stops behaving negatively. *Negative reinforcement* is *not to be confused* with *punishment.* We would like to emphasize that the two are very different. Negative reinforcement comes into play when individuals learn to avoid or escape negative consequences. For example, a child may stop a particular behavior to avoid more aversive parental behavior, thus reinforcing the parent's behavior.

Example 9.1: Negative Reinforcement

Parent to child sitting in front of a television set: Wally, come to the table. Supper is ready.
Wally: I don't want to. The Flintstones are on and I wanna watch it.
Parent (voice rising): I said come eat. Everyone is waiting for you.
Wally (voice also raising): NO! I'm gonna watch the rest of my program. Stop yelling at me and don't bug me.
Parent (clearly irritated, showing threatening behavior, and voice rising four more decibels): I am not going to tell you one more time young man. Get out here right this instance.
Wally: NO! Leave me alone. If you keep bugging me, I'm going to run away.
Parent (clearly at wits end, goes into the living room, pulls Wally by the arm and starts dragging him toward the kitchen to eat). GET IN HERE NOW!
Wally (resisting physically by now and clearly also upset, struggles to get free from the parent's grip and then sits again in front of the television set).
Parent: (Exasperated but gives up the struggle and leaves the room, allowing Wally to watch the rest of his show). I give up.

In this sequence, the parent has given into the child and for the child, the negative reinforcers work (removal of parents demands, thereby reinforcing child noncompliance). The parent has removed her negative behavior and the child gets what he wants. He feels good and has also learned to be disobedient because his mother will not follow through on her commands. If he resists enough, his mother will back off. The next time the parent asks Wally to do something, he has learned how he avoids complying with the parent's request in the future. He has thus learned, through his parents' removing their negative behavior, that he does not have to do what he is told and he now knows how to get what he wants in the future. This pattern becomes well established over time through the *ongoing repetition* of this pattern.

Punishment

Punishment is not the same as negative reinforcement. It involves the use of an aversive stimulus (punishment) *immediately* after the behavior occurs. Many parents believe that spanking (punishment) is an effective form of behavior control. We contend, however, that physical discipline is unskilled parenting where parents fail to pay close attention to positive child behaviors and therefore do not reinforce them. Punishment only requires intermittent attention to the child, such as when s/he does something "bad." Positive reinforcement, on the other hand, involves continuous observation and contact with the child. Frequent use of punishment leads the child to seek out more pleasure-inducing behaviors, not necessarily involving those activities related to the issue at hand. Punishment is necessary occasionally.

Exercise 9.3

Debate Spanking
(In Class)

A major social debate has erupted over the use of spanking to discipline children. Some countries, such as Sweden have outlawed spanking altogether. In this country, parents contend that spanking is a necessary parenting technique used to gain child compliance. Child abuse experts are less convinced. Take one side of the argument and together with others who believe the same thing debate with the opposite side the following: Spanking is an ineffective parenting technique and should be outlawed.

Again, the following sequence revisits the scenario with Wally:

Example 9.2: Punishment

Parent to child sitting in front of a television set: Wally, come to the table. Supper is ready.
Wally: I don't want to. The Flintstones are on and I wanna watch it.
Parent (keeping voice steady but remaining firm): I said come eat. Everyone is waiting for you.
Wally (voice also raising): NO! I'm gonna watch the rest of my program. Stop yelling at me and don't bug me.
Parent (irritated but determined): I am not going to tell you one more time young man. If you do not come to the table, I am going to turn off the television and have you sit on the chair for five minutes while you think about how hungry you are. Get to the table right now, please.
Wally: NO! Leave me alone.
Parent (firmly walks to the television set, turns if off and takes the remote control). Please sit on this chair for five minutes. I will come back in five minutes.
Wally (clearly displeased but remains on the chair).
Parent: (Places the child on a chair and makes certain that he remains there. After five minutes invites Wally to join the family for dinner).

In this sequence, the parent has remained firm and the child has learned that he must comply with his mother's request. The next time the parent asks Wally to do something, he has learned that she is serious and there will be no payoff for disobedience. Again, this pattern of parent-command-child-compliance entrenches through *ongoing repetition*. The parent has used *time-out* to punish the child and give him the message that disobedience has negative consequences.

Extinction

Extinction is another technique that can be used to eliminate *mildly* negative behavior. It occurs when parents ignore the child who is behaving inappropriately and refuse to reinforce the behavior. Extinction of a behavior occurs is a slow process that requires consistency and perseverance. All family members need to cooperate with the plan. If one parent ignores the problem but the other soothes the child, extinction will be ineffective.

Time-Out

Time-out is now a popular punishment technique that is used to eliminate unacceptable behavior and is preferred over physical discipline. It is a procedure whereby sources of reinforcement are removed or reduced for a specified behavior. It gives both parents and child space during which the tension and conflict between them is allowed to defuse. It allows parents to regain composure and involves removing the child from a provoking situation by placing him or her in a quiet and unstimulating setting. The setting might be in another room with a chair, or alternatively, it can be a quiet room.

For example, if a brother hits a sibling, rather than using physical punishment, the parents might place the child on a "time-out chair" in a different room for a specified amount of time (the length needs to match the developmental and cognitive abilities of the child). The use of Wally's example might not be as straightforward as we have presented it because children often resist time-out when it is first used and persistence is required to make it effective. For example, if the child leaves the time-out location, the parent should warn the child by saying that the clock is being re-set and the time is starting from zero. The clock will only tick for the time that the child complies and the child needs to know this.

Learning to use time-outs effectively can be exhausting, until the child learns the rules and the parents remain firm and consistent in enforcing them. In our example of the dinner refusal, parents must be prepared to have their dinner disrupted several times before Wally learns that his parents are serious and there are real and predictable consequences for noncompliance.

Some families use positive and negative reinforcers regularly. However, parents often reinforce the wrong behavior. For example, parents of aggressive children may inadvertently reinforce fighting, temper tantrums or resistance. They may also overly rely too much on aversive methods of behavior control (e.g., such as physical punishment) and fail to manage their child's behavior consistently or positively. Breaking down interactions between parents and children on a minute-to-minute basis could assist the family worker and parents come up with other ways of modifying behavior (and possibly reduce the risk of child abuse).

1. Parents use the time-out technique when a child breaks rules. A list can be made of what behaviors qualify for time-out programs and parents then tell the child what the expectations are ahead of time and the rationale. (Examples: hitting a sibling, temper tantrums, defiance, disobedience, and refusal to comply with a parent's request). Parents must select their battles carefully and choose only behaviors that are important and severe. Using a time-out for every infraction will create a power struggle.
2. The parent selects a quiet location that will be used every time for the time-out. The parent also plans ahead of time exactly when the time-out will be used.
3. *Immediately* after the child breaks the rule, the parent puts the child in the time-out spot. The length of time in the spot will depend upon the child's age. Parents are not to argue with the child while using time-out. The child must have settled down by the end of the time-out.

(continued)

4. When first using time out, parents should be prepared to take charge, since the child will not be familiar with this method of discipline. Children might resist the time-out and not comply with its conditions (e.g., keep jumping off the chair or leaving the time-out room). It is imperative that the parent show that s/he is serious and be willing to set the child firmly, but calmly back into the time-out location. This demands a lot of self-control on the part of the parent, who might have a low frustration tolerance in the first place. The first attempts at imposing time-out may be more stressful and exhausting than allowing the problem behavior to continue. Parents must be prepared for this and have a plan in place that will ensure that they follow through without resorting to their usual responses such as spanking or yelling. Parents should realize that if the child resists the time-out, keeping the child in the quiet spot for the duration is exhausting. They need to remain close to the child but distant enough not to stimulate the child any further.
5. Once the child becomes familiar with the consistent use of time-outs, he or she will become more compliant.
6. Consistency and persistence is the key.

Example 9.3: Basic Steps in Creating Behavior Change

A behavior change plan is structured following five basic steps (we go into more detail when we discuss Contingency Contracting):

1. *Decide upon the behaviors to reinforce.* This can include such behaviors as picking up toys, being nice to a sibling, or doing homework on time. In the scenario provided above, turning off the television set and coming to the dinner table are the targeted behaviors.
2. *Decide how to reinforce these behaviors.* Select the reinforcers (rewards) that will be used, after a parent-child discussion. The rewards should match the behavior and the parents should have no difficulty using the rewards. We find that children like to participate in selecting the reinforcers. Bloomquist (1996) recommends varying the reinforcer with a menu or even surprises. In our example, the parent might have a special food that the child especially likes but the child has to come to the table to eat it.
3. *List behaviors to ignore.* Behaviors to be ignored should be mild such as pouting or whining. (Although anyone who has been cooped up in a house for an entire day with a whining child might tell us that it is impossible to ignore). Again, using our example, if the child comes to the table and pouts throughout the meal, the parents can decide to ignore the pouting.
4. *Decide how to ignore negative child behaviors.* Ignoring some behaviors can be hard because the natural tendency is to let off steam by yelling. However, yelling only reinforces the behavior. Parents can decide to walk away or talk between themselves. In the example of Wally, they might change the topic to something more pleasant or interact with one another about an interesting event that happened that day, thereby ignoring the pouting.
5. *Use a formal parental self-monitoring and goal setting procedure.* The worker can help parents set up a chart to structure observations and responses more intentionally. They can write down every time they notice their child's behavior. Some use a chart on a fridge and place stars on it when good behavior is observed (Bloomquist, 1996, pp 56-57). After dinner, for example, the parents can debrief on the sequence of the interaction. They might make note on the chart that the child did come to the table when asked and place a star on the day and time.

Disobedience on the part of the child and allowing the child to get away with being disobedient can be the first link in a change of an ongoing sequence of behavior problems. Gaining children compliance to parent's requests can be exhausting, especially when children have learned that there are no consequences for being disobedient.

We refer to Bloomquist (1996, pp. 88-90) who offers a step-by-step approach of gaining child compliance:

1. *Give effective commands:* The commands must be clear, firm, direct, and simple. "Come to the table now. Supper is ready."
2. *Use effective warnings:* "If you do not come to the table now, I am shutting off the television set and you will sit quietly on the chair by yourself for five minutes."
3. *Give positive or negative consequences to the child for compliant or noncompliant behavior:* The consequences need to match the developmental age and child's ability to understand. Parents of younger children can use time-outs. Removing privileges is most effective with older children.
    a. (If the child comes to the table). "Thank you Wally for doing as you are told. I cooked your favorite vegetable for you."
    b. (If the child does not comply with the command). Wally, I am now turning off the television and you are to sit quietly by yourself for five minutes.
4. *De-escalate and stay cool.* Do not let the exchange become a power struggle. Be matter-of-fact and unemotional.
5. *Use charts to graph occasions when the child has listened and obeyed.*
6. *Persist.* Sometimes the behavior will get worse before it gets better.

Below is a simple example of behavioral chart for a child who refused to stay in bed at night. Every night when the child stays in bed all night, the child receives a happy face. Once 10 happy faces stars are earned, the parent will take the child to the zoo.

Emily's Sleeping Chart

Sunday	Monday	Tuesday	Wednesday	Thursday	Friday	Saturday
☺		☺	☺			
				☺		☺
	☺					
☺	☺		☺	☺	**ZOO**	

10 ☺ = one trip to the zoo

Exercise 9.4

Positive and Negative Reinforcement

(In Class)

The following scenario involves a young child who has done something that she should not have done. Give three examples of how negative and positive reinforcement and extinction in the following scenario can be used (be creative):

Five-year-old Ellie has left her toys strewn throughout the house. She is ready to go outside and play with Teresa, but knows that her mother has asked her to pick up her toys first. As she gets her coat on, without picking up her toys, her mother reminds her to pick up her toys before she goes out.

Positive Reinforcement:

1.

2.

3.

Negative Reinforcement

1.

2.

3.

Punishment

1.

2.

3.

Contingency Contracting: Putting It All Together

The family worker can teach parents to use a contingency contracting program, which involves designing a program where parents reward positive child behaviors and ignore, or punish behaviors that they want to discourage. It is based on the belief that behavior will change when contingencies or reinforcements are changed. Before this can happen, the family worker must first do a detailed assessment and find out how often the problem behavior occurs before the plan is implemented. In addition, the parents and worker should gather information on the antecedents (what happens immediately before) and consequences (what happens immediately after) of the problem behavior. Parents must define problems in concrete, observable, and measurable ways. Based on this information, strategies are devised to alter the antecedents and consequences of the behavior. To track change, the family worker or parent measures the frequency of the problem behavior before and after the intervention.

A contract can then be developed delineating what behaviors are expected. The contract outlines expected behaviors of each person involved in the contact. It also includes who is to do what for whom, as well as the circumstances. (Example: mother will not yell and the child will comply with mother's request within two minutes of being asked to do the dishes.) Once the targeted behaviors are spelled out, a reward system is developed that rewards both parties in the deal (Example: Child can play with friends for 30 minutes and mother will get to read a book).

We outline a four step-by-step procedure for producing behavioral change below (Collins, Jordan, & Coleman, 1999). This step-by-step procedure is generally accepted for developing a Contingency Management Program.

Step 1: Fact Finding: Defining the Problem Clearly and Precisely

Three components of the behavior must be identified and defined:

1. Identify and describe the antecedents of the events that occur immediately before the behavior (Example, the mother usually yells at the child to get him or her to do the dishes).
2. Describe the behavior in concrete, observable, and measurable ways (Example: The child says in a minute and proceeds to turn on the television set and does not do the dishes).
3. The family worker and parents select and implement consequences to the behavior, such as parental responses that reinforce it. (Mother yells at child again, but does the dishes herself).

The parents are key figures in identifying the targeted behavior because they are the most influential people in the child's life. The parents select the behaviors that should be increased or decreased with positive consequences. This can happen in one interview with the parents, through observing the family in their home, or by having parents videotape the sequence of the behavior. Parental input should be the focus of the first interview. Parents need to understand social learning theory and see that the child's behavior is learned within the context of their responses to the child. The child could attend the second session so that the worker can observe parent-child interaction. When the pertinent information has been gathered, some workers use observation rooms with one-way mirrors to observe and record family interaction patterns. When behavioral work occurs in the home, the worker is in the fortunate position of being present during these behavior sequences and can use "teachable moments" to work with parents and children.

Parents might identify problem behaviors yet have difficulty identifying what precipitated the behavior (antecedents). If antecedents are clear, the parents can remove them. For example, if the child always throws a temper tantrum at 5:00, the child might be hungry or tired. Videotapes are indispensable for pointing out the entire sequence of parent-child exchanges. The family worker must give the parents prompts to describe the sequences. For example, if the child refuses to go to bed, finding out how parents settle the child and what they do they do when the child gets out of bed provides much needed information about the behavioral chain of events. How does the child resist bedtime? Does it happen every night? What things typically happen before the child goes to bed? How do the parents respond? Parents need to provide information about the antecedents, the actual behavior, and the consequences. This information is not just for the family worker. It helps parents become more aware of what they are doing and how they are contributing to the problem.

In Step 1, parents learn to: (1) Observe and describe the antecedents of the behavior (that is, events that set the stage for the behavior). (2) Describe the behavior in concrete and measurable terms. (3) Assess the consequences of the behavior.

Step 2: Observing and Measuring Behavior

After the targeted behavior has been described, ways to track and record its frequency, intensity, and duration of the behavior must be developed. Awareness of these characteristics will enable parents to evaluate if there has been improvement. Parents can also start to collect detailed information by using charts to record the sequences of interactions and the child's behaviors. Tracking behavior in this way helps become more aware of their own behaviors (Example: A chart is devised that keeps track of every time the mother yells and every time the child is uncompliant with the request).

Events that occur outside the home may also reinforce the child's problem behavior. For example, peers may encourage the child to skip school. Problems outside the family require careful coordination with all involved parties to ensure that the response to the behavior is consistent (e.g., teacher and parents working as a team). The focus of family intervention is on changing parent-child interactions. The family worker should recognize and reinforce the family's efforts.

Step 3: Designing an Intervention

Measurement of the target behaviors does not stop here but continues throughout the program and after. A single case design could be used here (refer to your research course). The family must be capable of and committed to participate, and should not be distracted by their "noise" such as stress or marital conflict. The child also needs to understand and even select possible positive reinforcers.

Parents must develop the "habit" of responding *immediately* after the behavior occurs. They might slowly withdraw the reinforcers as the patterns becomes better established. The danger is that the withdrawal reinforcers behaviors might occur too early and the parents and children will fall back on old habits. If reinforcement is a social one, parents might consider keeping it going. Continuing the use of social reinforcers keeps the relationship on a positive keel and parents cannot withdraw or ignore their child as it requires ongoing monitoring. Changes in child behavior can be very rewarding for parents. (Example: The mother checks to see that the dishes have been done and then thanks the child and gives him or her permission to go out and play.

Step 4: Teaching the Family to Continue New Behaviors

An evaluation must focus on whether improvements occurred in the first place and whether they continued. If parents are to continue to use their new skills, they must learn to use them with different behaviors and with other children, when necessary. They must also keep the changes going in the face of stress that could erode gains they have made. Parents should recite what they have learned and how they expect to continue reinforcing the desired behavior. The worker can also arrange for "booster shots" through follow up at certain points after the program ends. (Example: The parent and child continue with their chart mapping out the frequency of yelling and noncompliance, or alternatively, asking nicely and complying with the request. The chart should cover at least one month's efforts.)

What a parent believes (cognitions) about a particular situation plays a large role in how they respond to a child. Thus, a parent who believes that their child is "bad on purpose to get at me" is apt to behave negatively toward that child versus a parent who believes that their child is "hungry, thirsty, or tired." Again, reflect back on the thoughts-feelings-behavior sequence on *Circular Causality* in Chapter 5. Imagine a child throwing a temper tantrum. The parent has a choice on what to believe about this temper tantrum. The exercise below is designed to help your explore different possible interpretations of a child's behavior.

Example 9.4: Example of a Behavioral Contract

Behavior Expectations	Privileges Earned	Privileges Lost
Do the dishes	watch tv for 1/2 hour	no TV that day
Take dog for walk	get a treat	no phone calls
Do my homework by 9:00	stay up 1/2 hour later	go to bed 9:30
play nicely with Jackie	Mom reads me a story	I don't get a story

Signed

____

____

____

Exercise 9.5

Stress
(In Class)

Take a piece of paper and make three columns. Reflect on your current life and then write down in the first column five of the most important roles in your life. In the second column, make a list of all the major stressors in your life. Once you have completed these two lists, make a third column identifying how this stress impacts each of the roles that you included in column one.

Important Roles in My Life	Stressors	Impact of Stressors
1.	1.	1.
2.	2.	2.
3.	3.	3.
4.	4.	4.
5.	5.	5.

Exercise 9.6

Different Meanings
(In Class)

Two year-old Cam has just started yelling and screaming, seemingly without provocation. The parent, Connie, just walked toward him in the room where he had previously been playing with his toys. Connie does not understand what is going on with him. She starts to wonder if he is mad with her for feeding him peas for lunch, which he hates. She begins to think that she is an incompetent parent and feels anxious and hurt. She also believes that Cam's temperament is difficult, just like that of her ex-husband Geordie. She begins to feel angry at Geordie philandering and subsequent departure from the family with his secretary. She begins to believe that Cam is trying to get back at her for his father leaving. She starts to yell at him.

This example shows one possibility of how Connie's thoughts-feelings process might come into play when approaching two-year-old Cam. Using this example, provide two other possible thoughts-feelings-behavior sequences that might be possible in this situation. How might the different meanings of how she sees Cam's behavior affect her feelings and behaviors toward him?

	Thought	Feelings	Behavior
1.			
2.			

In the thoughts-feelings-behavior sequence, several questions are important to consider:

1. What does the parent believe about the child? What meaning do they give to the child's behavior?
2. What is the impact of these thoughts and beliefs on the feelings that the parent is experiencing in this particular circumstance? How do these feelings affect their behavior toward the child?
3. What is the parent's response (behavior) toward the child? How are these behaviors the outcome of the parent's thinking-feeling sequence?
4. What beliefs can the parents change about their child? How will these beliefs make a positive difference child?

Included in beliefs is the need for parents to understand normal child development. Knowing about child development can interrupt this cycle by helping parents understand that for some behaviors, the real meaning of the child's behavior is vastly different from the meaning they gave.

Teaching Skills

One way of teaching parents is by sharing information. For example, a family worker counseling with new parents could provide them with information to help smooth the transition to parenthood. As mentioned in the previous chapter, each stage of the family life cycle brings with it upsets. Parents may not know what is "normal" at each stage. The family worker uses knowledge about child development and child abilities at each stage to help parents understand what to expect. Stories with examples can also be useful. Other times, parents are uncertain about how to use a particular skill and need help learning it. The family worker can walk a parent through learning and using a skill with a four-step program:

1. The family and worker together select the skill to be learned. The worker might point out to the parents, after observing them, that a different approach to the child's behavior might work better. Some families may find this a new approach because previous counseling experiences focused on analyzing their past. Opportunities for teaching and demonstrating skills can be identified "on-the-spot" when in the home, where the family worker capitalizes on "teachable moments" by using a crisis or other timely event as a catalyst for learning.
2. The worker then explains the rationale for learning and using the skill. Parents may want to understand how the new skill will benefit them. When the family is motivated, the worker models it and ask family members to describe what they saw. When a skill involves a series of complex behaviors, the skill can be broken down into simpler steps to allow the parents to learn each aspect of the skill. Modeling is used when family members lack the necessary skills or when they feel inhibited. Parents can view other models through videotapes or meetings with peers who have similar problems and have developed the skills to deal with those problems.
3. Parents then rehearse the skill with the worker giving them feedback.
4. Parents need to apply the skill to a real-life situation. They will be more likely to practice a skill when they see that it produces positive results. Afterward, the worker debriefs with the parent their experience of using the skills and the family worker offers positive comments and corrective suggestions.

Exercise 9.7

Creating a Contract
(In Class)

Write out a contract between a husband and wife, between a parent and teenager, between a parent and child.

Husband and Wife:

Parent and Teenager:

Parent and Child:

Compare your Contracts with your Classmates.

One of the most important skills a parent can have is the ability to set rules and follow through on these rules. Parents are often unskilled in knowing what rules are reasonable, how to create rules, and how to enforce them, leading to a chaotic and inconsistent form of behavior control (See Chapter 6). Rules are important to the child as it make them feel more secure, even though they might resist. Parents need skills at setting rules and creating limits for children. They need to know when rules are required and how to enforce them when children are disobedient. Rules must be enforced *consistently* (consistency is the key), with predictable consequences for breaking them. Reflecting back on the parenting styles outlined in Chapter 6, what kind of family would you think would have most difficulty creating and enforcing rules?

Setting rules occurs in five steps:

1. First, parents must decide what rules are reasonable. They can base the rules they set on knowledge about child development as well as the specific behaviors of their child. Families that are socially isolated may not be exposed to other parents, so they are not in a position to learn from them. Others families have boundaries that are too rigid and therefore do not have access or are not open to current parenting practices.
2. They then select an appropriate consequence. The consequence should be age appropriate and meaningful. The child might give the parents a list of possible consequences, which will engage the child in the intervention.

(continued)

3. The child must be informed about what the rules are and why they are being imposed. Ideally, the parents will sit down with the child and calmly and clearly explain the rules. Most children appreciate rules and see them as an indication that their parents care about them. Reasonable rules also make children feel secure (even teenagers). Parents might ask the child what s/he thinks are the reasons behind the rules. Parents should then list the consequences of inappropriate behavior. (The child could participate in choosing the consequences of breaking these rules).
4. The parent should issue a firm warning (if the behavior is not severe).
5. If the behavior happens again, the child is stopped and parents impose the consequence *on the spot*, not tolerating arguing. This procedure must be followed *every time* the child breaks the rule.

Exercise 9.8

Behavioral Intervention with a Family

(In Class)

Imagine your supervisor asks you to work with the Smith family, who are experiencing problems with thirteen-year-old Jackie. The problems center on Jackie's desire for more freedom and privileges. She would like to hang out downtown with her friends on Saturday night until 2:00 a.m., but her parents are worried that she is not old enough for this privilege. Jackie believes that her father is too bossy and domineering, while her mother is "out of touch and old fashioned." Jackie reports that her father spanked her when she stayed out late last week. Jackie also says that her brother Cam, age 14, is allowed to stay out late without adult supervision every Friday night. She claims she is being treated unfairly.
Working with a classmate, develop a plan for carrying out the following steps to address the problems of the Smith family:

1. Define the Problem;

2. Observe Behavior;

3. Design a Behavioral Intervention.

Additional Interventions

A wide variety of other specialized behavioral techniques can be used in family social work. The techniques should be tailored to the specific needs of each family. These interventions include role-playing, assertiveness training, parent training, relaxation training, modeling, and self-control training. Most of these involve practice a certain skill so that parents can use the skill in situations that are troubling them.

Exercise 9.9

Practice Modeling
(In Class)

List some appropriate situations when modeling would be a helpful technique. Pick one of these and practice it with a partner.

a.

b.

c.

d.

Exercise 9.10

Usefulness of Role Playing
(In Class)

Imagine that you have been invited for your first job interview involving working with families. Pair off with another student and stage a role-play interviewing for this position. One person plays the worker and the other person plays the role of the interviewee. The worker coaches the interviewee and gives him or her feedback about the performance. Now switch roles.

Case Example: Geordie

Geordie is an 11 year-old boy who was taken into care two years ago after showing severe behavior problems at school and at home. Geordie was adopted at birth. Geordie has been diagnosed with Tourettes, ODD, and FASD. His behavior escalated out of control and because of all of the school suspensions, his mother's job was in jeopardy. Geordie currently has no contact with his biological father and has not had any contact with him for a number of years. His mother, Margaret, is currently engaged to Darren. They reside together with Darren's daughter Jackie. Jackie's mother is not involved with her and she refers to Margaret as her mother. Geordie continues to do quite well in the treatment center, although he struggles with peer interactions, particularly in a group setting. Geordie occasionally does well with peers when he is one-on-one (depending on the peer) but as soon as he enters a group setting, he has a lot of difficulty interacting with peers.

Margaret and Geordie's biological father were married in 1990 and divorced two years later. One year after the divorce, Margaret met Darren and they are now living common law. Geordie's father was physically and verbally abusive to both Geordie and Margaret while he lived with them. Currently, Darren and Margaret are in the process of deciding whether they are capable of caring for Geordie in their home. Darren is skeptical about having Geordie return home.

Geordie has been spending a lot of time at home lately and really enjoys the visits with his family. Geordie often has little difficulty when he has home visits family even when the visits are long. Occasionally Margaret has reported that there are times that Geordie appears agitated but she is often able to redirect him.

Geordie continues to be seen in joint sessions with his mother and more recently his stepsister, Jackie. Geordie does well during therapy and has made a lot of progress. For example, when Geordie first came to see the worker, he refused to talk about anything pertaining to his treatment and instead, preferred to play with action figures. Geordie now appears to understand the purpose of coming to therapy and is able to talk more openly about issues that pertain to him.

Geordie and Jackie's first session focused on exploring how they saw the situation when Geordie came home. The sessions also served the purpose of developing an understanding of how Jackie felt about Geordie because of past incidents, specifically when he threatened her with a knife. Geordie identified earlier that he used to get very frustrated with Jackie because she bugged him. Jackie was able to say that she was frightened of Geordie, although she is less frightened of him than before. Family sessions also focused on their relationship. Jackie acknowledged that sometimes Geordie has temper tantrums and gets very angry. Jackie was seen individually once to explore whether or not there was anything she wanted to say that she may have had a hard time saying in front of Geordie. She reported that she was still frightened of him and in response, a safety plan was put into place because she did not know how to protect herself if Geordie got out of control again. Jackie expressed reservations about Geordie returning home because she was worried that things would be different because family members would act differently to accommodate Geordie's needs. She also said that she likes being the only child.

Geordie has also participated in one group therapy session. This group specifically focuses on anger management and assertiveness training. In the first group, members identified what happens when they are angry. Each member was asked to select, out of three characters (The Hulk, Luke Skywalker or Eeyore), who they most resembled when they become angry and why. Geordie was able to identify what happens when he becomes angry and said that he was most like The Hulk. The rest of the group agreed with him. Geordie stated that the reason he is like The Hulk is that he sometimes loses his temper and throws things which he called "a lose temper thrower hulk man."

Geordie continues to have extended visits with his family. These visits are apparently going well. Margaret has played an active role in Geordie's treatment.

Sharon, the family worker believed that Margaret would benefit from parent training before Geordie was returned home. She contracted with the mother and stepfather to implement a program to deal with Geordie's troublesome behaviors.

Exercise 9.11

Implementing a Parent Training Program for Margaret and Darren

(In Class)

Carefully read over the case notes provided on the previous page. You will be setting up two behavioral programs: one for Margaret and Darren, and another one for Geordie. Pair up with two other members of the class. Your first task is to work with Margaret and Darren to set up a behavior management program for the parents. First, discuss the case in a small group and develop and behavioral contingency contract with the parents, taking into account all of the details. It might help to write chart out your thoughts and plans in a systematic way. Then role-play an interview with Darren and Margaret.

Exercise 9.12

Implementing a Parent Training Program for Geordie

(In Class)

The next phase of the intervention is to work with Geordie to improve his behavior so that he can return home again. Again, read over the case notes provided. Then discuss the cases in a small group and develop a behavioral contingency contract with Geordie in the group home, taking into account all of the important details. It might help to write chart out your thoughts and plans in a systematic way. Then role-play an interview with Geordie in the group home, outline a plan to change his behavior.

Exercise 9.13

Putting It All Together

(In Class)

Now imagine that Geordie is set to return home. Meet with the entire family to establish a behavioral program that involves all the family members. You will need to form groups of five or six students so that all family members are represented. Assign one member the role of note-keeper and observer who will give feedback and offer coaching in the establishment of this plan.

Homework

Homework is the final behavioral intervention we discuss. It is an important part of all family work, for without it, families would not take what they learn and use it in day-to-day activities. Assigning homework strengthens a behavior that was dealt with in a family interview. It is usually assigned at the end of every family interview and it has the goal of ensuring that change continues between sessions. Behavioral assignments help family members to be mindful and place responsibility upon the family to implement what they learned. Doing so helps them transfer their learning to real-life situations.

Assignments should be based on the work done with the worker. The worker needs to spell out the tasks clearly. Examples of homework include following through on a contingency management program, charting behavior, or going for a real job interview after practicing a role-play. The worker expects the family to be accountable in the next session where parents report on their homework. If the family did not do the homework, the family worker needs to determine why. Children might be delighted to hear that their parents have homework also and remind the parents during the week about their obligations. Reasons may range from not understanding the instructions to a lack of commitment. Through regular homework assignments regularly, families learn to expect a task at the end of each interview.

Chapter Summary

In this chapter, we discussed the use of a behavioral family intervention. Behavioral family work can improve family relationships by making behavior, particularly the child's, more palatable to parents. It also helps children develop positive social skills. The use of positive reinforcement is encouraging, while negative reinforcement is eliminated. Parents learn how important their responses are in creating and eliminating certain behaviors. Techniques such as contingency contracting engages the whole family in a journey of behavior change.

Exercise 9.14

Weekly Family Work Assignment
Setting Up a Behavioral Intervention
(PBL Worksheet)

Today, you are going to set up a behavioral family intervention. Typically, this intervention will involve problematic family member behavior, but given that not all the families have problems other than child-related ones, you might have to use another problematic issue in the family. Select a (child) behavior related to some of the issues we talked about in class. Then work to increase family member involvement and positive reinforcement. To do this, follow the following procedures:

Stage One

Identify when parents are reinforcing undesirable or uncompliant behavior. Discuss examples of uncompliant or problematic behavior and how they can be changed.

Stage Two

1. List positive behaviors to reinforce
2. Determine how to reinforce these behaviors
3. List mild negative behaviors to ignore (extinction)
4. Determine how to ignore mild negative behaviors
5. Implement a formal parental self-monitoring and goal setting procedure
6. Set up a contract and chart to monitor the changes

Remember to pay attention to increasing parental involvement and positive reinforcement; improving family communication skills; helping the family problem-solve or dealing with family anger/conflict management. Instead of role-playing, an alternative is to work together as a group and configure one or two programs to change behavior.

Tip

Include all members of the family in this discussion. It is particularly important that everyone decide on what role they are playing in reinforcing the behaviors. Then everyone can be included in the contract for change. Use some of the charts from the class if you would like.

Exercise 9.15

Affective Involvement
(PBL Worksheet)

From your PBL "family" work group, list as many activities as possible that the family enjoys doing together. What kind of activities do the parents share with their children? Recall the section in the Family Categories Schema referring to *Affective Involvement.* Who does what activity with whom? Does everyone get their fair share of involvement with other family members? (This list will also help you identify the subsystems within the family that appeared in Chapter 5 on *Family Systems*).
Initiate a family discussion about what these activities mean to individuals and the impact it has on the family unit.

List of Activities

a.

b.

c.

d.

e.

Exercise 9.16

Increasing Affective Involvement and Planning for a Positive Thought-Behavior Sequence (PBL Worksheets)

In your PBL family work group have the parents and one child (preferably the IP) schedule an activity together. The activity can be anything, but examples include drawing a picture of the family, having the child read a short story to the parent, working with clay, or playing a game of cards. It is preferable to have the child select the activity. The family worker and the remaining family members will watch this parent-child interaction. (You might want to tape the exchange and show it back to the family).

Note parental activity such as praise, touching, laughing, asking questions, giving commands, or criticizing. Also pay attention to how long the parent can stay "in contact" with the child. Is the parent paying more attention to the "negative" versus "positive" behavior? Also, note how the child responds to the parent's behavior. After about 20 minutes, debrief, first with the parent-child dyad and then with the entire family. Show the tape if you have time. If the parent is responding more to negative child behavior, have the parent make a plan to become aware of his/her behavior and set new goals, with concrete recommendations.

Exercise 9.17

Family Homework: Tracking Positive Child Behavior (In PBL Groups)

The purpose of this exercise is to help the parents track and monitor positive child behavior. They will need to do this outside the session. For homework, have the parent(s) in your family work group keep a notebook. Pages of the notebook should be divided into 3 columns: date, behavior and parent response. When the parent notices a *good* child behavior, s/he should record it in the notebook, while at the same time telling the child what s/he is writing down. The parent is to tell the child that both the parent and child are being graded on this homework. They are to bring the notebook into the family sessions for now on.

Exercise 9.18

Listing Positive Reinforcers for Child
(In PBL Groups)

When using positive reinforcers, it is important that each family member "buy into" the plan. It is most important, however, that the child whose behavior is the target of change and the parents who have the primary influence be most committed to the program. In your family work groups, select a behavior that is troubling to family members. The family worker needs to get each family member to commit to working on the changes, without making any individual family member defensive about their role in the problem. Once the target behavior is identified, the parents must commit to working on changing their behavior in regards to the child's behavior. At the same time, the child must also understand the mechanics of the program.

The child and parents should work together to develop a list of positive reinforcement ideas. Ideally, these reinforcers should be social-interactional in nature (e.g., parents spending time with the child, praise, going to a movie, staying up late, praise, etc.). You can include a short list of material reinforcers (e.g., CD, if you would like, but we recommend that social reinforcers be used also.

In your family session, work with the family and develop a list of 20 possible positive reinforcers that can be used to reinforce the child's behavior:

1.	11.
2.	12.
3.	13.
4.	14.
5.	15.
6.	16.
7.	17.
8.	18.
9.	19.
10.	20.

Exercise 9.19

Reciprocating: Changing Parental Behavior
(In PBL Groups)

Sometimes a total focus on the child's behavior emphasizes the power imbalances in the family and makes the child feel that s/he is the family target. One way of equalizing the power imbalances is to make the interaction reciprocal. That is, the child can identify the behaviors of other family members to be changed. Get the child and parent(s) to identify parental behavior to be changed. (For example: The child may not like parents yelling at him or her and wish this behavior to stop.) Get the parents to list 20 behaviors that could serve as a reinforcer for them to stop their behavior. At the same time, it would be a good idea for parents to determine how to replace the yelling:

1.
2.
3.
4.
5.
6.
7.
8.
9.
10.
11.
12.
13.
14.
15.
16.
17.
18.
19.
20.

Chapter 10 **Table of Contents**

WORKING IN THE HOME & TREATING FAMILIES WITH CHILDREN IN CARE

Chapter 10

Working in the Home & Treating Families with Children in Care

Chapter Coverage

- Working in the Family's Home
- Characteristics of Home-Based Services
- The Process of Providing Home-Based Services
- Treating Families with Children in Care
- Case Examples

Working in the Family's Home

Following the line of least resistance, the older type of worker usually conducted First Interviews at his office desk, with record form before him and pen in hand.
- Mary Richmond (1917)

Intoduction

Home visiting is a practice through which a worker helps a family in its own environment (Wasik, Bryant, & Lyons, 1990). The history of home-based family work is grounded in health care, education, and social services. Social work, in particular, has a rich history of home visiting. Today, home visits may occur in several contexts. For instance, families might have a public health nurse or a homemaker visit their home. Doctors used to see patients in the home, although this is very rare now. Child welfare workers and social workers in other capacities also see a family in its natural environment. Recently, family support workers, parent teachers, and child and youth care workers have also focused on working within the home. Some home-based services target a specific problem area such as child abuse. Others services are preventative and broader because everyone qualifies. One example is the visit of a public health nurse after the birth of a baby.

At the turn of the twentieth century, Mary Richmond recognized that office visits sometimes created more advantages for *workers* than *families*. Almost a century ago, she argued in favor of interviewing families in their homes. Her reasoning was fourfold:

(1) Offices make clients defensive while homes make workers defensive. "The host and the hostess are at their ease" (1917, p.107).
(2) Homes answer questions of clients, and give information about material things as well as relationships.
(3) It is a natural environment for conversations about the family and family members.
(4) It emphasizes the personal side of people.

Exercise 10.1

List the Advantages and Disadvantages (to the Family) of Home Visits

(In Class)

Disadvantages and benefits of home versus office visits

Advantages	Disadvantages
a.	
b.	
c.	

List the advantages and disadvantages (to the worker) of home visits.

Advantages	Disadvantages
a.	
b.	
c.	

After you have completed both lists, choose a side and debate the issues in class.

We therefore see that home visits have been part of the family work landscape for at least a century. However, their popularity has ebbed and flowed with the times, and home visits are becoming popular once again. One of the first family workers, Mary Richmond, met with families in their homes most of the time, although she also spoke of the need to adapt the interview setting according to need. She envisioned a range of possible places where an interview could occur, and argued that the setting should be neutral. Above all else, interview settings, regardless of whether they occur in the home or office, should never erect barriers between the worker and family.

In the 1970s, investigators made an alarming discovery - too many children were removed from their families and placed in foster families and treatment centers. Many never returned home. Children drifted between foster homes and treatment facilities. Children were dislocated from their siblings since many foster homes take in only one or two children. When siblings were separated, little effort was made to reunite brothers and sisters. Visitation of siblings in care requires much in terms of resources and coordination by a numerous workers. Children could be placed in different communities many miles apart. These difficulties led to the enactment of legislation in both Canada and the United States mandating Permanency Planning for children. At the same time, attachment theory described the critical role of the parent-child bond and workers commented on how multiple moves disrupt important family relationships. Many of the state placements were considered unnecessary, particularly if services could be provided to keep children safely at home with their families. Ethnic minority children were at high risk of out-of-the home placement. Not only was out-of-home care damaging to many children, it was also more costly than keeping children with their families.

We recall the story of Richard Cardinal, a Metis child in northern Alberta, Canada. Child welfare removed Richard and his siblings from their family at a very young age and placed them in separate foster homes. Richard bounced around multiple foster families that were often in deplorable conditions, primarily because he wet his bed. He was lost and neglected by the very system designed to protect him. He had little contact with his biological family. Shortly before Richard turned 18 (the age of emancipation), Richard hung himself. He left a diary. A public investigation into his suicide showed a sensitive and talented young man who was harmed by the very system through his multiple moves and lack of family contact and continuity.

In response to similar tragedies across North America, new services emerged designed to keep children at home with their families, while the family receives intervention to solve the problems that put children in jeopardy. Institutions became smaller and more family friendly. Home-based services took three forms: (1) resource, support, and education; (2) family-centered supportive services provided on an extended basis, and; (3) intensive crisis oriented family-centered services (Fraser, Pecora, & Haapala, 1991). Other responses included kinship care (foster care with relatives), family reunification, and family preservation all designed to keep families intact or alternatively, create a permanent and stable life for children who could not return home.

Some home-base services attempt to prevent the unnecessary placement of children outside their families. Many are short term and crisis oriented, such as The Homebuilders Program. Workers usually enter a family at the first sign that a child is at imminent risk of being removed from the home. Family preservation workers go into a family's home with the goal of building upon a family's strengths. Many families are poor or disadvantaged.

Home-based services are driven by the philosophies about *empowerment, enhancement,* and *enablement* (Wasik, Bryant, & Lyons, 1990). We discussed empowerment in Chapter Two, but briefly mention it again here. Empowerment entails allowing families the power to make important decisions and take action on their own behalf and take control of accessing and controlling resources for themselves. They also have the right to self-determination, regardless of whether the family worker believes that they are the right ones. Nevertheless, no family has a right to harm a child. Families are active participants in the work, which has been a basic premise of this book. Enhancement follows from a strengths-based philosophy such that all families have inherent strengths that can be capitalized on. Finally, enablement involves locating resources that can help families function to its fullest. Combined, all three philosophies require that workers open up opportunities for families, recognizing that it is the family's responsibility to take advantage of these opportunities. In this way, the worker is a facilitator rather than being someone who does something *to* the family. The overarching goal is the development of family competence and self-sufficiency.

Providing services in a family's home has many advantages. Many families do not have the resources, such as transportation, to attend agency interviews on a regular basis. Some families may be ambivalent about participating in family work and the basic requirement of going to an agency might be enough to tip the scales in favor of not participating. Workers thus have a better chance of engaging reticent family members and ensuring that services are not disrupted by nonattendance.

A worker going to a family's home has a better opportunity of engaging the family in the work. Working in the home also gives workers insight into the "real life" issues that families face. When family work occurs in the home to prevent placement, the work is based upon the belief that children are best off with their parents but that parents can learn more effective child management skills to improve their family situation. In-home services also stem from the belief that the best way to help children is to help their parents. Part of helping parents involves addressing their basic life problems that prevent them from dealing effectively with their children. In addition, home services, as an outreach program, are useful for families that are experiencing a crisis (Wasik, Bryant, & Lyons, 1990).

Providing services in the home also has some disadvantages. Travelling can consume much of the worker's day. This is less of a problem when the family worker works with one family per day compared to working with four or five families in a single day. Home-based work also has many potential distractions such as telephones, televisions, and neighbors and friends visiting. Confidentiality might also be jeopardized when neighbors see family workers come and go from the home. Home-based family work can be intrusive to families as well in that many intimate details of a family's life cannot be hidden from view. Families decide what to reveal to workers in an agency, but they are more vulnerable when the worker enters their environment. Gaining entry into the home and engagement may also be difficult when services are involuntary. Child welfare workers, in particular, are familiar with the situation of going to a home only to discover that the client will not answer the door. Scheduling appointments might be difficult when one or both of the parents work, necessitating evening appointments. Home-based work can be an intense and intimate experience for workers who see families in their natural environment many hours at a time. They must make room for client independence and be sensitive when families are becoming overly reliant on their efforts. Finally, workers must be sensitive to boundary issues and guard against transforming the relationship from a professional to a personal one.

The Process of Providing Home-Based Services

The provision of services in the home parallels that of agency-based services. Issues related to engagement, rapport, relationship building, assessment, and intervention are similar. We recommend covering the following issues during the first home visit:

1. *Setting up the interview.* Setting up a mutually agreeable interview is complicated by the fact that the parents might work. This might necessitate that the worker use times outside of regular office hours in order to find a mutually agreeable interview time. Many workers, who have lives of their own, might be reluctant to give up personal time to visit families. Agency hiring practices will include expectations about work hour and overtime. The worker makes plans to travel to the home. Concerns include safety issues and making sure you know how to get there.
2. *Introductions, establishing rapport, engaging the members, and relationship building.* Workers must take extra care and recognize that the power difference is not the same as office-based interviews.
3. *Reviewing the purpose and goals of family work.* It is important that family members understand why you are seeing them. Sometimes the family will have little choice about the purposes and goals of family work. These are involuntary clients who have been referred to your agency due to child welfare concerns.
4. *Establishing clarity around the roles of the worker and the family.* Home-based work often involves the provision of concrete services and helping families navigate daily routines.
5. *Clarifying client expectations.* Before any work can proceed, you need to get a clear understanding of what you expect from the family and what the family expects of you. When services are voluntary, the family will be more influential in clarifying expectations. Expectations about who should be involved in family work must be spelled out at this point.
6. *Beginning assessment.* Assessment now can expand to include the family's concrete living arrangements.
7. *Establishing an initial contract, including times for visits.* The contract includes what goals will be worked on, the roles that workers and family members will play, and the frequency of visits. At this point, the worker outlines a tentative plan on how the issues will be addressed. If the work is to be done totally outside the office, this needs to be spelled out as well.

Workers must also be prepared to deal with practical issues in working with the family in its home. We mentioned issues related to scheduling and timing. Some families are very mobile and you may have difficulty locating them. Other families will not have a telephone or have an unlisted number, making the first contact tricky. You should also be prepared to address safety concerns. The cardinal rule is to never go into a home if you feel unsafe. Sometimes homes are located in unsafe neighborhoods. Sometimes, a family member might have a substance abuse problem or difficulty handling anger and you need to know this ahead of time. You might want to schedule the first visit accomplished by another worker. We recall a friend, a child welfare investigator, eight and one half months pregnant, who went to a home one morning to apprehend three children. The father, a big burly man, irate at the possibility of losing his children, held the worker hostage for eight hours. She had not told anyone where she was going or how long she would be gone for. This incident prompted the agency to develop new safety policies for its workers. We relate this story not to frighten new workers. Rather, we emphasize that caution and back up plans are necessary when working in unfamiliar environments. The agency has a responsibility for making policies and training workers pertaining to safety concerns.

Exercise 10.2

Safety Issues
(In Class)

Learning how to handle threats to personal safety is an important part of providing home-based services. Pair off with another classmate and role-play one of the following scenarios. Report back to the class on what you have learned.

A father who is intoxicated
A very angry mother who is threatening to throw things at you
Visiting a home where there is a pit bull
Walking down a dark street to get to the home
Entering a home where several people are high on coke
An adult who is sexually provocative toward you
A family where there is a lot of anger being expressed
A parent who abuses a child in front of you
Make up your own scenario

You will also be armed with materials designed to make the work go smoother. This might include play materials for younger children, assessment tools, a list of important phone numbers, the referral form, and possibly agency notes (although you must take precautions not to lose them). In addition, a cell phone is indispensable. Interruptions are a fact-of-life in home-based family work and you will need a plan on how for handling interruptions. You might want to ask at the start of the interview whether the client has time to meet with you for an hour without interruption, thus conveying the message that your time together should be focused on the work. Privacy and confidentiality are harder to preserve in home-based visits. You might bump into other clients on the way to the family's home. Friends and neighbors might knock at the door while you are there. You will need to be prepared to deal with these situations.

Exercise 10.3

Handling Confidentiality
(In Class)

Role-play one of the following scenarios with two other classmates. Report back to the class on how you handled the situation.

You and your family are talking about an intimate family matter. A family friend knocks at the door and is invited in.

You are walking to a client's home and bump into a former client while you are knocking at the door.

You are meeting with a family and one of the children's friends, who you know from a previous contact, is there.

Create a scenario of your own.

Exercise 10.4

Personal Versus Professional Boundaries
(In class)

Working in a family's home can contribute to blurring of professional and personal boundaries. Beside each scenario presented below, give a possible professional and personal response.

	Professional Response	Personal Response
Death of a family member		
Needing transportation		
Going to a movie		
Dating		
See drinking in the home		
Other events that might blur relationships		

Characteristics of Home-Based Family Work

Workers operate from an ecological perspective and believe in the importance of plugging the family into needed community supports, both formal and informal. While in the home, workers can see first hand the basic needs of the family and how well it meets its needs. Thus, the provision of concrete services becomes a necessary focus. Meeting families in their home requires both the same skills and a different set of skills than are needed for office visits. Some families may feel empowered that the worker cares enough to go into the client's home. On the other hand, home visits can also be intrusive, in that what can be hidden through office visits is exposed in the home. Home-based services share common characteristics. Many of these characteristics are important aspects of this book:

1. Services are family centered. Family systems theory directs the interventions used with the family. Family systems theory is discussed in more detail in Chapter 5. A focus on family systems means that workers are sensitive to the context in which people live - and the most important context is the family. It also means that family members are affected by and affect one another, often in *patterned* sequences of behavioral interactions. Understanding family systems theory helps maintain a worker's focus. Family systems theory also provides and framework in which interventions can be developed and understood. While it means that the family is the client, family systems thinking also helps workers understand that a change in one person will have a domino effect such that every other member of the family will be affected.
2. Services are strengths-based. Family work in the home recognizes the importance of recognizing family strengths and avoiding pathologizing families. Workers recognize that families do the best they can with what they have at a particular time.
3. Services are designed to respond to the unique needs and resources of individual families. Assessment is therefore a vital component of the home-based work.
4. Services are ecologically based and workers provide multi-layered services to, including concrete resources as well as social support. Some home-based workers, for example relate stories of helping clients with the dishes or packing for a move to a new location. Lewis (1991) identified 25 of the most common concrete services provided by one intensive family preservation program, the most common of which is providing transportation. Other concrete services included arranging cleaning services, providing material resources, securing childcare and providing food. Family workers believe in the importance of plugging the family into needed community supports, both formal and informal. While all people need social support, some families have greater difficulty accessing it and knowing how to use it. Social support or the lack of it makes an enormous difference for a family's well being. Social support contributes to better emotional and physical health, and decreases social isolation. People with strong social support systems also have better access to resources such as information and problem-solving assistance. Thus, the provision of concrete services is a necessary focus. Understanding the importance of social supports makes it necessary for workers to help families navigate their social environment. It also requires that workers help coordinate the formal resources available to the family so that they do not overlap or work at cross-purposes. Case management will also ensure that there is no gap in services (discussed in Chapter 5).

(continued)

5. Social learning theory, skill development, and teaching child management skills are also intrinsic to home-based family work. Chapter 9 presented the key elements of social learning theory. Perhaps the best fit occurs between the use of social learning theory and working in the home. Lewis (1991) reported on a wide range of clinical services offered to families in a family preservation program. While too extensive to list here, services included social learning approaches such as assertiveness skills, tracking and charting behaviors, the use of time-outs, and improving child compliance. Skills were not confined to social learning theory and instead spanned a range of theories again reinforcing the importance of generalist practice.
6. Service coordination and case management. In Chapter 5, we presented how the use of Ecomaps facilitates case management services on behalf of the family. Case management activities, apart from service coordination, included consultation, advocating, and referral to other agencies.
7. Services include crisis intervention and long term planning term. Crisis intervention can include defusing crises, problem solving, and support.

Exercise 10.5

Social Support
(In class)

Make a list of the types of social support you receive from those now around you. Using Maslow's (1967) hierarchy of needs, make note of which need each source of social support provides you. Finally, speculate on what would happen if you did not have each source of social support in your life.

Source of Social Support	Need Met	What Would Happen Without This Support
a.		
b.		
c.		
d.		

Exercise 10.6

Ripple Effect
(In Class)

Listed below are several possible individual behaviors or events that can affect an entire family. Beside each behavior or event, speculate on how it might affect other members of the family. Are all the impact statements positive to the entire family or do different members benefit more than others? Share your responses with the rest of the class.

Changed Behavior	Family Impact
A parent stopping drinking	
Stopping spanking and replacing it with time out	
A parent finding employment	
A child being removed from a family	
Decreased parental arguing	
Increased parental arguing	
A child who throws bad tantrums	
Select a behavior or event of your own	
Removing a child from the home	

Case Example: Eddie

Eddie has been diagnosed as having ADHD, ODD, and brain damage due to mother's drug use during pregnancy, specifically, crack cocaine and marijuana. He was taken into state custody because of domestic violence. Kayley, his mother, admits to extensive alcohol and drug use during pregnancy and in the present. She has been ineffective in instituting house rules. The first trouble with Eddie surfaced eight years ago when Kayley reported concerns about Eddie's out-of-control behavior. Five years ago, Eddie disclosed that his mother's boyfriend, Brad, sexually abused him. His mother was out drinking at the time. Even after the disclosure of sexual abuse, Kayley still left Eddie alone at home with Brad.

Kayley received Family Preservation five years ago, but Kayley failed to follow through on the recommendations of an earlier psychological assessment. Four years ago Kayley was assaulted by Brad and Eddie found her at the bottom of the stairs which led to Brad's immediate apprehension. At first Kayley would not leave Brad because she could not afford the rent. At the time, Kayley was unaware of the amount of emotional distress that Eddie was experiencing. By November of last year, the state had taken temporary custody of Eddie. At that time Kayley was tested for drugs and the results were positive for alcohol, marijuana and crack cocaine. Kayley failed to follow through on a drug treatment program and was uncooperative with a family support worker. A Child and Family Functioning Assessment was completed by a family worker three years ago, identifying resistance and minimization on the part of Kayley with regard to the issues of domestic violence, and the drug and alcohol abuse. Since then, Eddie has been caught with a pipe after returning from a home visit.

A case conference was held with the treatment staff, family support worker, addiction counselors, child welfare and Eddie's teacher. Kayley did show up for this conference and one year ago, the state assumed permanent guardianship over Eddie.

Kayley was physically and sexually abused by her second oldest brother as a child. She also has an extensive history with multiple abusive partners, some of whom were emotionally and physically abusive of Eddie. One partner was incarcerated for domestic violence. A psychological assessment suggested that she may not have a drinking problem but is prone to alcohol abuse in times of stress. She has little to say about how her behavior affects Eddie. She tends to minimize Eddie's negative behaviors, reporting that she acted that way when she was younger.

Exercise 10.7

Making a Home Visit
(PBL Worksheet)

Read over the case example of Eddie. Once you understand the issues, break into groups of three and discuss issues that might arise as the result of doing a home visit. What are the advantages and disadvantages? What steps do you need to take for your own safety? How would you engage this mother? What would be the obstacles to providing services to Kayley in the home and how can you address these obstacles?

Role-play starting the first interview with Kayley. Take approximately 15 minutes. What issues did you encounter?

Exercise 10.8

Doing a Home Visit with Your PBL Family
(PBL Worksheet)

If time and circumstances allow, plan a home visit with your PBL family. You will need to decide ahead of time where to meet. Compare this visit with the office-based visits you have had with your family. What are the similarities and differences for the worker and family? What were the obstacles? Which setting do you prefer to work in? Debrief in the larger class.

Treating Families with Children in Care

You leave your disabled child parked with us for a while, and when your child is fixed we'll call you to come and pick him up
(Minuchin, Colapinto, & Minuchin, 1998, p. 185).

At times, children are removed from their families and placed in settings such as foster care, residential treatment, detention centers, and psychiatric facilities. Reasons for a child's removal vary. Some children might have behavioral or psychiatric problems that put themselves or others at risk. Other children might be at risk of abuse and need to be removed and placed in a safe environment. Megan's example illustrates this point. Megan was born to low functioning parents and they abandoned her in a park at the age of three months. A child welfare worker took Megan and placed her in foster care. Five year-old Brad was discovered by a neighbor weighing only thirty pounds and he was placed in a hospital first and then moved to foster care. A loving family later adopted him.

Yet other children are placed by their parents who do not believe that they are capable of handling the child's behavior, or alternatively, that the child should be taken out of the family environment to be "fixed." Younger children are usually removed from their families because of safety concerns, while older children who are given up for unmanageable behavior are often teenagers, although this is not a fixed and fast rule. Adolescents are also abused and parents sometimes have difficulty managing younger children's behavior. We have had to apprehend two teenage sisters, Crystal and Charlotte, whose father locked them out of their home with their bags packed after he decided he could not tolerate their behavior any more. They were interfering with his relationship with his new wife. Another young person showed up on the doorsteps of an agency, again with his bags packed by his adoptive parents, after they decided they could not manage his behavior. His parents decided that they tried their hardest with him, but after his behavior became unmanageable, decided to return him to the state. Thirteen year-old Wendy's behavior was very difficult. She ran away from home uncountable times and child welfare decided to apprehend her and place her in residential treatment from which she continually went AWOL. Her child welfare worker received as many as two missing person reports a day. The police would locate her and return her to the treatment center, only to have her run away within an hour. A shortage of closed facilities hindered work with Wendy and she was placed each time in the same open facility, but with little success. After a lengthy time of this repetitive pattern, she disclosed that her father, a single parent, had been sexually abusing her over a number of years. Wendy finally settled down and the child welfare worker thought she had a breather. Shortly after, Wendy's brother started running away! Other children have severe emotional difficulties necessitating that they be placed in a protective environment while their issues are addressed.

There has been a bias about children being placed outside the family home. "The tendency to separate difficult children from their parents through institutional placement is more pronounced ... when families are poor and involved with social services" (Minuchin, Colapinto, & Minuchin, 1998, p. 158). Middle class or wealthier families have access to more resources, allowing them to make their own arrangements for out-of-home care assistance. In addition, there might be a subtle prejudice against poor families accompanied by the belief that they are incompetent in every aspect of their lives.

Sometimes workers encounter families whose children are placed outside of their home because of parents' requests. For example, when a child's behavior is unmanageable, parents will willingly seek out the assistance of Child Welfare. In these situations, the parent may come in with several different mind-sets. For example, the parent(s) may blame the child alone for the behaviors and not perceive the problem as a family issue. When this occurs, children often feel blamed, rejected and their behavior may even regress. As a result, many of these situations are best dealt with by dealing with the family as a whole. Questions of how to get the parent(s) to realize that the situation has to be handled by the family as a whole may be running through your head. What if each member blames another member for the situation at hand? How do we support families in managing the child's behavior while also having the families work collaboratively? The case example on page 260 explores a situation in which none of the members of this three-person family wish to take any responsibility.

Once children are placed outside the home, the facility has a number of philosophical decisions to make about family involvement. How does the institution make families feel welcome? What is the social distance between the staff and the families? One of the authors worked in a psychiatric facility where children were placed in "cottages." The term "cottage" is a misnomer in that it had vaulted ceilings, was elegantly furnished, and each child had a private bedroom. The impact of placing children in settings far removed from what they are accustomed has far-reaching implications for children.

Two assumptions are behind placing children in special settings. The first assumption is that the families cannot control their children. Tied in with this assumption is the belief that parents are unable to provide a healthy family environment *and* maybe, they are the source of pathology. The second belief is that the best way or perhaps the only way for children to get better is to remove them from their pathological environment and move them to a safe and neutral place (Minuchin, Colapinto, & Minuchin, 1998, p.158). The belief seems to be that once the child's behavior is controlled, the child can return home.

These stories, and there are too many more, are tragic, both for the families and the children. Although each of these stories is different, the children all share similar issues. In addition to whatever trauma they experience, they also experience the emotional trauma of removal from a familiar environment and from loved ones. Most children, despite the treatment they receive from families, still care for family members. The authors have worked in residential treatment, child psychiatry, and child welfare, and have witnessed many such stories of children being removed from their families. Most of the reasons for removal were legitimate and we are convinced that these facilities are necessary. Child welfare is an overburdened system, and workers rely on foster families and a range of child-serving facilities to help children and families overcome their difficulties.

Involving the families after children have been removed from their care is relatively recent. We now recognize that out-of-home placements need to be more family friendly. Now, the system is moving towards more family-friendly interventions in which families are recognized as playing a key role in a child's life, even after children are removed from their care. Families play an important role in shaping who the child is and what experiences they have. Taking a child into care is a major transition for children and their families, disrupting familiar family patterns. When children enter an out-of-home placement, most families continue to have ongoing rights and responsibilities. Other times, parental rights and responsibilities are overlooked. The goal of family work when the child enters care is to reduce trauma to the family and child, build upon family strengths, and increase the probability of family reunification (Minuchin, Colapinto, & Minuchin, 1998).

Out of home placement disrupts family functioning, rupturing familiar patterns and attachments. As soon as a child enters care, a new triangle is formed, consisting of the agency, the family, and the child. Work done with children without recognizing the context of their behavior and the attachment they feel to their families does a disservice. Collaboration and coordination is imperative in order for intervention to be handled successfully and the problems resolved. Collaboration also demands constant family-center contact while working toward a common goal - the well being of the child.

Without a strong working relationship with the family, returning the child home becomes difficult. How the family and institution view each other is an important determination of success. There are two general attitudes. The first is when a decision is made by an authority to place the child. The process is unpleasant for the family and the center becomes the enemy, interfering with the partnership working on behalf of the child. The second attitude is where the parents see the institution as the answer to their problems. The institution will fix the child and return him or her home in better shape and their family problems will be over (Minuchin, Colapinto, & Minuchin, 1998).

In addition, some attitudes hinder partnerships with families. Most institutions offer services based on a child advocate philosophy and this philosophy hinders the development of a collaborative relationship with parents who are seen as the reason for the child's difficulty in the first place. The motives of institutional staff are good - they want to protect the child from further harm and injustice. These good intentions bring with them the difficulty that parents become the enemy; parents are the ones who harmed the child in the first place. And, while children are rescued in the centers, family dynamics and structures change, making reunification more difficult. What is the impact on children and their families who are separated from each other for lengthy periods? Children form attachments in their immediate living environment and families move on.

Residential staff must reflect upon their attitudes toward the parents of children in their care. What messages are they giving parents about their involvement? For example, do they subtly convey the message that parents are intruders in the treatment plan? Do they see parents as the "bad guys" who hurt their child and therefore do not deserve to parent anymore? Do they discourage visits by the parents or convey to them that the center will take care of the child without requiring their involvement? It is important to remember that, despite family conflict and hurt, most family members have a bond with one another.

Messages about parental involvement should begin at intake. When possible and feasible, parents should be partners in the treatment team. A statement of goals and a contract should be signed by the staff and the family (Minuchin, Colapinto, & Minuchin, 1998). The contract should cover what is needed in terms of commitment and involvement of the family and how the center will nurture that involvement. Ongoing communication also needs to be part of the contract. Will the parents be brought into the center for regular family sessions, or alternatively, will the worker accompany the child to the family's home for family sessions? What are some ways that centers can involve parents in the activities of the center and in the treatment plan?

Other issues are unique to residential treatment centers. Consider the impact of the structure of the center on ongoing involvement with the family in terms of:

- Shift work
- Distance of the center from the family's home
- Social distance between the center staff and the family
- Beliefs about the nature and cause of the problem
- Involvement or lack of involvement of family
- Changes in the family system
- Beliefs about parents - the cause of the child's difficulty or a healing resource
- Estimates of risk to the child
- The social structure of the therapeutic milieu
- Distance in terms of time separated from a family

The question of home visits is an integral part of the treatment plan. The danger of residential treatment without family involvement makes returning the child home more difficult. Recall the components of family systems theory. Out-of-home placement can affect the family system in each of these six areas:

1. The family as a whole is greater than the sum of its parts.
2. The family maintains a balance between change and stability.
3. A change in one family member affects the other family members.
4. Family members' behaviors are best understood from circular rather than linear causality.
5. A family system is part of a larger social system and is also comprised of many other smaller subsystems.
6. A family functions according to established rules of governance.

Exercise 10.9

Out-of-Home Placement and Family Systems Theory

(In Class)

Beside each premise of family systems theory, write down how out-of-home placement will affect the family system. What are the implications for (1) intervention, and (2) returning the child home?

Premise	Impact of Out-of-Home Placement	Issues of Returning Home
1. The family as a whole is greater than the sum of its parts.		
2. The family maintains a balance between change and stability.		
3. A change in one family member affects the other family members.		
4. Family members' behaviors are best understood from a circular rather than linear causality.		
5. A family system is part of a larger social system and is also comprised of many other smaller subsystems.		
6. A family functions according to established rules of governance.		

A concern about residential treatment is the impact of prolonged estrangement upon the child, the parents and family relationships.

Case Example: Jerry Barlow

Jerry is an eleven-year-old boy who has been in a residential treatment center on and off for the past three years for aggressive behaviors toward his mother and 14-year-old brother, Mark. Jerry has a lengthy history of behavior problems, dating back to when he was 4 years old. His mother, Sharon, described him as "out of control" and impulsive while in her care. His father, Randy, committed suicide three years before Jerry's admission to the center. Mrs. Barlow has had in home supports on and off since her husband's death. Jerry has since been in and out of the care of his mother and was readmitted in the treatment home in one year ago. Jerry's mother, Sharon, is a 40-year-old woman who works full time at a local library. Jerry was diagnosed with Attachment Disorder, Severe Oppositional Defiant Disorder and Conduct Disorder. His intelligence falls within the Borderline range. Although Jerry can be physically defiant, the residential center has found that overall his behaviors at home are manageable. Sharon continues to struggle with managing the behaviors of both of her children and her main mode of behavior control is yelling.

Mrs. Barlow does not have much in terms of social support. Her former husband's friend Aaron, provides some support to her and takes the boys dirt biking on weekends.

This family has received multiple services including individual and family counseling, grief counseling, an in-home support worker, and a youth worker for the children. A parenting assessment was completed when Jerry was 9 highlighted concerns about Sharon's ability to parent her children. It is apparent that she loves both children, but is unable to manage their behaviors and keep them under control. Sharon was a foster child when she was younger and moved to five different homes. Sharon had a poor relationship with her mother and could not live with her. Her IQ is in the low to average range. The IQ assessment revealed that Sharon had problems understanding abstract concepts and is a concrete learner. Sharon also has problems processing information.

Jerry has stated that he does not want to become a Permanent Ward of the State. Sharon's child welfare worker explained to her what Permanent Guardianship/Joint Guardianship was and she was adamant that she does not want to relinquish custody of Jerry despite her difficulty handling his behavior. Sharon has difficulty parenting one child but when the two children are together, she has made several calls to the treatment center to pick up Jerry. If there is no change noted in the next three months, the child protection worker intends to apply for Permanent Guardianship. There has been no change to date and in fact Jerry has become more defiant and aggressive with his mother.

The family members blame the situation on one another. For example, Sharon thinks that the boys are the cause of all of the problems and that she has nothing to do with the situation, even though she still is open to receiving support in a family setting.

Exercise 10.10

Returning Jerry Home

(In Class)

Read over the case example of Jerry. Break into groups of three. Clearly, both Sharon and Jerry want him at home. Looking at the treatment plan, try to make a plan to return Jerry to his family. Are there any additional steps that have not been taking to assist Jerry? What about Sharon? What about the family as a whole? Develop the best-case plan that you can in order to return Jerry home. Make sure that you use the assumptions of family systems theory in your plan.

Plan:

Family workers have several options in working with children and their families. One option is to work with families in their home. Home-based visiting is becoming more popular these days, but it carries both disadvantages and disadvantages. At the opposite end of the spectrum is when children are removed from their families and placed in treatment centers. The risk of removing a child from his or her family is that ongoing family systems patterns will be so disrupted that returning a child home is difficult. Involving families in their treatment is imperative if children are to be helped to return to their home.

Exercise 10.11

A Missing Family Member

(PBL Worksheet)

Imagine that your PBL family has lost a member for three months (either through hospitalization, imprisonment, work or through placement in a residential treatment facility). Select the family member who was gone. Spend 20 minutes creating new patterns and then for the next 40 minutes try to integrate that person back into the family. What was the impact of the removal as well as return to the family?

Chapter Summary

Chapter 10 discusses the advantages as well as disadvantages of working in a family's home. Key issues related to home-based services are presented along with the key components or characteristics of home-based family work. The final part of the chapter provides a context for treating families with children in care. In addition, we discuss issues related to out of home placement and its impact on the family.

Chapter 11 **Table of Contents**

SPECIALIZED FAMILY APPROACHES

Chapter 11

Specialized Family Approaches

Chapter Coverage

- Structural Family Therapy
- Communicative/Experiential Family Therapy
- Solution Focused Model
- Narrative Family Therapy
- Feminist Model: Gender Sensitive Practice

Introduction

Now that you understand a generalist approach to working with families, we bridge the gap of moving from a generalist to a specialist approach to family work. Thus, we provide a thumbnail sketch of five different specialized approaches. Some of the concepts and techniques will be familiar to you since they are integrated into the generalist practice approach described in this book. There are numerous family therapy approaches available to present yet we have selected we believe five of most commonly used ones.

We start our presentation of five different approaches to working with families with the Structural Family Therapy approach. The structural family therapy approach views problems from the social systems assumption that *the family is the problem*. Thus, the focus on intervention is on family patterns of interaction.

1) Structural Family Therapy Approach

Historical Background

Salvador Minuchin developed structural family therapy in the 1960s through his work at the Wiltwyck School for Boys. In the 1970s, structural family therapy became one of the most widely practiced forms of family therapy in North America. (Minuchin, 1974, 1981, 1981, 1992)

Major Concepts

Three major concepts underpin structural family therapy: 1) Family Structure and Hierarchies; 2) Subsystems, and 3) Boundaries.

1. **Family Structure and Hierarchies**: Rules create a family structure that determines how, when, and to whom family members relate. Functional families have a structure that places the parents at the top of the hierarchy, in a position of power and authority over their children.

2. **Subsystems:** Subsystems are units within a family, created because of characteristics such as sex, age, or interest". There are three major subsystems: the spousal/marital, the parental/executive, and the sibling subsystems. The spousal/marital subsystem includes the two individuals who have come together as a couple. The parental subsystem is made up of those persons in the family who have authority over the children. People are often both part of the parental subsystem and the spousal subsystem.

3. **Boundaries:** Boundaries are the invisible barriers within a family and between a family and its environment that regulate the amount of contact that individuals, subsystems, and entire family units have with each other. Boundaries fall on a continuum ranging from rigid to diffuse, with "clear" being the midpoint.

Rigid boundaries are restrictive and inflexible. They limit transactions between different family subsystems, creating "disengaged" families. In disengaged families, members are so separate, they are unaware of how their actions affect each other. Relationships between family members can be cold or indifferent and members uninvolved with each other's lives.

Clear boundaries are firm and flexible, and permit individual autonomy. They also support and nurture family members. For example, family members may be close to each other while having healthy and age-appropriate levels of individual freedom.

Diffuse boundaries are blurred and family members are over involved with each other, which results in "enmeshment." Enmeshed relationships occur where family members are so tightly locked that individual autonomy cannot be expressed. For example, the family members are not allowed to be involved in any activities outside of the home.

Goals of Structural Family Therapy

The goal of Structural Family Therapy is "to change dysfunctional aspects of a family system to a more adequate family organization structure, one that will maximize the growth potential of each family member" (Minuchin, 1981, p. 446). The goals with the following types of families include:

- The goal with enmeshed families is to clearly define and strengthen individual and subsystem boundaries to allow individual autonomy. For example, asking each family member how they perceive who makes the rules in the family: "Who decides where this family will go on vacation? Do the children have some say in vacation planning?"
- In disengaged families, the goal is to increase closeness and involvement of family members with each other. That is, the family worker is not there to solve the family's presenting problem, but rather to teach the family new interactions so that the family can solve its own problems. The family worker works on changing family structure to allow the family to access their repertoire of under used problem-solving skills. It is important that the family worker understand interactions between all members of the family. The family worker might sit quietly and observe family patterns. When an interaction occurs three times this usually indicates a family pattern.
- In trying to deal with "life threatening symptoms," the structural family worker might employ techniques from other therapies. For example, in the case of anorexia, the family worker might use a behavioral technique such as reinforcement to get the person to eat.

Techniques

The following are the most commonly used techniques in Structural Family Therapy:

- **Accommodation**: Accommodation involves using the skills necessary to achieve a therapeutic alliance with the family. Accommodation is part of the engagement phase of working with families.

  There are three ways to accommodate (adjust to) a family:

  1. **Joining**: The therapist establishes rapport with family members, temporarily becoming part of the family system. For example, the family worker might try to understand the family members' feelings by saying: "I hear you are feeling very angry. I wonder if there might be sadness underneath that, too. "

  2. **Maintenance**: The family worker supports a part of the family structure while analyzing it. For example, the family worker will observe how the family members act toward on another while trying to get an understanding of what is really going on.

  3. **Mimesis**: The worker parallels a family's mood or behavior. Often the family worker will mimic the way a client sits and matches their tone of voice and pacing of their speech momentarily to "join" with the client. For example, the family worker may temporarily suck his thumb if a child is.

- **Boundary Making**: Structural therapists will work to realign boundaries through increasing either proximity or distance between family members and subsystems. For example, in a family with a seating arrangement where the parents do not sit beside on another, the family worker would have the parents move their seats. The family worker would say, "John, I notice that you are sitting with the children and Linda is here by herself. I would like you to move your chair over next to Linda." For example, if a parent and child were having a discussion and the parent keeps sspeaking with the family worker instead of with the child, the family worker might direct the parent by saying: I want you to tell Jasmine, not me."

- **Intensity**: The family worker focuses on drawing out underlying feelings to intensify family patterns. For example, the worker may say, "I sense a lot of sadness in this family."

- **Unbalancing**: Occasionally a family worker might want to shake up the family system. One way of doing this is through unbalancing where the worker joins and supports one member or subsystem at the expense of others. For example, the family worker might momentarily take sides with one family member against another, usually done by stopping a family member interrupting who the family worker is talking to and having the family worker continue to pay attention more to one family member over another.

- **Enactment**: Perhaps the most important intervention used with families is enactment. A worker stimulates a family enactment by getting members involved in acting out a transactional pattern. For example, the family worker may instruct a family to discuss a certain topic in the interview. Family workers do this in order to flush out dysfunctional or problematic transactions between family members, and to provide an environment conducive to practicing more functional ways of interacting. Once an enactment is presented and the difficulty becomes apparent, the worker intervenes by either commenting on what went wrong, or pushing members to continue.

Case Example of Structural Approach with the Stone Family

Assessment and Intervention

Based on the information that the family worker received on this family, the worker as a Structural Family Worker would try to understand the family's structure, boundaries, and subsystems. The worker would interpret Michael's actions as a symptom of this family's structure that is no longer working. In particular, Mr. Stone, as a stepparent has not assumed a parenting role with Michael, leaving the parenting solely to his spouse. As well, Mrs. Stone's depression would be seen as a marital subsystem that is not working well.

Techniques with Brown Family

1. Enactment - The family worker would first get the family to engage in an enactment in order to determine their interactional patterns. For example, the worker could say, "I would like to see how you problem solve. John and Linda, could you talk to each other about how the two of you could work better together as parents."
2. Manipulating Physical Space - In family work, the worker would manipulate physical space by placing John and Linda together, and Michael and Mary opposite to them.

3. Unbalancing - the worker would side with John to support him in showing the children that although he is a stepfather; he needs to take an active role in parenting of the children. For example, if Michael turns to his mother for advice, he would be instructed, instead, to ask his stepfather first for his opinion.

By using these techniques, the worker hopes to re-establish clear and appropriate boundaries, structure, and subsystems in the Stone family. Once this is achieved, the family should be able to problem-solve on its own.

Exercise 11.1

Structural Approach

(PBL Worksheet)

In the PBL groups try interviewing your PBL family using the structural family approach (30-40 minutes). In the large class, discuss this experience.

2) Communication/Experiential Model Approach

In this section, we present the communication/experiential model primarily developed by the late social worker Virginia Satir. The emphasis of this model is the use of clear, direct, open, and honest communication, particularly of feelings of caring to each other in the family (Satir 1967, 1976; Satir & Baldwin, 1983).

Experiential therapy is a form of family work, which is based on becoming aware of feelings in the here and now. Families are viewed more as groups of individuals than as a system. Experiential therapy focuses on the *immediate* interactions between family members in an attempt to help with the problems the family has brought to the family worker. The underlying belief is that the expression of honest feelings will lead to personal and family fulfillment. That is, individuals who feel cared for and loved will have a high sense of self-esteem and will act in worthwhile ways. The major system for individuals to receive these messages of caring and love is the family system.

Historical Background

The experiential model arose from the humanistic psychology of Gestalt and client centered therapy. The two main developers of the experiential model were Virginia Satir and Carl Whitaker. Satir strongly believed in the healing power of love and the centrality of communication. Whitaker emphasized that self-fulfillment depended on family cohesiveness. Both are united in their use of spontaneity, creativity, and risk-taking as a means to conflict resolution.

The communication/experiential model is effective in helping family members get in touch with their affective blocks so that a healthier family unit can exist. Techniques such as Family Sculpting, role-play, and body contact (discussed below) are particularly effective in helping family members get in touch with their feelings. Various techniques may be utilized in order to reach the family's goals. These techniques provide the family the opportunity to become aware of unhealthy and dysfunctional patterns and move onto more healthy functional patterns of behavior.

Satir attempted to connect with people for she believed that they all have the basic need to feel loved and valued. The experiential model attempts to get to the core of people's unhappiness and move towards a healthier functioning. In this therapy, the family worker is an active change agent and acts as a role model to teach clear and concise communication. Hence, family workers need be aware of their own emotions as well as being in tune with the family's emotions.

Major Concepts

Five concepts are fundamental to the communication/experiential model of family work: 1) focusing on affect; 2) family worker as change agent; 3) self-worth; 4) communication; and 5) marital relationship.

1. **Focusing on affect or feelings**: People have a basic need to feel valued and loved. For example, the family worker wants to ask each member of the family, "what do you want?" or "what problems do you see in the family?" (Satir & Baldwin, 1983, p. 35). Symptoms are caused by lack of emotional expression (dysfunctional families are often disengaged from each other). For example, "It seems to me like the members in this family don't feel comfortable with expressing how they feel and this might be part of the reason the family is having difficulties."

2. **Family worker as an important change agent**: Family workers should utilize and voice their own reactions and personal experience in helping the family reach their goals. This can be done through appropriate self-disclosure. For example, if a member of the family is talking about a death, the family worker might disclose that she has also experienced the death of a loved one or the family worker knows of someone who has gone through a similar painful experience.

3. **Self-worth**: Communication style and overall functioning is closely linked to an individual's self-concept and self-esteem. The premise is that if one gets in touch with one's emotions, change will occur. The family worker wants to increase awareness through labeling. For example, "John, I noticed that when you talk about your father you become sad, are you aware you do this?" The family worker wants to listen carefully, normalize feelings, and stay away from blaming. For example, the statement "whenever we get mad" implies anger is a universal feeling (Satir & Baldwin, 1983, p. 23).

4. **Communication**: Communication, to be effective, must be clear and direct face-to-face interaction (in the here and now). For example, "I want to make sure I understand what you are saying right now, are you saying ...." Openness and honesty lead to trust and the family worker wants to emphasize that this is a safe environment by stating, "When the family comes into this room I will do all I can to make sure that everyone feels safe." Communication needs to be congruent both verbally and non-verbally. The family worker needs to teach the family to check on nonverbal cues when they are communicating. An example is " you have a look on your face ... I am not sure what you are feeling right now" (Satir & Baldwin, 1983, p. 48).

Indirect communication tends to be a sign of dysfunction (Satir, 1967, p. 17). In some families there are implicit rules regarding talking about one's pain. For example, "I knew I couldn't tell my mother I was feeling sad. These things just weren't talked about."

5. **Marital relationship**: Partners are considered to be the "architects" of the family and influence family homeostasis (Satir, 1967, p. 1). It is believed that when the marriage or couple relationship is strong and healthy, the family unit is also stable. Dysfunctional parenting tends to be a result of marital difficulties. For example, "I am sensing that Mary and Dan as a couple are not relating to each other as they would like and this may cause a conflict when parenting decisions need to be made."

Goals of the Communication/Experiential Model:

- **Growth of family members**: Family members who become more aware of feelings within the family and are able to share their feelings will have a better sense of self. Increased self-esteem and self worth is a form of growth. To increase the family's awareness, members need to take risks in sharing vulnerable feelings. It is believed that maintaining the status quo generally does not lead to a stronger family unit. For example, "I am aware that sharing feelings may not be the way you would do this at home, however I would like you to try it." It is hoped that increasing the sharing of feelings in a supportive family environment will also related to congruence between feelings and behaviors. Family members become aware that there are choices in the way one can communicate and/or behave. For example, "There is another way you can let Michael know you are upset with him.
- **Family Comfort**: The worker helps the family feel at ease with talking and expressing their feelings. Using appropriate humor can do this, as it helps to diffuse the tension and attempts at connecting people. For example, "There seems to be a lot of fighting going on in this family. I wonder if sometimes it doesn't feel like a wrestling match." Workers also enhance sensitivity to individual and family needs and encourage appropriate sharing. It is important to let each person speak for themselves, whenever possible. For example, "Mary I noticed you haven't said anything, I am wondering how the fighting between your brother and mother makes you feel." It is important for the family worker instill a sense of hope in the family. For example, "If everyone is willing to support each other the situation will get better."
- **Directive Therapy**: The working style is described as involved, active and directive. For example, "I am going to have the family stand up and show me what happens at home." The family worker models clear and open communication. For example, "Is it clear what I am asking you to do?" Emphasizing the importance of relationship building and maintaining respect with each family member, can be done through reframing for a more positive understanding, or hopefully a less negative connotation. For example, "The word temper has been changed to 'the way of bringing out his thoughts' (Satir & Baldwin, 1983, p. 37).

Techniques

- **Role-Playing**: Family enactment of roles and situations. When possible, the family worker moves chairs so that members face each other and encourage interaction through stating, "Can you show me Jane and Sally how you talk to each other when you are at home?" It is believed true feelings come out through acting realistic issues. For example, "I never knew you felt that way."

- **Family Sculpting**: This is a physical arrangement of the family by one selected family member or by the family worker in order to depict an interpretation physically of what is going on within the family. If the family worker is directing the session, it is important for the participants to be aware of what the family worker is doing. For example, "I am going to physically arrange the different family members into positions I see them having within this family." Family sculpting helps members gain further insight into family dynamics and interactions through visual illustration. Again, it is important to confirm if the picture is an accurate perception of the family. "Is this how you view yourself in the family?" Also family art therapy or drawing is commonly used to stimulate unexpressed feelings, particularly when working with younger children.

- **Body Contact**: Encouraging body contact helps members become aware of deep emotions of love and affection through physical touch, as well as being physically close. For example, "Would you please move your chair closer and I would like Linda and John to hold hands." (It is important for the family worker to first assess if physical touch would be helpful for this family). For example, when there is sexual abuse in the family, the family worker would want to try to help family members distinguish between "good" and "bad" touch.

- **Family Life Chronology**: The worker places more emphasis on the marital relationship than on the "identified patient." There is an assumption that the marital system needs to be healthy in order for people to be good parents (This is often the case with most families who come in for therapy, although this is not necessarily always true). For example, a child sucking his or her thumb may initiate the parents to fight. The underlying issue may be that the couple does not want to talk about (or admit) problems in their marriage, therefore the focus is shifted onto the child. The family worker gets an idea of how decisions are made by asking the parents what the relationship was like with their own parents (i.e., what beliefs they learned?). For example, "It seems to me Linda's relationship with her father was very healthy and positive and as a result, Linda expects her marriage with John to be the same."

Case Example of Communication/Experiential Approach with the Stone Family

A straightforward approach would be to ask Mr. and Mrs. Stone to role-play. Remember the concept of detriangulation as forcing two people to talk to each other directly, preventing triangulation. "I would like Linda and John to turn your chairs facing each other and for the two of you to talk about the feelings you are having about your relationship, I know this may be difficult but I would like to see if you can share your feelings." As the family worker, you want to look for circular communication patterns being mindful of the range of feelings shared. Eventually you will model and coach the couple to share feelings in a clear, direct, open, honest, and supportive manner if they are unable to do so.

Exercise 11.2

Communication/Experiential Model
(PBL Worksheet)

In your PBL groups try the communication/experiential model with your PBL family (30-40 minutes). In the large class, discuss this experience.

3) Solution Focused Approach

In this section we present first the solution-focused model. The following model, the narrative model, is somewhat related to the solution focused approach.

Historical Background

Solution-focused Therapy is committed to brevity, de-emphasizes history, and gets the family to concentrate on solutions that have worked for members in the past. From its roots in Strategic Therapy, it has moved away from a focus on problems. The primary developer of this therapy was Steve de Shazer. His background includes working in Palo Alto with the MRI group where he was influenced by their brief approach. His wife, Insoo Berg, substantially contributed to the theory, training most of its leaders. (de Schzer, 1983, 1991)

Major Concepts

1. **Focus on Solutions:** Rather than over-explain problems or describe family dynamics, this theory focuses on solutions. There is an assumption that clients really want to change. Family workers use techniques that steer clients away from "problem talk" to "solution talk," as language is reality. Thus, family members identify their own goals, resources, and exceptions to their problem. Solution-focused family workers believe that people already have the skills to solve their problems but have lost sight of this ability. Their problems loom large, crowding out their strength in dealing with them. This calls for a simple shift in what they are already doing that works, or searching for abilities they are not currently using in dealing with life's difficulties.

2. **Brevity:** It is not necessary for the whole family to attend - just those interested in coming. Intake information is limited, as Solution-focused family workers prefer to focus on the future. The therapy itself is brief, which makes it a favorite of the managed care industry.

Goals of Solution Focused Family Work

The family worker works from the family's understanding of the problem. Therefore, the concern is only with the family's presenting complaint. Because Solution-focused Therapy is not designed to reorganize personality or family structure, modest goals are standard. A small change is usually all that is needed because that change tends to snowball.

Techniques

- **Starting the Interview**: At the first session, the family worker asks, "What can I do that would be helpful for this family?" or "What would you like to see different for this family coming out of this interview?" These questions stimulate the family to identify what they want help with specifically. It also sets the stage for the negotiation of an achievable goal.

During the sessions, several techniques are used to initiate and maintain problem-solving faculties in clients:

- **"Miracle question"**: "Suppose one night while asleep a miracle happens and the problem is solved. What would this look like? How would you know? What would be different?" By asking these questions, people are producing a clear definition of their goal.

- **"Exception question"**: "During times in the past or present when the problem was not present when it ordinarily would be, what was different"? This produces clues in order to expand those times of exception. It demonstrates that the problem can be changed, controlled, or eliminated.

- **"Scaling question"**: "On a scale of I to 10, with 10 being the best you can feel, how far are you today on your way to 10? What do you need to do to get to (the next number)"? This nurtures small changes and disarms resistance. It also identifies and measures concrete changes and goals when dealing with vague topics such as depression and communication.

- **"Coping question"**: When a client recalls surmounting difficult situations, and is asked how they did so. This question seeks out demonstrations of a client's competence and coping skills.

- **Formula First Session Task**: At the end of the first session, the client is instructed to observe and write down what happens in their life or relationships that they would want to continue. This helps them focus on their strengths, creating a more positive outlook. This is the "Formula First Session Task."

Solution-Focused Therapy Techniques with the Stone Family

The following are examples of questions that could be asked to the Stone family:

"What can I do to be helpful to you?" (Stimulates the client to identify what they want help with specifically).

"How did you cope with your depression?" (Coping question, seeking a demonstration of competence).

"Have you experienced anything like this before?" (Looking for past success to build on).

"On a scale of I to 10, with 10 being not worried at all, what number would you say represents the worry you feel for Linda at this moment?" (Using a "Scaling Question" for measuring steps toward a goal and change).

"Now I would like you to think of what would need to happen in order for that 4 to be bumped up to a 5 or even a 6." (Encourages development of concrete goals).

"Linda, let's look at what number, on a scale of I to 10 with 10 being not depressed, you feel you are today, right now". (Scaling Question" is especially effective in identifying change and goal of ending depression).

"And what steps would move that 3 to a 4? Or even a 5?" (Again encouraging concrete steps toward the goal of ending depression).

"It is important to just concentrate on one step at a time. You both have mentioned a goal of improving Linda's sleeping patterns. That's a good first step for what we can begin to work on. Linda, I'm glad you're here trying to do something about your depression. It shows me that you know when to go for help. It shows strength on your part, and that's very good. Can you recall a time in, say, the last six months that you didn't feel depressed? (Encouraging incremental goals - small changes." Affirmation of first steps toward solution followed by an "Exception Question" to demonstrate the client's ability to change, control or eliminate a problem).

"If one night a miracle happened and you awoke the next morning with your depression gone, how would you know? What would that be like? Tell me about that." ('Miracle Question " is used to produce a fine-tuned definition of Linda's goal).

(Turning to John) "Now the same questions for you. One night a miracle happens in your life and you wake up the next morning and your worry over Linda is gone. How would you know? And what would that be like?" ("Miracle Question " to seek John's definition of the goal).

"I want to compliment you both on how well you are able to share what's been going on. Your communication skills are great, and I sense tremendous warmth and caring between the two of you. Our time is coming to a close now, so I would like to suggest that each of you think about something in the next week before we meet again. I want you to write down what it is in your lives and in your relationships that you would want to continue. Then we'll discuss these things when I see you again." (Session is ended on an affirmative note highlighting their resources. The "Formula First Session Task" will help then focus on their strengths, which will then create more hope that a solution is not far away and that they are capable of finding it).

Exercise 11.3

Solution Focused Model
(PBL Worksheet)

In your PBL groups try the solution-focused model with your PBL family (30-40 minutes). In the large class, discuss your experience with this model.

4) Narrative Therapy Approach

We are born into stories: the stories of our parents, our families, and our culture. These made meaning, which predate us and envelop us upon our arrival into the world, can be constraining, even imprisoning, or they can be freeing and liberating....Born into the cradle of familial and cultural stories, we begin to construct personal narratives not long afterward, with all the idiosyncratic features that this many entail
(White & Murray, 1992).

Historical Background

Narrative therapy is one of the most recent approaches to family work in North America. Michael White and David Epston are two principal contributors to the development of narrative therapy. In its most basic form, it involves the listening and telling or retelling of stories about people and the problem they are experiencing (White, 1990, 1995).

Major Concepts

Focus on stories: Stories are the reality in which we exist. There is no reality, only stories we tell about reality. The role of the family worker is to listen to the family members' stories and identify openings for them to rewrite the story into a preferred outcome. Through the process of telling their story, family members are able to examine their lived experiences in a meaningful and fulfilling way (Freedman & Combs, 1966). The past can be changed by constructing new *narratives* or stories.

Goals of Therapy

Narrative Therapy assumes that the person is not the problem. *The problem is the problem.* This means that the problem is seen as separate from the individual, not as part of the individual. In narrative therapy, it is believed that each person's experience can be interpreted in many different ways, and there is no single 'truth.' Through clients sharing their interpretation of a situation, the narrative family worker is able to draw upon exceptions and use these exceptions to reshape the client's story. Although somewhat an individual focus, narrative therapy not only encourages individual stories, but also invites the family to listen and rewrite the stories together as they are the experts on their family experience.

Techniques

- **Beginning therapy**: Family workers find out from clients how they usually spend their time in order to get an idea of how they see themselves. The family worker may also use circular questioning, that is, questions that connect relationships. In narrative therapy, circular questioning is used to create interdependence between the client and their stories. When doing this, the family worker pays much attention to the client's talents and competencies. This is often accomplished through placing exaggerated importance on these things when the client mentions them. For example, a family worker may say such things as, "Oh, that's so great that you are able to spend time with your son!" or "That's wonderful that you are able to balance all the things in your life so well!"

- **Externalizing the Problem**: The family worker asks the clients to tell their stories, including their problems. When the family worker has a sense of what the family has been going through, the family worker begins to ask questions that will externalize the problem. Externalizing the problem means looking at the problem as a separate entity that is outside the person or relationship. This may be done through techniques such as naming or personifying the problem. For example, a problem may be named the "Anger Monster" or may be personified through the family worker using such phrases as "When Anger comes to visit… "or "When you feel Anger nearby." This shows the problem as an intruder that tries to dominate family member's lives.

- **Mapping Influence**: Next, the family worker maps the influence of the problem by examining how the problem has affected family members' lives and relationships. This may be done using a relative influence question such as, "How does the Anger Monster affect your life Michael?" or "What does Anger make you do?" As well, the family worker maps the influence of the person, which involves examining how the client has been able to control the problem. An example of a relative influence question here may be, "Can you remember a time when Anger tried to control you but you didn't let it Michael' or "Is Anger with you in the shower? Does Anger follow you to the gym?" Questions such as these may uncover unique outcomes, which are times that do not fit the client's presented pattern, as the problem is not present.

- **Re-Authoring the Story of Lives and Relationships**: At this stage, the family worker uses unique outcomes as a starting point from which to develop a new story. By focusing on these victories over the problem, clients realize that they do have options and that they are able to control the problem. Eventually, the client's entire identity will be reshaped around a new, more positive story.

- **Reinforcing the New Story**: The client's new story is celebrated and affirmed. In order to maintain this new story, outside support is needed. Thus the client may be asked such questions as, "Is there anyone that you would like to tell about this new direction you are taking?" to encourage the development of such support. As well, the family worker may get the client involved in letter writing, in which s/he formally documents the changes in their life story. After the final session, the family worker may also use this technique by writing the client a letter in which the worker commends the client for the control s/he has over things in their life, in order to again re-affirm the client's new life story.

- **Questions**: Narrative therapists ask questions to generate experience rather then to gather information (Freedman & Combs, 1996). From the narrative perspective, the purpose of using questions is to elicit, clarify, and enhance descriptions of times the problem is not influential in the family members' life (Chang & Phillips, 1993). In asking questions, the family worker highlights times in the family members' lives when they have been able to cope successfully with adverse situations because of their own experiences. This process allows family members to highlight the abilities and competencies they are drawing to assist them with the presenting problem(s). For example, "When in your life have you experienced happiness?" By using externalizing questions, uncovering unique outcomes the problem's tactics and strategies can be more readily understood and therefore, more likely to support the client in finding the answers to disable the problem's influence on their life.

Narrative Approach Techniques with the Stone Family

Working from a narrative perspective, the family worker would first spend some time finding out how Linda sees a depression episode as occurring. From this, the family worker would be able to determine Linda's perception of the events. The family worker would encourage Linda to tell her story, including her problems, after which the family worker would start to ask questions that would help externalize the problem. Examples of such questions would include, "Can you till me what happens when you feel Depression taking hold of you?" or "How do you think Depression is coming between you and your husband?"

Questions such as these demonstrate how the problem has influenced Linda and John's lives, while reaffirming that Depression is a separate entity, outside both. The family worker would also look for unique outcomes, to determine how Linda has been able to take control of Depression in the past. This would be done through posing questions such as, "Can you think of a time when Depression tried to get a hold of you but you didn't let it?' Examining these victories over Depression allows Linda to realize that she is able to control Depression. Proving Linda's competencies allows the authoring of a new narrative to begin.

Exercise 11.4

Narrative Approach
(PBL Worksheet)

In your PBL groups try the narrative approach with your PBL family (30-40 minutes). In the large class, discuss this experience.

5) Feminist Model: Gender Sensitive Practice Approach

It is imperative that family workers be sensitive to issues of power and oppression in families. Power is manifested in many ways in families and is an unavoidable facet of family life. Power is embedded in every conflict situation and sensitivity to it will help in the resolution of conflicts. It is the misuse of power that must be contained since power is unavoidable. Another reason for paying attention to power and gender issues within the family is that without an awareness of the theoretical and personal biases of family workers, family workers will overlook subtle gender stereotypes and gender-based oppressions.

Historical Background

Until recently, family practice and other forms of helping were gender blind. That is, gender roles, gender-based oppression, and family responsibilities, were ignored or discounted. Family therapy also had a biased approach toward gender in the family, perpetuating beliefs that created the oppression. Goldner and Hare-Mustin in particular, challenged existing theories and pointed out gender bias and oppression.

In the 1980s, family systems theory was criticized for its sexist beliefs, particularly the belief that all participants in a family system contribute to the problem and each member fills a position of equal power. Circularity is especially troublesome and how it is described in contributing to family violence. Feminist therapists insisted that women are not equally responsible for their own abuse and circular causality was seen as "blaming the victim" and keeping the status quo going.

Further, systems' explanations were criticized for ignoring the larger social, cultural, historical, and political basis to gender inequality. Feminists also attacked concepts of neutrality and complementarily. Neutrality emphasized that family members contribute equally to the production and maintenance of problems (power differences become invisible and individual responsibility is removed). Beliefs about the complementarily of sex roles cloud problems of power and domination by appealing to the democratic belief about separate but equal.

Exercise 11.5

Theoretical Biases
(In Class)

Break into groups of two. Each member is instructed to reflect back on some of the theories that you have taken in the program. From a critical stance, identify how these theories promote gender bias. What are the implications for family work? Share your results with the rest of the class.

Theory	Gender Bias
a.	
b.	
c.	
d.	

Exercise 11.6

Personal Biases
(In Class)

Break into groups of two. Reflect back on some of the beliefs about gender that you learned as you were growing up. The beliefs might originate in your family of origin, in your religious teachings, in your educational background, your culture, or in your community. List these beliefs about gender. How might these beliefs affect your work with families? How have things changed since your beliefs were formed? Share your discussion with the rest of the class.

Belief	Affect of Belief on Family Work
a.	
b.	
c.	
d.	

Changes since beliefs formed:

Major Concepts

1. **Understanding Gender Roles:** By understanding the social context of gender roles, the family worker can learn to understand why family violence occurs. Additionally, they understand that some women remain in relationships, though powerlessness, helplessness, and lack of control over their lives. Feminist workers strive for political, economic, and social justice of all people, inside and outside the family. When translated into marital relationships, a gender sensitive philosophy strives for equality in decision-making, economics, and in shared participation in household tasks and childcare. Feminist workers connect social conditions and socially constructed gender roles with what is occurring within family relationships. Consciousness-raising within a feminist context creates awareness of the impact of classism, racism, sexism and other forms of oppression within intimate relationships.

Exercise 11.7

Supportive/Educative Approach
(In Class)

Consider the Stone family once again, and team up with a partner to design a strategy for understanding how gender biases may be influencing their choices and creating problems for them. Use the issues listed below and apply them to the Stones.

Issue 1: Destructive Consequences of Stereotyped Roles and Expectations -

Issue 2: Dependency and Submissiveness for Women -

Issue 3: Build Women's Self-Esteem; Encourage Men's Interaction with Household/Child Duties -

2. **Family Homeostasis:** As mentioned in Chapter 5, family homeostasis is a central assumption of family systems theory. When viewed in this way, the risk is the elimination if individual responsibility since behavior becomes an attempt to maintain homeostasis.

Family workers should take special note of how homeostasis is interpreted in the development of family problems, particularly when the problem involves victimization. For example, family systems conceptualization of intrafamilial sexual abuse has described the father's behavior in positive terms (i.e., to show affection), while the mother is seen negatively, (i.e., mothers should be assessed for inhibited sexual desire or collusion). In the words of Goldner (1985b): "Insofar as all roads lead to Mom, her excesses and deficiencies will indeed make an enormous difference in how life flows around her and how the children develop" (p.40).

3. **Power:** From a feminist perspective, marriage is a relationship based upon an unequal distribution of power — usually with the male as the dominant partner. The husband is a member of the privileged gender. His status is validated politically, economically, and physically and men have access to power, knowledge, and resources that are often inaccessible to women. Feminist theory acknowledges the core inequality inherent in spousal relationships and through legal sanction, power from gender norms, power from education and resources, power stemming from personality differences, power from life circumstances (age, location, or life-stage), and power from emotional factors.

   Family work empowers women and children by increasing awareness of available options. Women and children also are encouraged to eliminate self-demeaning attitudes, counter submissive behaviors, and eliminate negative attitudes. Several intervention techniques are suggested including encouraging and underscoring women's competence.

   The most prevalent gender sensitive intervention is education. Defining the family problem to include power and gender, or introducing and discussing gender issues are just two of the approaches of educating. A fundamental aim of feminism is to make certain that power in family relationships is appropriate and healthy. While primarily concerned with women, gender sensitive practice also addresses the role of men in social change.

4. **Spousal Relationships:** Relationships might often start out as a partnership but change after the birth of the first child. Women, who remain at home with an infant even for short periods, often fall behind in their careers. Child rearing removes women from public roles while men gain more social power. Marriage and family life also have a differential impact on men and women. Regardless of the labor status of the partners, females continue to do most of the work within the home (Coleman, 1992).

Goals of Gender Sensitive Family Work

Family workers must be sensitive to issues of gender, power, and oppression. Doing so requires fostering equality at every opportunity. Feminist practice is a strong philosophical foundation upon which to base family work because it calls for sensitivity to all family members to deal with abuse of power. Thus, family workers must develop self-awareness to avoid rigid, traditional gender roles, and acknowledge power inequities.

Family workers model egalitarian relationships to their families. They must be aware of situations (such as abuse) in which neutrality supports inequality. The family worker must work with the family in nonsexist ways, while helping members make choices that transcend gender. The goal of feminist practice involves how gender role stereotyping operates in the family.

Feminist practice focuses on patriarchy, power, and sexism, recognizing that families take come in different forms and that no one structure is superior to another. Judgments about the desirability of a particular structure and composition is made solely in terms of their effects on family members, not in terms of rigid gender roles (Carruthers, 2001; Silverstein, 2003; Zimmerman, 2002).

Gender sensitive family work does not promote dependency and submissiveness. Women often feel their role is to nurture and support others, rather than to assert themselves and have been taught to take care of others first. As a result, they often have difficulty meeting personal needs. Many women are exhausted after working one shift at work and another shift at home, demands resulting in "burnout."

Techniques

Many of the techniques of feminist practice are philosophical assumptions that guide behavior. In fact, feminist workers may use the techniques from other models, but they use these techniques with feminist principles in mind.

- **Creating an egalitarian relationship:** An egalitarian relationship is established between family worker and family whenever possible. Workers are catalysts for families. The feminist family worker works toward eliminating dominant-submissive relationships.
- **Recognizing the social context of behavior:** The worker and family assessing the social and cultural restraints that limit women's functioning, because the personal is political.
- **Consciousness-raising:** The feminist family worker helps women understand the negative impact of social values on their lives.
- **Family worker self-disclosure**: The family worker can share personal information, generally in the form personal emotional reactions or the disclosure of value positions regarding women, indicating that therapeutic goals would be compatible and allow families to decide if these are personally desirable. Feminist family workers might also share a history of oppression and vulnerability to the same stresses and conflicts that families experience.
- **Conveying the belief that women are the experts in their lives**. To do this, therapy becomes a political experience in that the social environment has conveyed that men are the experts.
- **Avoidance of labeling and pathologizing:** Feminist workers discourage diagnosing or labeling behavior. In addition, they find some DSM IV-R diagnoses are sexist.
- **Reframe and re-label**: Reframing and re-labeling can be used to shift the conceptual or emotional perspective of a situation by countering common social messages. Normality describes the ability to demonstrate the positive aspects of female traits.
- **Models, encourages the power of female relationships, works toward the development of more androgynous sex roles, emphasizes balance between work and interpersonal relationships.**
- **Sharing case notes with clients:** Feminist workers have little hesitation sharing case notes with clients. Doing so is a concrete way of equalizing in the relationship.
- **Including fathers in parent-child interactions:** Doing so will ensure that both parents are actively involved in the lives of the children. Mothers are not the source of family dysfunction. Both parents must be included when looking at child issues and change. The father must be involved in all aspects of assessment, history taking, and intervention.
- **Bring gender-related issues into family work**: This might involve looking at the time that men and women spend on domestic chores. It will also entail a look at family power arrangements. The family worker should be especially alert to abuse of power such as domestic violence and sexual abuse.
- **Look for the strengths and optimize client power and ability to choose**: It is easier to pathologize women because of the extent of their involvement in so many aspects of family life. However, raising two children is the equivalent of at least two other full-time jobs for women.
- **Be aware of personal biases**. Confront your personal agendas and become tune into blind spots related to gender.

Feminist Approach with the Stone Family

The gender sensitive family worker must point out that there are two key ingredients for a satisfying marriage:

A good marriage requires a supportive, nurturing relationship involving genuine commitment and caring for each other. This is an indirect way of saying that relationships need intimacy in order to achieve marital satisfaction.

A satisfying marriage also requires sharing of instrumental tasks within the household. When children are involved, a nurturing relationship by both parents is necessary, with the sharing of parenting tasks. For example, assisting children with homework, taking children to appointments, and spending playtime with children, all involve consistent, creative, and involvement by both partners. The time invested in childcare needs to have a stronger value than it has currently. Furthermore, the male's role in raising children has to be enhanced to that of an equal participation with the female partner. This means that men can no longer select the less time consuming and more "glamorous" household roles.

In practice with the Stone family, the couple would be asked about the sharing of instrumental household tasks. In another session, child-care tasks would be explored. The Stone couple would compile a checklist of major household tasks and would be assisted by the family worker in dividing these tasks equally. For example, who is responsible for the cooking, cleaning the kitchen, vacuuming, etc. and these tasks would be divided in a fair manner.

Exercise 11.8

Traditional Versus Flexible Gender Roles

(In Class)

Think about your family as you were growing up. What was the gender role arrangement in your family? How did family structure affect the expression of gender roles? What roles defined as traditional, were shared? What roles did the children assume? In what circumstances were roles shared? What is the implication of these childhood patterns on your life today in relationships? Share your answers with the class.

Exercise 11.9

Gender Sensitive Interventions
(In Class)

Break into groups of two. Pick one of the values listed below and role-play it with a partner for approximately ten minutes. How did you show the particular skill or value? How is it unique in feminist practice?

1. Shifting the power balance between men and women
2. Skill training
3. Use of self
4. Consciousness-raising
5. Showing equality in the relationship

Exercise 11.10

Role Allocations Based on Gender[1]
(In Class)

Compare your family of origin with another family of your choosing. Then complete the following list of household chores, allocating percentages to who performed these tasks. Beside each one, indicate whether this has become a gender expectation in your present thinking:

Chore	Family of Origin	Current Family
Cooking		
Vacuuming		
Scrubbing the bathroom		
Assuming responsibility for finances		
Dishes		
Taking out the garbage		
Lawn work		
Taking care of the car		
Fixing things around the house		
Change the beds		

If there are children, look at who does each of the tasks and comment on the implication for gender.

Stay home when children ill
Shop for clothes
Take children to appointments
Attend school functions
Attend school interviews
Help children with homework
Discipline
Feed the pets
Put the children to bed
Other (please list below)

[1]Adapted from Collins, Jordan & Coleman (1999)

Exercise 11.11

Nonsexist Child Rearing
(In Class)

Under the categories of male and female children, provide a list for each about what approaches/behaviors would not be appropriate for the other gender. For example, many people would find it inappropriate to allow male children to play with dolls. Provide a reason why the approach/behavior would be inappropriate.

Male Children	Female Children
a.	
b.	
c.	
d.	

Exercise 1.12

Feminist Practice Debate
(In Class)

Some argue that feminism is a middle class movement that ignores the social oppression of economically disadvantaged women. Others also charge that feminist practice is insensitive to different cultural groups where patriarchy is part of the culture. The other side of the argument is that feminism is about anti-oppressive practice and therefore applies to everyone. Pick one side of the argument and join the group that takes your side. Students take 15 minutes to prepare their argument and debate in class for 30 minutes.

Exercise 11.13

Gender and the Family
(PBL Worksheet)

Today you are going to examine gender roles in your family. What are the hidden messages about gender? How closely does gender adhere to common social stereotypes? How are the children socialized into gender roles in this family? What family rituals have evolved and how closely do these rituals prescribe gendered behaviour?

The role of the family worker is to engage family members in a discussion of these issues. The idea is to understand how these issues relate to this particular family.

Tip

It might be a good idea to find out how the family functions in its day-to-day operations. Also, discuss gender in terms of public-private, power, caretaking, responsibility for the well being of members and their emotions.

Exercise 11.14

Redefining Family Problems to Include Gender Sensitive Explanations
(PBL Worksheet)

In the PBL groups assess the family using a feminist lens. How would you assess this family's' problems? Make sure you have defined the problems including dimensions of power and gender.

Exercise 11.15

Feminist Model
(PBL Worksheet)

In your PBL groups try the feminist model with your PBL family (30-40 minutes). In the large class, discuss this experience.

Chapter Summary

Chapter 11 helps family work students to become aware of some of the many different specialized family therapy theories and approaches available to complement and expand what we can do to help families. We present a brief outline of the key points of five of these specialist approaches to family work: 1) Structural family therapy; 2) Communicative/Experiential family therapy; 3) Solution focused model; 4) Narrative family therapy; 5) Feminist model: Gender sensitive practice. Each theory is accompanied by a brief historical background, the major concepts, therapeutic goals, techniques, and application to the Stone family.

Note to Instructor: It may be impossible to cover this whole chapter in one class. Instead, each of these models could constitute one class and the chapter could be spread out over a number of classes.

Chapter 12 **Table of Contents**

TERMINATION

Chapter 12

Termination

Parting is such sweet sorrow.

Chapter Coverage

- Loss Counseling
- Termination as a Loss Issue
- Termination of Client Involvement
- Termination Stages
- Termination Tasks

Introduction

We start this chapter with a discussion of loss counseling. Issues pertaining to loss are often mimicked in termination. Indeed, if the family worker and client family has been a meaningful relationship, there may be feelings of loss generated due to the ending of the family work.

Loss Counseling

Since all of us have experienced losses over our lifetime, we can be of great assistance to clients by helping them learn how to deal with loss. When experiencing loss, clients often face a range of emotions, including, denial or avoidance, sadness, anger, guilt, and acceptance. The key skills in helping clients deal with loss are:

1. To allow clients to experience the range of loss emotions in a safe and supportive environment. It is important that clients do not stay "stuck" on one emotion but are able to express a range of emotions;
2. To normalize the grieving or loss process;

(continued)

3. To educate clients about the grieving process, which includes: recognizing the here and now grief while still instilling hope by letting clients over time and with support, finally deal with their feelings to the point they can reach acceptance of their loss. The family worker can let clients know that often with grievous loss of a significant other, it takes about two year of grieving before acceptance is reached. However, they may remain in a relationship with the significant other forever, although the nature of the relationship changes. This does not mean we will forget the significant other or stop missing this person. It may mean that when we think of our loss, we are no longer overwhelmed by our grief but have slowly learned to terms with it.

The role of the family worker is to facilitate the client expression of feelings. The worker actively listens, shows great warmth and caring, and makes it safe for the client to express any feelings they might be experiencing. Remember, in family work to allow appropriate time for all family members to express their feelings. Family members experience loss in different ways. Some people may avoid their feelings, others feeling immense sadness or anger, while others may have arrive at a sense of acceptance. The family worker needs to let all family members talk about the loss experience, to reminisce, and let out the many feelings they may have about their loss.

It is important for the worker to allow this sharing in a safe, comfortable way, and to validate feelings. Grieving is painful. The worker can let members know that it feels like you will cry for ever, but it usually occurs that you cry for twenty minutes, the next time nineteen, the next eighteen, and eventually the tears are replaced by acceptance. The process of 'letting go' of the pain can take months or even years. As stated above, the grieving process often takes a couple of years to arrive at the acceptance stage. Nevertheless, it is important to allow people to grieve in their own ways and not superimpose a model of "what is supposed to happen." Grief is normal and people experience it in ways that are unique to them. Loss counseling allows the grieving process to unfold.

Exercise 12.1

Loss Role-Plays
(In Class)

Break into groups of two, one member is the worker and the second is the client. Select one scenario from the list of examples and role-play it for

Role-play a client who is grieving the loss of a love one through death and is having difficulty sleeping etc. because of this grief.

Role-play the loss of a relationship through separation or divorce.

Role-play the anger stage of termination of interviews.

Role-play the loss of health, with a client finding out they have cancer.

Termination as a Loss Issue

The termination of work with a family can involve many mixed emotions. Depending on the nature and intensity of the involvement, termination can be a loss for families. Dealing with termination provides an ideal opportunity to model dealing with loss to the family. We hope that the family will generalize their learning to other loss situations.

For family workers, termination can also stir up a range of emotions about their professional competence and feelings about the family. If all has gone well, the family worker will undoubtedly feel pleased about the progress that has been made, but like the family, may feel a of loss and grief in the parting. In addition, the family worker may also find that termination has stirred up mixed feelings about the quality of their work: guilt about not having done a better job with the family and concern about the family's efforts to move forward independently.

In the final disengagement, family workers might want to make it clear that the door to future work is open, that they will be available for future problem-solving (if permitted by their agency), and if not, the worker will find an appropriate agency for further work and follow-up. Workers should assure their client families of their continued interest in them and of their belief in the family's ability to move on to other goals and other efforts. It is often useful to mark the last contact with a symbolic gesture, such as a family party or other type of celebration. In some instances, a formal letter or award signifying accomplishment of the goals may be very meaningful.

Families may also present with a range of behaviors and emotions at termination. They might return to earlier patterns or introduce new problem situations and tasks. Another reaction might be that of explosive behavior in which the client says that the worker was wrong when the worker thought that the client could go it alone. Anger might be expressed directly or indirectly. Alternatively, clients might precipitate a break in the relationship as though to say that the client will leave before the worker leaves the client.

Exercise 12.2

Loss Counseling
(PBL Worksheet)

In your PBL groups, define one of the family problems as a loss issue and engage the family in the loss counseling process (30-40) minutes. Debrief experience in large class.

Termination of Client Involvement

All work must eventually end and family work might end in several ways. Families may terminate the work prematurely, before the goals have been reached and before the time agreed upon in the contract. Reasons for premature termination vary. The family might not be interested or motivated in continuing or one or two family members might be more reluctant to continue than others. Often reluctant members are those in positions of power, such as a parent. Alternatively, they might feel satisfied with what they have accomplished even though the worker might believe that more work needs to be accomplished. Perhaps family members do not believe that the work has been effective and they do not want to invest any more time. They might not show up for scheduled appointments or, if the work is home-based, not be at home when the worker shows up for the scheduled appointment.

Alternatively, the family worker may terminate prematurely. Possibly the worker does not believe that the family is investing enough energy resolving issues. The worker might be leaving the agency and need to refer the family to another worker. Whatever the reason for termination, a thorough review of what transpired in family work is an important learning experience.

Research suggests that early termination is associated with environmental factors, hence the need for an ecological perspective in working with families. Two such factors include lower household income and ethnicity (Clarkin & Levy, 2004; Kadzin, 2004). Other factors include some personality characteristics of clients, particularly negative attitudes towards the work, initial hostility, or a poor relationship with the worker. These two characteristics speak to the need for attention to the Stage of Change that clients are in as well as the need for strong engagement and goal setting skills to minimize attrition. Marital problems or single parent status in addition to high parental stress adds to the stress of remaining in the work (Kadzin, 2004). Case management services reduce the risk of early dropout. Finally, it appears that workers are keener to recommend intervention when clients are more likely to decide that intervention is not needed (Clarkin & Levy, 2004). Keeping children and families in work is a challenge for workers and the dropout rate ranges between 40 and 60 percent (Kadzin, 2004, p.551).

Exercise 12.3

Termination Reasons
(In Class)

List some reasons why you might choose to advise a family to terminate family work.

1.

2.

3.

4.

Would there have been any way of circumventing any of the problems you listed above?

Reviewing Family Work

What is involved in reviewing the course of family work? A review of the work between the worker and family should cover:

Summarizing Family Work

One of the first steps in reviewing family work is to summarize what was done. This involves starting with the first contact and review why the family became involved in family work in the first place. Families and workers can share first impressions and funny stories about their first contact. They can then talk about what goals they set up and how well their goals were met. Talking about what transpired during the family work will shed light on the process of family work. Clients might confess some surprising things at this time, such as they did not like what you were wearing or they thought you were too young (or too old!) to help them. You can laugh with the clients about their funny stories. Workers, too, can share their first impressions of the family and how their impressions changed over the course of family work. One of the workers was amused to hear from a client that she thought that the worker was "too normal" to help her with her problems. We had a good chuckle about her impressions in the final session together.

Reviewing and Evaluating the Process

The door is now open to discussing the intricacies of the work. You will need to include the successes of the players in the process. Has the family met its goals? If so, how did that happen? What were the roles that everyone played over time? What did the worker do that helped and what did not help? What was accomplished during family work (the outcome, meeting of the goals)? The information provided by the family will be invaluable to the worker who will go on and work with more families in the future. This is an informal evaluation of the work, although the worker might also want the family to fill out a formal evaluation as well.

Preparing for the Future

Just as important as looking at the past is looking to the future. Clients need to discuss what obstacles they see in the future, talk about their fears and excitement and make plans for what they must do to prevent sliding back into old patterns. Making plans for the future, such as transfer to another worker, referral, or self-directed tasks should also be discussed. The worker can plant seeds for the family about how the experience can be transferred to other problems and situations in the future. As mentioned in Chapter 3, one concern is how the family can prevent sliding into previous patterns that created the difficulty in the first place. This will necessarily entail looking at the contributors to the problem such as stressors and lack of skills. It may mean that the worker and family review any of the theoretical issues from this book, describe how it applies to their particular situation, and how they can identify when they are starting to slide back into old patterns. Finally, the worker needs to know what to do at the first sign of relapse and take immediate action if they see this happening.

Reviewing the Relationship

The family will want to speak about how members viewed the relationship with the worker. Likewise, the worker can give his or her impressions of the family and family members, focusing primarily on positives. This is also a time for unfinished business or loose ends to be addressed. Maybe a comment from the worker or family member was left unexplored and now is the time to ask and seek clarification. Dealing with unfinished business is an important learning for the family member as they can learn to do the same thing in other important relationships. A question such as, "What did you want to happen that did not occur?" will provide useful feedback to the worker and give the opportunity to tie up any loose ends. The worker might use a scaling question, such as, "On a scale of one to ten, with ten being most satisfied, how satisfied were you with the family work." If the response is less than ten, the worker can explore what could have happened to make the experience a ten.

Evaluating the Work

Some of the comments described above provide an informal mechanism through which to evaluate the work. Client narratives about work that has been done provide useful information to workers, although the nature of the feedback will depend on the openness and trust in the relationship. Some agencies might have more formal evaluation procedures and the worker might be required to administer an evaluation instrument in the final session. As mentioned Corcoran and Fischer (2000) provided two volumes of assessment measures that can be used with children and families. Some agencies might have their own evaluation form.

Exercise 12.4

Evaluating Family Work
(In Class)

Get together in groups of three. Brainstorm what kinds of questions you can ask families in the final session to get accurate feedback from the family about the impact of family work. Now role-play a final interview.

Closing the Door

The final step is closing the door. The worker should encourage the sharing of feelings about saying goodbye. Likewise, the worker can share his or her feelings about walking out of the door for the last time. Above all, the worker should credit the family for its efforts in resolving problems and re-affirm family strengths. If needed, the worker should ensure that necessary supportive resources are in place for the family and help the family link to these resources.

Exercise 12.5

Summarizing Accomplishments
(In Class)

Using the Stone family as a case example, practice summarizing the family's accomplishments. List some examples of positive gains you want to acknowledge.

Positive Gains

a.

b.

c.

d.

Termination Process: Four Stages

Ideally, the termination process starts at the beginning of the family work, when the family worker first meets with the family. At that time, the work that is bounded by a time limit that matches the goals and the contract that have been established. Issues related to termination should be formally addressed within the last four sessions of family contact. Four stages usually occur when termination is neared: 1) avoidance, 2) anger, 3) sadness, and 4) acceptance.

Termination Session 1: Avoidance

First, the worker raises with the family that only four sessions remain before the final termination. Often the family shrugs off the news of the pending end of services. For family work where a strong relationship has been established and where the family has made significant progress, there may be denial or avoidance. What is perhaps most significant, however, is that the family worker has raised the issues of termination and brought it to the family's awareness. A deeper discussion of termination is not usually required at this point, but the seed has been planted and the family can reflect on termination issues until the next session.

Termination Session 2: Anger

In this session, the family worker might again raise the issue, pointing out that only three sessions remain. Often families who over the past week have thought about the end of their helping relationship with the family worker might now express anger at the pending termination. They may say things like "How can you stop counseling now as you are the only person we have been able to open up to?" or, "We are not ready to terminate as we have so many other issues to work on." These comments can instill feelings of guilt about ending the relationship. It remains important to raise the termination issue and allow the family's feelings to the surface. At this point, it is important to have an open and honest discussion of feelings, both the family's and worker's.

Termination Session 3: Sadness

In this session before the final appointment, raise the pending termination again. If in the previous session the family worker and the family openly and honestly discussed their feelings, particularly feelings of anger and disappointment, families might now express sadness about the upcoming termination. They might want to discuss the importance of the family work, which is a very meaningful and rewarding expression of their feelings.

Final Session 4: Acceptance

In this final meeting with a family, it is imperative again to discuss the ending of the work, including a discussion of the worker's relationship with the family. If the previous three sessions have unfolded well, families will have accepted the loss of a family-worker relationship. Ideally, they will be able to construct concrete plans for their future outside of family work. Their plans beyond family work might include involvement with outside support systems. This final session is the time to reflect and evaluate the work that has been done.

At this time, it is also important to move the family toward maintaining the gains they have made in counseling. Lambert and Ogles (2004) urge workers to make systematic efforts to help clients solidify the gains they made in their work. They can do this by exploring the meaning of the improvement and develop ways of coping with future challenges. Few studies follow clients beyond termination of work to determine how long families maintain their gains, but it is reasonable to conclude that some families do maintain their gains indefinitely while others relapse more quickly. Closely related to maintaining gains is whether to follow-up clients for "booster shots" after the work ends.

Exercise 12.6

Positive Gain Suggestions
(In Class)

List some suggestions you might make to a family to help them maintain positive gains in the future.

1.

2.

3.

Exercise 12.7

Termination
(PBL Worksheet)

Today you will complete the termination phase with your family work groups.

Tasks to be sure to complete in your family work groups:

Summarize your family work to date;

Address any unfinished business;

Evaluate whether the presenting problem has been resolved;

Discuss the accomplishment of goals and the movement toward the family vision;

Ask if the family is satisfied with the outcome;

Ask the family "What did you find most helpful during our work together?' and;

"What did you want to happen that did not occur?";

Encourage the sharing of feelings concerning saying goodbye;

Credit the family for its efforts in resolving problems and re-acknowledge family strengths;

Ensure supporting resources are in place;

Identify community resources and;

Help the family link to these resources.

Summarize and review your learning from this group experience.

Was the family ready to terminate?

What new skills did you develop in working with this family?

The best work seemed to be…

We could have improved our experience by…

Provide final feedback to members on their contribution.

Celebrate your family's accomplishments!

Celebrate your work group success!

Just as it is important to arrive at closure with your family work, it is also necessary for you to reach closure with this class. For some, the experience has been exhausting. For others, it has been exhilarating. We hope that for all, it has been a valuable learning experience. Nevertheless, it is important to debrief your experience with your small work group and say good-bye. We have had students who have held onto their pretend family name throughout the time they were in our program. They would joke around with us in the hallways about their experiences and reminisce with one another when they met outside of classes. We thank you, our students, for making our job easy and enjoyable. To you, our students, we offer your gift to others. Go and change the world!

Exercise 12.8

Reflection for Next Family PBL Groups
(In Class)

(Your feedback will be passed along to the next family class)

What did you learn during your family work groups that surprised you the most?

How well did your group work together? Why is group research important in an activity like this?

How did the handouts help you complete this activity?

Would you use the handouts differently?

The next time you do an activity such as this, what might you do differently?

What worked well? What would you like to recommend for future students?

Chapter Summary

Closing a family file might occur for several reasons. Perhaps the worker or family ended the work early. Most ideal is the situation where the work was completed as planned and the case is closing because the goals have been accomplished. In this situation, termination can be a loss issue for families and workers. Workers will need to review the process of family work, summarize the activities and talk about the positive changes. An evaluation, whether it is formal, informal, or both, is an essential step in termination. Saying good-bye can be a celebration as well as time to say how important the relationship was.

References

Abudabbeh, N. (1996). Arab families. In M. McGoldrick & J. Giordano. *Ethnicity and family therapy* (pp. 333-346). New York: The Guilford Press.

Ahrons, C. (1999). Divorce: The unscheduled family transition. In B. Carter & M. McGoldrick, (Eds). *The expanded family life cycle: Individual, family, and social perspectives, 3rd ed.* (pp. 381-398). Needham Heights, MA: Allyn & Bacon.

Almeida, R. (1996). Hindu, Christian, and Muslim families. In M. McGoldrick & J. Giordano. *Ethnicity and family therapy* (pp. 395-423). New York: The Guilford Press.

Bandler, R. (1976). *Changing with families: A book about further education for being human.* Palo Alto, CA: Science and behavior books.

Barker, R. (1995). *The social work dictionary* (3rd ed.). Washington, D.C. NASW.

Barrows, H. (1985) *How to design a problem-based curriculum for the preclinical years*. New York: Springer.

Berliner, K., Jacob, D., & Schwartzberg, N. (1999). The single adult and the family life cycle. In B. Carter & M. McGoldrick, (Eds). *The expanded family life cycle: Individual, family, and social perspectives, 3rd ed.* (pp. 362-372). Needham Heights, MA: Allyn & Bacon.

Blacker, L. (1999). The launching phase of the life cycle. In B. Carter & M. McGoldrick, (Eds). *The expanded family life cycle: Individual, family, and social perspectives, 3rd ed.* (pp. 287-306). Needham Heights, MA: Allyn & Bacon.

Bloomquist, M. (1996). *Skills training for children with behavior disorders*. New York: The Guilford Press.

Bowen, M. (1978). *Family therapy in clinical practice.* New York: Jason Aronson.

Carruthers, P. (2001). *A feminist family therapy: Therapeutic invitations to egalitarian family relationships.* Unpublished doctoral dissertation. The University of Calgary.

Carter, B. (1999). Becoming parents: The family with young children. In B. Carter & M. McGoldrick, (Eds). *The expanded family life cycle: Individual, family, and social perspectives, 3rd ed.* (pp. 249-273). Needham Heights, MA: Allyn & Bacon.

Carter, B., & McGoldrick, M. (Eds.). (1999). *The expanded family life cycle: Individual, family, and social perspectives, 3rd ed.* Needham Heights, MA: Allyn & Bacon.

Carter, B., & McGoldrick, M. (1999). Overview: The expanded family life cycle: Individual, family and social perspectives. In B. Carter & M. McGoldrick, (Eds). *The expanded family life cycle: Individual, family, and social perspectives, 3rd ed.* (pp. 1-26). Needham Heights, MA: Allyn & Bacon.

Carter, B., & McGoldrick, M. (1999b). The Divorce Cycle: A major variation in the American Family Life Cycle. In B. Carter & M. McGoldrick, (Eds). *The expanded family life cycle: Individual, family, and social perspectives, 3rd ed.* (pp. 373-380). Needham Heights, MA: Allyn & Bacon.

Carter, B., & McGoldrick, M. (1999c). Coaching at various stages of the life cycle. *The expanded family life cycle: Individual, family, and social perspectives, 3rd ed.* (pp. 436-454). Needham Heights, MA: Allyn & Bacon.

Chang, J., I Phillips, M. (1993). Michael White and Steve de Shazer: New Directions in Family Therapy. In *Therapeutic Conversations.* S. Gilligan & R. Price (Eds.). New York: W. W. Norton & Company.

Clarkin, J., & Levy, K. (2004). *The influence of client variables on psychotherapy.* In M. Lambert, Handbook of psychotherapy and behavior change, (pp.194-226). New York: Wiley & Sons.

Coleman, H. (1992). *The family ideal and the alignment of therapies*. Unpublished paper.

Coleman, H., & Collins, D. (2003). Problem-based learning and social work education. *International Journal of Learning*, (9), 689-703.

Coleman, H., & Collins, D. (1997). The voice of parents: A qualitative study of a family-centered, home-based program. *Child and Youth Care Forum* (Special Edition on Research in the Field of Child and Youth Care). 26(4), 161-178.

Coleman, H., Unrau, Y., & Manyfingers, B. (2001). Revamping family preservation services for native families. *Journal of Ethnic and Cultural Diversity in Social Work, 10*(1), 49-68.

Collins, D., Jordan, C. & Coleman, H. (1999). *An introduction to family social work.* Itasca, ILL: Peacock

Coontz, S. (1996). The way we weren't: The myth and reality of the "Traditional Family." *National Forum*, 76(4), 45-58.

Corcoran, K., & Fischer, J. (2000). *Measures for clinical practice.* New York: The Free Press.

Daughhetee, C. (2001). Using genograms as a tool for insight in college counseling. *Journal of College Counseling*, 4, 73-76.

de Shazer. S. (1991). *Putting difference to work.* New York: Norton.

de Shazer, S. (1983). *Patterns of brief family therapy: An ecosystemic approach.* New York: Guilford.

Eichler, M. (1997). *Family shifts*. New York: Oxford University Press.

Epstein, N., Baldwin, D., & Bishop, S. (1983). The McMaster family assessment device. *Journal of Marital and Family Therapy,* 9, 171-180.

Epston, D., & White, M. (1992). *Experience, contradiction, narrative, and imagination: Selected papers of David Epston and Michael White, 1989-1991.* Adelaide Australia: Dulwich Centre Publications.

Falicov, C. (1999). The Latino family life cycle. In B. Carter & M. McGoldrick (Eds.). *The expanded family life cycle: Individual, family, and social perspectives, 3rd ed.* (pp.141-152). Needham Heights, MA: Allyn & Bacon.

Franklin, C., Hopson, L., & Ten Barge. (2003). Family systems. In C. Jordan & C. Franklin (Eds.) *Clinical assessment for social workers.* (pp. 255-312). Chicago: Lyceum Books.

Fraser, M., Pecora, P., & Haapala, D. (Eds.) (1991). *Families in crisis*. New York: Aldine de Gruyter.

Freedman, J., & Combs, G. (1996). *Narrative therapy.* New York: W. W. Norton & Company.

Friere, P. (1970, reprinted in 2000). *Pedagogy of the oppressed.* New York: The Continuum International Publishing Group Inc.

Garbarino, J. (1982). *Children and families in their social environment.* New York: Aldine de Gruyter.

Garcia-Preto, N. (1999). Latino families: An overview. In M. McGoldrick & J. Giordano. *Ethnicity and family therapy* (pp. 141-154). New York: The Guilford Press.

Garcia-Preto, N. (1999b). Transformation of the family system during adolescence. In B. Carter & M. McGoldrick, (Eds). *The expanded family life cycle: Individual, family, and social perspectives, 3rd ed.* (pp. 274-286). Needham Heights, MA: Allyn & Bacon.

Geismar, L., & Krisberg, J. (1966). The Family Life Improvement Project: An experiment in preventive intervention. *Social Casework*, 47, 563-570.

Gerhart, C. (1990). *Caring for the chronically mentally ill.* Itasca, ILL: Peacock Press.

Giordano, J., & McGoldrick, M. (1996). European families: An overview. In M. McGoldrick & J. Giordano. *Ethnicity and family therapy* (pp. 427-441). New York: The Guilford Press.

Good, G., Gilbert, L., & Sacher, M. (1990). Gender aware therapy: A synthesis of feminist therapy and knowledge about gender. *Journal of Counseling and Development*, 68, 227-234.

Goldner, V. (1985a). Warning: Family therapy may be hazardous to your health. *The Family Therapy Networker*, 9(6), 18-23.

Goldner, V. (1985b). Feminism and family therapy. *Family Process*. 24(1), 31-47.

Green, R., & Herget, M. (1991). Outcomes of systemic/strategic team consultation: III. The importance of therapist warmth and active structuring. *Family Process*, 30, 321-336.

Greene, R., & Kropf, N. (2003). A family case management approach for level 1 needs (pp. 85-103). In Kilpatrick, A., & Holland, T. (Eds.). *Working with families* (3rd ed.) New York: Allyn Bacon.

Hanson, S. (1986). Healthy single-parent families. *Family relations*, 35, 125-132.

Hardcastle, D., Wenocur, S., & Powers, P. (1997). *Community practice: Theories and skills for social workers.* Oxford University Press.

Hardy, K., & Laszloffy, T. (1995). The cultural Genogram: Key to training culturally competent family therapists. *Journal of Marital and Family Therapy*, 21(3), 227-237.

Hartman, A., & Laird, J. (1983). *Family-centered social work practice*. New York: Free Press.

Holman, A. (1983). *Family assessment*. Newbury Park, CA: Sage Publications.

Ivanoff, A., Blythe, B., & Tripodi, T. (1994). *Involuntary clients in social work practice*. New York: Aldine de Gruyter.

Jackson, D. (1972). Family rules: Marital quid pro quo. In G. Erickson & T. Hogan (Eds.), *Family therapy: An introduction to theory and techniques* (pp. 76-85). Monterey, CA: Brooks/Cole.

Johnson, T., & Colucci, P. (1999). Lesbians, gay men, and the family life cycle. In B. Carter & M. McGoldrick, (Eds). *The expanded family life cycle: Individual, family, and social perspectives, 3rd ed.* (pp. 249-273). Needham Heights, MA: Allyn & Bacon.

Jordan, C., Hunter, S., Rycroff, J., & Vandiver, V. (2003). Assessing families who are multistressed. In C. Jordan & C. Franklin (Eds.). *Clinical assessment for social workers*, 2nd ed. (pp.313-350). Chicago, Ill: Lyceum Press.

Kadushin, A., & Kadushin, G. (1997). The social work interview (4th ed.). New York: Columbia University Press.

Kadzin, A. (2004). Psychotherapy for children and adolescents. In M. Lambert, (Ed.). *Handbook of psychotherapy and behavior change* (pp. 543-589). New York: John Wiley & Sons.

Kliman, J., & Madsen, W. (1999). Social class and the family life cycle. In B. Carter & M. McGoldrick (Eds.). *The expanded family life cycle: Individual, family, and social perspectives, 3rd ed.* (pp.88-105). Needham Heights, MA: Allyn & Bacon.

Lambert, M., & Ogles, B. (2004). The efficacy and effectiveness of psychotherapy. In M. Lambert, (Ed.). *Handbook of psychotherapy and behavior change* (pp. 139-193). New York: John Wiley & Sons.

Lee, E. (1996). Asian American families: An overview. In M. McGoldrick & J. Giordano. *Ethnicity and family therapy* (pp. 227-248). New York: The Guilford Press.

Mahmoud, V. (1996). African American Muslim families. In M. McGoldrick & J. Giordano. *Ethnicity and family therapy* (pp. 112-138). New York: The Guilford Press.

Maslow, A. (1967). *Toward a psychology of being*. New York: Van Nostrand Reinhold.

McCowan, W., & Johnson, J. (1993). *Therapy with treatment resistant families*. Binghampton, NY: The Haworth Press.

McGoldrick, M. (1999a). Women through the family life cycle. In B. Carter & M. McGoldrick, (Eds). *The expanded family life cycle: Individual, family, and social perspectives, 3rd ed.* (pp. 109-123). Needham Heights, MA: Allyn & Bacon.

McGoldrick, M. (1999b). Becoming a couple. In B. Carter & M. McGoldrick (Eds.). In B. Carter & M. McGoldrick, (Eds). *The expanded family life cycle: Individual, family, and social perspectives, 3rd ed.* (pp. 231-248). Needham Heights, MA: Allyn & Bacon.

McGoldrick, M., & Gerson, R. (1985). *Genograms in family assessment.* New York: W.W. Norton & Company, Inc.

McGoldrick, M., Giordano, J., & Pearce, J. (1996). *Ethnicity & family therapy*. New York: The Guilford Press.

McGoldrick, M., Watson, M., & Benson, W. (1999). Siblings throughout the life cycle. In B. Carter & M. McGoldrick, (Eds). *The expanded family life cycle: Individual, family, and social perspectives, 3rd ed.* (pp. 153-168). Needham Heights, MA: Allyn & Bacon.

McKeachie, W. (2002). *Teaching tips*. Boston, MA: Houghton Mifflin Company.

Miller, S., & Duncan, B., & Hubble, M. (1997). *Escape from Babel*. New York: W.W. Norton & Company, Inc.

Minuchin, P., Colapinto, J., & Minuchin, S. (1998). *Working with families of the poor*. New York: The Guilford Press.

Minuchin, Salvador (1992). *Family healing: Tales of hope and renewal from family therapy*. The Free Press.

Minuchin, S. (1974). *Families and family therapy*. Cambridge, MA: Harvard University Press.

Minuchin, S. (1984). *Family kaleidoscope.* Cambridge, MA: Harvard University Press

Minuchin, S. (1981). *Family therapy techniques.* Cambridge, MA: Harvard University Press.

Minuchin, S. (1981). Structural family therapy. In R.L. Green and J.L. Framo (Eds.), *Family therapy.* Madison, CT: International Universities Press.

Moore-Hines, P. (1999). The family life cycle of African American families living in poverty. In B. Carter & M. McGoldrick, (Eds). *The expanded family life cycle: Individual, family, and social perspectives, 3rd ed.* (pp. 327-345). Needham Heights, MA: Allyn & Bacon.

Moore-Hines, P., & Boyd Franklin, N. (1996). African American families. In M. McGoldrick & J. Giordano. *Ethnicity and family therapy* (pp. 66-84). New York: The Guilford Press.

Moxley, D. (1989). *The practice of case management.* Newbury Park, CA: Sage Publications.

Orlinsky, D., Ronnestad, M., & Willutzki, U. (2004). Fifty years of psychotherapy process-outcome research: Continuity and change. In M. Lambert, (Ed.). *Handbook of psychotherapy and behavior change* (pp. 307-390). New York: John Wiley & Sons.

Patterson, J., Williams, L., Grauf-Grounds, C., & Chamow, L. (1998). *Essential skills in family therapy.* New York: The Guilford Press.

Piercy, F., & Sprenkle, D. (1986). *Family therapy sourcebook.* New York: Guilford Press.

Prochaska, J., DiClemente, C., & Norcross, J. (1992). In search of how people change: Applications to addictive behaviors. *American Psychologist*, 47, 1102-1114.

Prochaska, J. & Norcross, J. (2003). *Systems of psychotherapy: A transtheoretical analysis.* Pacific Grove, CA: Brooks/Cole.

Richmond, M. (1917, reprinted 1964). *Social diagnosis.* Philadelphia: Russell Sage Foundation.

Rothman, J. (1994). *Practice with highly vulnerable clients: Case management and community-based services.* Englewood Cliffs, NJ: Prentice-Hall, Inc.

Rosen, E. (1999). Men in transition: The "New Man." In B. Carter & M. McGoldrick (Eds.). *The expanded family life cycle: Individual, family and social perspectives, 3rd ed.* (pp.124-140). Needham Heights, MA: Allyn & Bacon.

Satir, V. (1967). *Conjoint family therapy.* Palo Alto, CA: Science and Behavior Books, Inc.

Satir, V., & Baldwin, M. (1983). *Satir step by step: A guide to creating change in families*: Palo Alto, CA: Science and Behavior Books.

Satir, V. (1976). *Helping families to change.* New York: Aronson.

Silverstein, L. (2003). *Feminist family therapy: Empowerment in social context.* Washington, DC: American Psychological Association.

Tomm, K. (1987). Interventive interviewing. *Family Process*, 26, 3-13.

Tomm, K., & Wright, L. (1979). Training in family therapy: Perceptual, conceptual, and executive skills. *Family Process*, 18, 227-250.

Truax, C., & Carkhuff, R. (1967). *Toward effective counseling and psychotherapy: Training and practice*. New York: Aldine de Gruyter.

Walsh, F. (1999). Families in later life: Challenges and opportunities. In B. Carter & M. McGoldrick, (Eds). *The expanded family life cycle: Individual, family, and social perspectives, 3rd ed.* (pp. 307-326). Needham Heights, MA: Allyn & Bacon.

Wasik, B., Bryant, D., & Lyon, C. (1990). *Home visiting: Procedures for helping families*. Newbury Park, California: Sage.

Watzlawick, P., Beavin, J., & Jackson, D. (1967). *Pragmatics of human communication*. New York: W.W. Norton & Co.

White, M. (1990). *Narrative means to therapeutic ends*. New York: Norton.

White, M. (1995). *Re-authoring lives: Interviews and essays*. Adelaide, Australia: Dulwich Centre.

Winawer, H., & Wetzel, N. (1996). German families. In M. McGoldrick & J. Giordano. *Ethnicity and family therapy* (pp. 496-516). New York: The Guilford Press.

Wright, L., & Leahey, M. (1994). *Nurses and families: A guide to famil'1y assessment and intervention*. Philadelphia: F.A. Davis.

Zimmerman, T. (2002). *Integrating gender and culture in parenting*. New York: Haworth Press.

Appendix 1.1: Sample Course Outline for Family Class

University
Faculty
Date

COURSE Number:
Course Name:
Times of class:
Classroom:
Instructor: Name of Instructor:
Office: Number:
Office phone:
Email:

COURSE OUTLINE

SYLLABUS STATEMENT AND COURSE DESCRIPTION

This course provides knowledge about family work practice. It focuses on conceptual skills, conceptual-perceptual integration skills and basic assessment/intervention tools. The course is designed to give students an introduction to family dynamics, family systems and beginning family practice skills.

LEARNING OBJECTIVES

This course will provide a conceptual foundation and practice approach for human service workers engaged in work with families. This course emphasizes the practice of generalist family work, with an emphasis on dynamics of family systems and how the development of repetitive interactional patterns can create a dysfunctional and non-nurturing process in families. It will look at a generalist family practice approach and will assist in the development of beginning intervention skills. Problem-Based Learning (PBL) is used with an experiential focus. Students will be expected to:

1. Construct a conceptual framework composed of biological, analytic, learning, social-interactional and belief system concepts to understand and assess problems presented by families;

2. Gain foundation knowledge of a family systems practice approach;

3. Gain an overview of a range of traditional and emerging family practice approaches;

4. Integrate practice theory with practice behaviors.

5. Critically analyze the use of family theory as it pertains to practice issues.

6. Use theory and skills of family intervention critically and in an analytical manner.

7. Develop skills of independent learning.

8. Feel prepared to work with families in a practice setting. Students are expected to create opportunities for learning transfer from the classroom to practice settings.

9. Develop skills related to independent learning through a problem-based learning course format.

Students will be involved in a theoretical and experiential learning process that will give them an opportunity to examine and explore the dynamics of family systems as well as transfer learning from the class to client situations. Through tapes, simulated families and experiential learning, we will look at family repetitive patterns and how the skill of a family worker can impact for change on family process, and discover ways of moving families beyond their blocks.

RELATIONSHIP TO OTHER COURSES

Though the course is designed for the beginning family practitioner, a foundation in generic human service work methods is required.

CLASS SCHEDULE

The 1st class starts the week of____________

Class 1	Introduction to generalist family work practice, family diversity, defining a family, challenges to traditional family discourse, diverse structures
Class 2	Diversity
Class 3	Beginning work with the family
Class 4	The Genogram
Class 5	Family systems theory and circular causality
Class 6	Family categories schema & Defining problems
Class 7	The Ecomap & Case Management
Class 8	Family Life Cycle Assessment
Class 9	Behavioral Approach
Class 10	Working in the Family Home & Treating Families with Children in Care
Class 11	Specialized family approaches
Class 12	Termination

ASSIGNMENTS

1) There are a number of possible assignments for this class. Several are described below:

Assignment # 1

Weekly log of experiential work and the integration and transfer of theory: Class participation and log of team's work: Students will work in teams of approximately six students. The team will work together on weekly problems in a role-play format. The first step is to construct a family with which students will work over the term. In this small group work, students will assume roles within a particular family as determined through group discussion and decision-making. One student will play the role of family worker and the other students will play a role in the family. Family teams will spend the first two weeks "forming" their family. Each week, family teams will meet in the lab section of class and work with their family. The family structure and composition will be determined by each team. Each family member have a name and a history by the group.

All assignments for this course will be centered around the family experience and dynamics that occurred in each weekly session. Each member's participation in the family role-plays will be assessed by the team. Students are expected to write a weekly log of their family experience and relate it to the class sessions and family theory. Each weekly log will be approximately two typed paragraphs long. Each weekly log shall identify the family members present and when appropriate identify the impact of missing family members upon the family session as well as what can be done to better engage the missing family member. The inclusion of relevant theory from the text, outside readings and classroom lectures is necessary to receive full marks for a log.
Due Date: ____ **Logs must be handed in before class.**
Weight: 30%, 2.5 points per log, including attendance (total of 12 logs).

Assignment # 2

Comprehensive Assessment: A comprehensive assessment of the family formed in your work groups. One approach to assessment will be discussed further in class. Students will base their family assessment on the theories and assessment models presented in class and outside reading. Weight: 30%
Due Date:

Assignment # 3

Intervention Plan: Students will develop a plan for creating change in this particular family. Keep in mind all the assessment tools taught.
Weight: 10%
Due Date:

Assignment # 4

Major paper: This final assignment is a major paper examining and *critically analyzing* the research and the literature surrounding a selected family problem or family issue. The paper should be 15 pages (excluding references) and include, as a major feature, critical reflection about the issue at hand. The paper should be referenced according to APA standards. Grading criteria for term papers and assignments are presented at the end of this course outline. [Please refer to the criteria for grading papers at the end of the course outline]
Due Date: The beginning of the last class. For further information about writing a term paper, please refer to the following web site:

http://www.nutsandboltsguide.com

Due Date: The beginning of the last class. Weight: 30%.

LATE ASSIGNMENTS

Late assignments will be accepted without penalty **only** if there are extenuating circumstances, for example, illness. No extensions are available for workload reasons.

Assignments late by two days after the due date will be penalized a 1/3 letter grade. In other words, if an assignment is due on Tuesday by 4:00 p.m., a student will lose 1/3 letter grade if the assignment comes in before 4:00 p.m. by the next Wednesday. Assignments more than two days late will lose a full letter grade. After two weeks, assignments will not be accepted.

INSTRUCTOR AVAILABILITY

Appointments with the instructor may be made in person or by telephoning either the instructor's office, [phone number and email address] or by dropping in during the office hours posted at the top of the course outline.

Messages may be left on the instructors' office phone answering machine. When leaving a message, leave your name, telephone number and when you may be reached. Alternatively, the instructor's email address is: [email address].

REQUIRED TEXT

Coleman, H., Collins, D., & Collins, T. (2005). *Generalist Family Work: A Problem-Based Learning Approach.* Peosta, Iowa: Eddie Bowers Publishing Co.

RECOMMENDED READINGS

Collins, D., Jordan, C., & Coleman, H. (1999). *An Introduction to Family Social Work.* Itasca, Illinois: F.E. Peacock.

Epstein, N.B., Baldwin, D., & Bishop, S. (1983). The McMaster family assessment device. *Journal of Marriage and Family Therapy*, 9, 171-180.

Garbarino, J. (1982). *Children and families in their social environment.* New York: Aldine de Gruyter.

Goldenberg, J. & Goldenberg, H. (2002). *Family therapy: An overview* (6th ed.). Pacific Grove, CA: Brooks/Cole.

Gurman, A. (1981). *Handbook of family therapy.* New York: Brunner/Mazel.

Nichols, M., & Schwartz, R. (2002). *Family therapy: concepts and methods* (6th ed.). Toronto: Allyn & Bacon.

McGoldrick, M., Giordano, J., & Pearce, J. (1996). *Ethnicity & family therapy.* New York: The Guilford Press.

Miller, S., & Duncan, B., & Hubble, M. (1997). *Escape from Babel.* New York: W.W. Norton & Company, Inc.

Minuchin, P., Colapinto, J., & Minuchin, S. (1998). *Working with families of the poor*. New York: The Guilford Press.

Satir, V. (1964). *Conjoint family therapy.* Polo Alto: Science and Behavior Books.

Tomm, K., & Wright, L. (1979). Training in family therapy: Perceptual, conceptual and executive skills. *Family Process,* 18(3), pp. 227-250.

Von Bertalanffy, L. (1966). General systems theory and psychiatry. In S. Arieti (Ed.). *American Handbook of Psychiatry*, 3. New York: Basic Books.

Watzlawick, P., Beavin, J.H., & Jackson, D.D. (1967). *Pragmatics of human communication.* New York: W.W. Norton.

Wright, L., & Leahey, M. (1994). *Nurses and families: A guide to family assessment and intervention* (2nd ed.). Philadelphia: F. A. Davis.

Criteria for Evaluating Written Assignments

Content - 40%

- Organization of the paper; with introduction, body, conclusions, all interconnected.
- Clearly stated purpose, putting the issues within a clear context, introduction of the issues; body with breadth, depth of examination of subject.
- Clear presentation of theory and the development of arguments backed up with research and theory. Student must be able to distinguish between values, opinions, theory, and research.
- **Critical thinking and use of ideas.**
- Domain of the substantive area comprehensively sampled. Literature is adequately represented. This cannot be counted. The literature review must be thorough and include major authors in a selected area.
- Development of a theme or an argument.
- Ability to understand concepts and to integrate these concepts into a coherent critical presentation.
- Conclusions address the implications of the arguments presented in the text and connect logically to the purpose, flow logical from the body of the paper.

Synthesis and integration - 40%

- **Critical and analytical thinking**
- Summarization when needed
- Logical flow of ideas.
- Ability to critique research, theory, and concepts based on knowledge of the practice, policy and research process.
- Balance in paper of arguments.
- Integration with conceptual framework, research and theory.
- Ability to identify and highlight key issues, linkage of themes throughout the paper.
- Ability to draw conclusions or make critical argument based on the soundness of the evidence reviewed.
- Ability to identify limitations of various stages of the review and research process for the articles used.

Technical 20%

- Clarity of writing and expression
- Coherent flow of ideas
- Economical and "crisp" use of language to express ideas.
- Non-sexist language, spelling, grammar, punctuation.
- Use of APA, citation and references.

Appendix 1.2: Family Definitions

(Collins, Jordan, & Coleman, 1999)

Family of Orientation: Most individuals belong to at least two family systems over a lifetime. All have belonged to families of orientation that is the family of origin. This is the family into which one was born and/or raised. Sometimes it is possible to come from two or more families of orientation; for example a child adopted at birth was, even for a brief time, part of a family of orientation with a birth mother. Nevertheless, in the child's mind, the family of orientation would likely be that of adoptive parents. Foster children or permanent wards have often lived in a number of different family units. Others might have been raised in institutional settings. Grandparents, aunts and uncles or even family friends can also raise children.

Family of Procreation: The family of procreation consists of a couple, who through self or state sanction have children. The basic family unit might be a mother and children.

Extended Family: The extended family is a combination of two or more family units, across generations. For example, a grandmother living with her married son, his wife, and their children would be considered extended family. Grandparents are the most common family extension others such as aunts, uncles or cousins may be included in the extended family is important in many ethnic families (Lum, 1992).

Blended Family: A blended family or stepfamily consists of two people, perhaps one or both with children from a former relationship, who are currently residing together. The two adults may also have biological children together.

Adoptive Family: An adoptive family has members through adoption, or another process through which parents have a legal commitment to parent the children of others. The parent or parents may also have biological children.

Single parent Family: A single parent family is one with of one parent and one or more children. The parent can be either male or female. Singlehood can happen because of death, divorce or desertion or having never been in a relationship before.

Family Defined

Eichler's (1988) definition of family guides this manual:

> A family is a social group that may or may not include one or more children (e.g., childless couples), who may or may not have been born in their wedlock (e.g., adopted children, or children by one adult partner of a previous union). The relationship of the adults may or may not have its origin in marriage (e.g., common-law couples); they may or may not occupy the same residence (e.g., commuting couples). The adults may or may not cohabit sexually, and the relationship may or may not involve such socially patterned feelings as love, attraction, piety, and awe (p. 4).

Cultures vary on how they define "family". The dominant Anglo definition identifies the nuclear family whereas aboriginal families include an expanded kin network. Asian focus on ancestors and Italians look at several generations of extended kin (McGoldrick & Giordano, 1996). In minority families, relationships with extended family and kin networks are based on interdependence, group orientation and reliance on others (Lum, 1992). Cultural values about family practices are important to ones worldview. Family values may diverge dramatically from mainstream culture.

Minority families are often formed by a "vertical hierarchy of authority" (Lum, 1992). Thus, authority is often paternal or may be shared by other males or elders as head of the household. Difficulties may arise when minority members encounter different beliefs and practices in the dominant culture. Not knowing those issues can make family workers who show biases towards families whose backgrounds are diverge from their own. The family worker may not understand the parents and be unable to overcome barriers created by differing social backgrounds. Another danger is that the family worker will make inaccurate assessments. Thus, family workers must be honest about prejudices and blind spots.

A broad definition of family is needed because family lifestyles and forms are fluid and evolving. Most people can create clear description to fit their own particular family. Working definitions of families can be made for most people. Basically then, a family is what a person in a family says it is. The experienced 'family' reality is what is important to family work.

Appendix 1.3: Problem-Based Learning Questionnaire

What did you like the best about the problem-based learning approach?

What did you like the least about the problem-based learning approach?

What was the most difficult aspect of problem-based learning?

Problem based learning required small group discussions about specific problems. Could you please comment on your experience with these small group discussions?

Problem-based learning is intended to create an active learning experience for students. To what extent did you feel that your learning was aided by this approach?

In problem based learning, the professor/instructor needs to take on a facilitator role in this approach and allow students to take the leadership. Please comment on the instructor's role in this class.

Compared with other courses, how much responsibility did you assume for your own learning as a result of this approach?

The problem based-learning approach is supposed to help students connect theory with practice. Please comment on how well this connection occurred.

How well did the problem-based learning approach help you integrate your learning in your program?

The problem-based learning approach requires the instructor and students to generate clear realistic problems for students to critically analyze. In the case of this class, the problems centered on families created for the purposes of this course. How well did this occur?

Any other comments you would like to make?

Index

F

G

H

I

L

M